Holiday Stress-Free Solutions

Holiday Stress-Free Solutions

Matthew Petchinsky

Holiday Stress-Free Solutions: A Survival Guide to Thriving During the Festive Season
By: Matthew Petchinsky

Introduction: Navigating the Holiday Maze
Overview of the Problem

The holiday season is often portrayed as a time of joy, warmth, and celebration, but for many, it can also be a period filled with stress, pressure, and overwhelming demands. Beneath the twinkling lights and festive music lies a complex web of challenges that can drain our energy, test our patience, and leave us feeling anything but merry.

Financial pressures skyrocket as we juggle gifts, holiday meals, and travel expenses, all while trying to maintain a budget that's already stretched thin. The rising cost of living makes it increasingly difficult to meet the expectations we or others set for the perfect holiday experience. This strain can easily overshadow the joy of giving, replacing it with anxiety over debt and financial mismanagement.

Family dynamics often intensify during the holidays, bringing unresolved conflicts, unmet expectations, and emotional baggage to the surface. Whether it's tension between relatives, the pressure of maintaining appearances, or the emotional toll of strained relationships, navigating these interactions can be mentally exhausting. The pressure to create harmony in a potentially volatile environment can weigh heavily, leading to stress and emotional fatigue.

Time management is another critical challenge. The endless to-do lists, from decorating the house to shopping for gifts and attending gatherings, leave little room for personal downtime. Many of us find ourselves rushing from one event to the next, burning out before the season even ends. The balancing act of maintaining work, home responsibilities, and social commitments becomes overwhelming, turning the holidays into a race rather than a time of reflection and enjoyment.

Mental well-being, too, is often overlooked in the holiday hustle. Feelings of loneliness, grief, or seasonal affective disorder can surface during this period, amplified by the social pressure to be constantly cheerful. For some, the holidays can be a reminder of lost loved ones or the absence of meaningful connections, leading to feelings of isolation. The constant comparison to others' seemingly perfect celebrations, amplified by social media, can contribute to a sense of inadequacy.

In short, the holiday season, while a time of potential joy, is also a maze of financial strains, emotional stress, time constraints, and mental health challenges. The weight of these issues can leave us feeling disconnected from the true spirit of the season.

Purpose of the Guide

This guide was designed with one clear purpose: to help you navigate the holiday maze with confidence, ease, and, most importantly, joy. It provides practical, actionable solutions to the common stressors of the holiday season, allowing you to reclaim the magic and meaning of this special time of year.

Rather than simply offering generic advice, this guide dives deep into the specific problems many face during the holidays. Whether you're struggling with financial stress, overwhelmed by family dynamics, or simply trying to find balance amidst the chaos, this book offers strategies tailored to your needs. We understand that everyone's holiday experience is different, and this guide embraces that diversity by providing customizable solutions that fit your unique situation.

Our aim is to help you move from surviving the holidays to truly thriving in them. You'll discover tools to manage your finances, create healthier boundaries with family, streamline your time, and prioritize your mental well-being. The solutions we provide are not just short-term fixes but strategies that will serve you well beyond the holiday season, fostering healthier habits that can be carried into the new year.

This guide isn't about perfection; it's about creating a holiday experience that reflects your values, your well-being, and your capacity to enjoy the season. We aim to help you strip away the unnecessary pressures and rediscover the joy and peace that the holidays can offer.

What You'll Learn

In this guide, you'll find a wide range of tools, techniques, and strategies designed to address the most pressing challenges of the holiday season. Here's a preview of what you can expect:

1. **Financial Mastery for the Holidays**

   Learn how to budget effectively for gifts, meals, and travel without sacrificing your financial health. We'll explore creative gift ideas, money-saving techniques, and tips for avoiding holiday debt. You'll also discover how to prioritize spending on what truly matters, helping you enjoy the season without the stress of overspending.

2. **Managing Family Dynamics**

   Navigating family gatherings can be tricky, especially when emotions run high. We'll cover techniques for setting healthy boundaries, dealing with difficult conversations, and managing expectations without losing your peace of mind. Learn how to create a more harmonious holiday atmosphere, even in the most challenging family settings.

3. **Time Management and Planning**

   The holiday season is a whirlwind of activities, but it doesn't have to leave you feeling burnt out. You'll learn how to organize your time efficiently, set realistic goals, and prioritize tasks so that you can enjoy the festivities without feeling overwhelmed. We'll share strategies for balancing work, social engagements, and personal time so that you can enter the new year feeling refreshed rather than exhausted.

4. **Mental Well-being and Self-Care**

   The holidays can be an emotional rollercoaster, but you'll discover practical ways to safeguard your mental well-being. From mindfulness practices to coping mechanisms for dealing with holiday-induced stress, we'll provide you with tools to stay grounded and emotionally resilient. Whether you're dealing with grief, loneliness, or anxiety, this guide will help you find peace and joy in the present moment.

5. **Creating a Holiday that Reflects Your Values**

   In a world of consumerism and high expectations, it's easy to lose sight of what the holidays mean to you. You'll learn how to create a holiday season that aligns with your personal values, focusing on connection, gratitude, and meaningful experiences. We'll explore ways to simplify and de-commercialize the holidays, so you can focus on what truly brings you joy.

6. **Practical Stress-Relief Techniques**

   From breathing exercises to quick relaxation methods, you'll learn practical techniques to relieve stress in the moment. We'll also dive into long-term strategies for managing holiday stress, including how to structure your days to create more space for relaxation and enjoyment.

By the end of this guide, you'll have a personalized roadmap for navigating the holiday season with ease, joy, and purpose. No longer will the holidays be something to endure—they'll be something to celebrate, in a way that honors your well-being and the true spirit of the season.

Part 1: Managing Financial Stress

Chapter 1: Understanding the Financial Triggers of Holiday Stress

The holiday season is often marked by celebrations, gifts, and gatherings, but beneath the festive exterior, many people experience a profound sense of financial pressure. This chapter explores how overspending, societal pressures, and expectations contribute to holiday stress, and how these factors intertwine to create a seemingly inescapable cycle of anxiety.

The Burden of Overspending

One of the most significant financial triggers of holiday stress is the tendency to overspend. With marketing campaigns urging consumers to "go big" during the holidays and sales events like Black Friday and Cyber Monday dangling irresistible deals, many find themselves trapped in a spending spree that extends far beyond their budgets. The combination of these enticing discounts and the desire to provide loved ones with memorable gifts leads many to reach for their credit cards without a second thought.

This overspending often spirals out of control. What starts as an attempt to buy just a few thoughtful gifts can quickly become a full-blown shopping spree, with people purchasing unnecessary items, adding on last-minute gifts, or upgrading to more expensive options because it "feels right for the occasion." The pressure to ensure that every family member, friend, and coworker feels appreciated through material goods pushes us to spend far more than we originally planned.

The consequences of overspending extend beyond the holiday season. When the festivities end and the credit card statements arrive, the financial hangover begins. Many individuals find themselves grappling with debt that can take months—or even years—to pay off, contributing to ongoing stress long after the holiday cheer has faded. The short-term satisfaction of gifting the "perfect" present is overshadowed by the long-term anxiety of mounting debt.

Societal Pressures and Consumerism

Societal pressures play a critical role in shaping how we perceive the holidays and our financial responsibilities during this time. Holiday advertising, media portrayals, and cultural expectations paint an idealized picture of the "perfect holiday," complete with lavish meals, mountains of gifts, and extravagant decorations. These images reinforce the belief that material abundance is a marker of holiday success and personal generosity.

Marketers know how to tap into our emotions, encouraging us to spend in the name of love, joy, and connection. Advertisements portray a heartwarming narrative where happiness is directly tied to the amount of money spent on gifts, décor, and experiences. As a result, many feel compelled to conform to these societal standards, even when doing so stretches their financial limits.

The rise of social media has further intensified these pressures. Platforms like Instagram, Pinterest, and Facebook are flooded with images of perfectly decorated homes, elaborate gift exchanges, and luxurious holiday vacations. For those scrolling through their feeds, it can feel like everyone else is having a picture-perfect holiday season, adding to the sense of inadequacy. This "holiday comparison trap" leads many to spend beyond their means in an attempt to keep up with what they perceive as societal norms, often resulting in financial strain.

At the core of this issue is the conflation of material wealth with emotional connection. We're taught to believe that the more we spend, the more love we show—and that if we don't spend enough, we're somehow failing our loved ones. This mindset can create an internal conflict where we know we shouldn't be spending excessively, but we feel that to do anything less would be to disappoint those around us.

Unrealistic Expectations and Gift-Giving Obligations

Gift-giving is one of the central elements of the holiday season, but it's also one of the primary sources of financial stress. Many feel obligated to buy gifts for an ever-growing list of people—immediate family, extended relatives, friends, coworkers, neighbors, and even casual acquaintances. As the list expands, so does the associated cost. It's easy to lose sight of the original intent of giving—an expression of gratitude and care—and instead become fixated on the need to fulfill expectations.

These expectations don't just come from external sources; they are often self-imposed. We set the bar high for ourselves, feeling the need to top last year's gifts or to present a certain image of ourselves as generous and thoughtful. We may also feel pressure to meet or exceed the gifts we anticipate receiving, creating a reciprocal cycle of spending that becomes difficult to break. In many families, there is an unspoken competition of who can give the most extravagant or impressive gift, which adds to the financial burden.

Holiday gift exchanges and Secret Santa traditions, which are meant to be lighthearted and fun, can also contribute to stress when people feel the need to participate regardless of their financial situation. The pressure to spend money on coworkers or acquaintances for whom meaningful, affordable gifts are difficult to find can add up, further straining the budget.

Moreover, expectations aren't limited to gifts alone. The desire to host the "perfect" holiday gathering, with lavish decorations, gourmet food, and festive entertainment, can be just as financially taxing. The pressure to ensure that everything looks and feels magical for guests can drive people to spend money on expensive party supplies, catering, or home décor that will only be used once, adding to the overall holiday expenditure.

The Emotional Toll of Financial Stress

The financial pressures of the holiday season often lead to anxiety, guilt, and shame. Many people feel embarrassed about their inability to meet societal or familial expectations, especially when they believe that others around them are able to do so with ease. This sense of inadequacy can erode self-esteem and contribute to feelings of failure.

Guilt is another common emotional response to financial stress during the holidays. Many feel guilty for not being able to provide their loved ones with the gifts or experiences they believe they deserve. They may also feel guilty for spending money they don't have, knowing that they'll face financial repercussions in the future. This guilt is often compounded by a deep-seated desire to create happiness for those they care about, leading to a cycle of spending, regret, and anxiety.

The emotional toll of holiday financial stress doesn't just impact individuals; it also affects relationships. Tensions can arise between partners or family members when financial priorities differ, leading to arguments over spending habits. Financial stress can also dampen the overall holiday experience, making it difficult to enjoy time with loved ones when money is a constant worry.

Breaking the Cycle of Financial Holiday Stress

Understanding the financial triggers of holiday stress is the first step in breaking free from their grip. Awareness of how overspending, societal pressures, and unrealistic expectations contribute to financial anxiety allows us to approach the holiday season with a more mindful and intentional attitude.

This book will provide you with strategies to regain control over your holiday spending, establish healthier boundaries, and shift your focus from materialism to meaningful experiences. From budgeting tips to alternative gift-giving ideas, the upcoming chapters will offer practical solutions to help you navigate the financial maze of the holiday season without sacrificing your well-being or financial stability.

The key to a stress-free holiday isn't in spending more—it's in spending wisely, with intention and care. By breaking the cycle of overspending and resisting the societal pressures that equate financial outlay with love, you can redefine what the holidays mean to you and create a more joyful, fulfilling experience for both yourself and those around you.

Chapter 2: Creating a Holiday Budget That Works

The foundation of a stress-free holiday season is rooted in a well-thought-out budget. Without a clear spending plan, the whirlwind of holiday expenses—from gifts to travel, decorations to meals—can quickly spiral out of control, leaving you facing a financial hangover once the festivities end. In this chapter, we'll walk you through a step-by-step process to create a realistic, achievable holiday budget that not only meets your financial limitations but also allows you to enjoy the season without unnecessary stress.

Step 1: Reflect on Past Holiday Spending

Before diving into the creation of a new budget, it's essential to take a step back and reflect on your past holiday spending habits. This is where you'll gain invaluable insight into patterns, mistakes, and successes that can help guide your approach this year.

- **Review Last Year's Expenses:** Gather credit card statements, receipts, or bank records from last year's holiday season to get a clear picture of where your money went. Categorize these expenses into gifts, travel, food, decorations, entertainment, and miscellaneous purchases.
- **Identify Problem Areas:** Were there categories where you spent more than anticipated? Did you buy too many last-minute gifts or decorations? Identify areas where you may have overspent or made purchases that didn't contribute to your holiday joy. Recognizing these patterns helps prevent repeating the same mistakes.
- **Acknowledge Wins:** On the flip side, reflect on what worked well last year. Did you find ways to save money on gifts or decorations without sacrificing quality? Did you host a low-cost yet memorable gathering? Identify what went right so you can replicate those successes.
- **Set a Realistic Expectation for This Year:** Based on your review, consider what a realistic holiday budget looks like this year. Are there any specific financial goals or limitations you need to account for? Perhaps you're dealing with tighter finances or want to avoid going into debt. Define the broad financial boundaries you'll be working within for the season.

Step 2: Set a Total Budget Cap

Once you've reviewed your past spending, the next step is to set a clear total budget cap for the holiday season. This is the maximum amount of money you can comfortably spend without jeopardizing your financial stability. When setting this number, consider:

- **Your Current Financial Situation:** Take stock of your income, savings, and any other financial commitments you have, such as bills or debt payments. Your holiday spending should fit into your overall budget without creating additional financial strain.
- **Avoiding Debt:** As tempting as it may be to splurge during the holidays, one of the key principles of a successful budget is to avoid going into debt. Determine how much you can spend without relying on credit cards or loans. If you must use a credit card, make sure you have a plan to pay off the balance quickly to avoid interest charges.

- **Savings Goals:** Keep your broader financial goals in mind as you set your holiday budget. Whether you're saving for a house, a vacation, or an emergency fund, ensure that your holiday spending doesn't derail your long-term goals.

Once you've set a total cap, write it down. This number will serve as your guiding star throughout the holiday season, helping you stay on track and avoid overspending.

Step 3: Break Down Your Budget into Categories

With your total budget in mind, the next step is to break it down into specific spending categories. This helps you allocate your funds more effectively and ensures that no single area eats up more than its fair share of your budget.

Here are the most common categories you'll want to consider:

1. **Gifts:** This is typically the largest holiday expense, so it's crucial to define how much you're willing to spend on gifts. Create a list of the people you'll be buying for and allocate a specific amount to each person. Be realistic about what you can afford—sometimes a thoughtful, homemade gift can be more meaningful than an expensive one.
2. **Travel:** If you'll be traveling to see family or friends, this can be a significant expense. Consider the cost of flights, gas, accommodations, and food. Factor in any extra costs, such as pet boarding or house-sitting fees, and set aside enough funds to cover these expenses without exceeding your cap.
3. **Food and Entertaining:** Whether you're hosting holiday dinners or contributing to potlucks, food can be a major budget item. Estimate how much you'll spend on groceries, dining out, or catering, and be mindful of hidden costs, like alcohol, party supplies, or serving utensils.
4. **Decorations:** Many people love decking the halls with festive decorations, but these costs can add up quickly. If you already have decorations, you may not need to spend much this year, but if you plan to buy new ones, set a clear limit on how much you're willing to spend.
5. **Holiday Cards and Wrapping Supplies:** Don't forget to account for smaller expenses like holiday cards, postage, wrapping paper, and gift bags. These seemingly minor costs can add up if not budgeted for.
6. **Miscellaneous:** Leave room in your budget for unexpected expenses that may arise, such as last-minute gifts, charitable donations, or impulse purchases. A small buffer (around 5-10% of your total budget) will give you some flexibility.

Step 4: Prioritize Your Spending

With your categories defined, it's time to prioritize. Not all holiday expenses carry the same weight, and it's important to focus your resources on what truly matters to you. Ask yourself:

- **What Brings the Most Joy?** Reflect on what aspects of the holiday season are most meaningful to you. Is it giving thoughtful gifts? Hosting a memorable gathering? Spending time with loved ones? Prioritize spending in areas that align with your values and contribute to your enjoyment of the season.
- **What Can Be Trimmed?** Look for areas where you can cut back without sacrificing the quality of your holiday experience. Do you really need to buy new decorations, or can you repurpose last year's? Can you swap an expensive trip for a local staycation or a virtual gathering with faraway relatives? Trimming unnecessary expenses will free up funds for what truly matters.
- **Are There Affordable Alternatives?** Consider creative, budget-friendly alternatives to some of your bigger expenses. For example, instead of buying expensive gifts for each family member, suggest a Secret Santa or gift exchange where everyone buys just one present. Homemade gifts, potluck dinners, and DIY decorations can also help you save without compromising the festive spirit.

Step 5: Track Your Spending in Real Time

Once your budget is set, the real challenge begins: sticking to it. One of the most effective ways to stay on track is to monitor your spending in real time. Here's how you can do it:

- **Use a Budgeting App:** There are numerous budgeting apps available that allow you to categorize your expenses, set spending limits, and track your holiday purchases in real time. Apps like Mint, YNAB (You Need a Budget), or even simple spreadsheets can help you keep tabs on where your money is going.
- **Set Alerts for Your Spending:** Many banking apps offer features that allow you to set alerts when you reach certain spending thresholds. These alerts can serve as reminders to rein in your spending when you're approaching your budget limits.
- **Review Your Budget Weekly:** Schedule time each week to review your holiday budget and compare it to your actual spending. This weekly check-in will help you catch any overspending early and make adjustments before it becomes a problem. If you find yourself exceeding your budget in one category, look for ways to offset it by cutting back in another.

Step 6: Prepare for Emergencies and Adjustments

No matter how carefully you plan, unforeseen expenses are bound to arise during the holidays. Whether it's a last-minute trip, an unexpected gift, or a forgotten event, having a contingency plan in place is crucial for keeping your finances in check.

- **Emergency Fund:** Set aside a small emergency fund as part of your holiday budget. This can be 5-10% of your total budget, depending on your circumstances. This fund will give you peace of mind knowing you have a financial cushion for any unexpected costs.
- **Be Willing to Adjust:** Flexibility is key to successfully navigating holiday spending. If you go over budget in one area, be willing to make adjustments elsewhere. For example, if you spend more than anticipated on travel, you might decide to cut back on gifts or forgo new decorations. The goal is to balance your budget without adding unnecessary stress.

Step 7: Plan for Next Year

One of the most effective ways to ease holiday financial stress is to plan ahead for the following year. By preparing in advance, you can avoid the last-minute rush and spread out your expenses over several months, making the holiday season much more manageable.

- **Start a Holiday Savings Fund:** After the holiday season ends, consider setting up a dedicated savings account for next year's holiday expenses. Contribute a small amount each month so that by the time the next holiday season rolls around, you already have a cushion to cover your spending.
- **Shop Sales Throughout the Year:** Take advantage of sales and discounts throughout the year to purchase gifts and decorations at lower prices. By spreading out your purchases, you can avoid the holiday rush and reduce the financial burden in December.

Conclusion

Creating a holiday budget that works is all about preparation, mindfulness, and flexibility. By setting a realistic budget, prioritizing your spending, and tracking your expenses in real time, you can enjoy the holiday season without the stress of financial strain. Remember, the goal isn't to create a picture-perfect holiday based on societal expectations—it's to craft a holiday experience that brings you joy, aligns with your values, and keeps your financial health intact. With the right budget in place, you can enjoy the magic of the season while avoiding the post-holiday financial hangover.

Chapter 3: Mindful Gifting on a Budget

Gift-giving is one of the most cherished traditions during the holiday season, yet it can also be one of the most stressful and financially draining aspects. The pressure to find the perfect gift for everyone on your list can quickly lead to overspending, especially when you feel compelled to match or surpass previous years' gifts. However, mindful gifting allows you to give meaningful, heartfelt presents without breaking the bank. This chapter will explore strategies for low-cost, thoughtful gift-giving that prioritize meaning and connection over price tags.

The Power of Thoughtful, Meaningful Gifts

One of the most important lessons of mindful gifting is recognizing that the value of a gift is not measured by how much it costs, but by the thought, care, and attention behind it. A gift that reflects the recipient's interests, needs, or desires shows more appreciation and effort than a flashy, expensive item that lacks personal meaning. Mindful gifting focuses on the quality of the sentiment rather than the price, making the exchange more special and memorable.

In this chapter, we'll explore how to create personalized, meaningful gifts that show you care, while keeping your budget in check. Whether you're looking to craft DIY presents, give experiences, or make creative use of resources you already have, these strategies will help you embrace a mindful approach to holiday giving.

Strategy 1: Embrace DIY and Homemade Gifts

Homemade gifts are among the most thoughtful and personal presents you can give, and they don't have to cost much. The time and effort you invest in making something by hand demonstrates a level of care and thoughtfulness that a store-bought gift might not convey. Here are some ideas for DIY gifts that are both budget-friendly and meaningful:

- **Baked Goods:** Whether it's cookies, breads, or cakes, homemade treats are always appreciated, especially during the holiday season. Personalize the gift by packaging it in a festive tin or wrapping it with a ribbon. You can even include a handwritten recipe card, making it a gift that keeps on giving.
- **Crafted Gifts:** If you enjoy knitting, crocheting, or sewing, handmade scarves, mittens, or blankets can be both practical and personal. Tailor the colors and patterns to the recipient's tastes, adding a personalized touch.
- **Customized Photo Gifts:** Photos capture memories and emotions, making them perfect for meaningful gifts. Create a personalized photo album or frame a special picture that has significance to the recipient. You can also create DIY calendars with family photos or a photo collage that reflects shared moments.
- **Memory Jars or Scrapbooks:** A memory jar filled with notes about shared experiences or a scrapbook filled with photos and mementos is a deeply personal and sentimental gift. These types of presents show the recipient how much you value your relationship, making them priceless in meaning despite their low cost.

- **Homemade Spa Kits:** Assemble a spa kit with homemade bath bombs, scrubs, and candles. These items are easy and inexpensive to make, and you can tailor the scents and ingredients to the recipient's preferences.
- **Customized Playlist or Mixtape:** While not physical, a carefully curated playlist of songs that remind you of the recipient or reflect their musical tastes can be a highly personalized and thoughtful gift. You can present it with a handwritten note explaining why you chose each song, adding a personal touch to the gesture.

Strategy 2: Give the Gift of Time and Experiences

In today's fast-paced world, many people value experiences and time spent together more than material possessions. Offering your time, skills, or an experience can be one of the most meaningful gifts you can give—and it often costs very little.

- **Experience-Based Gifts:** Instead of giving a physical gift, consider gifting an experience that the recipient will enjoy. Experiences can range from movie nights at home, hiking trips, or DIY wine-and-paint nights. You could offer to host a holiday brunch, cook a special meal, or organize a day of fun activities tailored to the recipient's interests.
- **Personal Coupons or Vouchers:** Create a personalized coupon book offering services or experiences, such as babysitting, pet sitting, helping with household chores, or cooking a homemade dinner. These gestures not only save the recipient time and effort but also offer a way to connect and spend quality time together.
- **Gift of Learning:** If the recipient is interested in learning something new, consider offering an experience that helps them explore their hobbies. You can find free or low-cost online courses, tutorials, or even free local workshops that align with their interests. Gifting a "skill-sharing session" where you teach them something you know—like baking, crafting, or photography—can be a valuable experience.
- **Outdoor or Nature Experiences:** Plan a low-cost outdoor adventure such as a picnic, hike, or stargazing session. These experiences provide opportunities for connection while enjoying nature, and they create lasting memories without any need for material gifts.

Strategy 3: Re-Gift Thoughtfully and Sustainably

Re-gifting, when done mindfully, can be a sustainable way to pass on items you no longer need or use while ensuring they go to someone who will appreciate them. Here's how to re-gift in a way that is thoughtful and considerate:

- **Assess the Item's Value:** Only re-gift items that are new, unused, and in good condition. Make sure that the item is something the recipient would actually enjoy or find useful. Avoid re-gifting items that were clearly given as part of a personalized or sentimental gesture, as this can be seen as impersonal or inconsiderate.
- **Add a Personal Touch:** Even when re-gifting, you can make the item feel more personal by adding a note or packaging it in a unique way. For example, if you're re-gifting a book, include a handwritten note about why you think the recipient will enjoy it.
- **Be Honest (If Appropriate):** In some cases, it's okay to acknowledge that the gift is something you received but never used. This can be framed positively, such as, "I thought of you when I received this, and I think you would enjoy it more than I have."

Strategy 4: Opt for Group Gifts or Secret Santa Exchanges

If you have a large family or friend group, buying individual gifts for everyone can quickly become overwhelming and expensive. Instead, consider organizing a group gift exchange, which allows everyone to receive one thoughtful gift without the burden of buying for multiple people.

- **Secret Santa or White Elephant:** Suggest a Secret Santa exchange where each person draws a name and buys a single gift for one person. Set a reasonable price limit to ensure everyone stays within budget. For a more playful approach, a White Elephant exchange can add fun and creativity to the gift-giving process, especially if you encourage participants to find unique, inexpensive, or humorous gifts.
- **Group Gift for a Loved One:** For more expensive gifts, consider pooling resources with other family members or friends to purchase a larger, more meaningful present. This approach allows you to give something special without each person having to stretch their budget.

Strategy 5: Shop Smart and Maximize Savings

If you do decide to purchase gifts, mindful shopping is essential for staying within your budget. By planning ahead, using sales wisely, and taking advantage of discounts, you can save a significant amount while still finding quality presents.

- **Make a Gift List and Stick to It:** One of the simplest ways to control your holiday spending is by making a list of the people you need to buy for and brainstorming gift ideas for each person before you start shopping. Set a specific spending limit for each gift, and avoid impulse purchases by sticking to your list.
- **Shop Sales and Use Coupons:** Take advantage of seasonal sales, such as Black Friday, Cyber Monday, and holiday promotions. Use coupon codes, cashback apps, or loyalty points to maximize your savings. Many retailers offer significant discounts leading up to the holidays, so plan your shopping strategically to get the best deals.
- **Buy in Bulk for Lower Prices:** If you're buying multiple gifts for friends, coworkers, or neighbors, consider purchasing items in bulk and personalizing them. For example, you can buy a set of candles, mugs, or ornaments, and customize each one with the recipient's name or a personal message.
- **Consider Secondhand or Vintage Gifts:** Vintage or secondhand items can make unique and meaningful gifts, often at a fraction of the cost of new items. Thrift stores, antique shops, and online marketplaces like eBay or Etsy can be treasure troves for finding one-of-a-kind presents that have history and character.

Strategy 6: Focus on the Meaning Behind the Gift

Ultimately, the key to mindful gifting on a budget is shifting your focus from the monetary value of the gift to the meaning and thought behind it. A carefully chosen or handmade gift, no matter how inexpensive, can have a profound impact when it reflects the recipient's personality, interests, and needs.

Here are a few ways to ensure your gifts are meaningful, even on a tight budget:

- **Personalization:** A personalized gift shows the recipient that you've put thought into their unique tastes and preferences. Whether it's a customized piece of jewelry, a monogrammed item, or a gift that reflects their hobbies, adding a personal touch makes the gift feel more special.
- **Thoughtful Presentation:** How you present a gift can enhance its impact. Even a simple or inexpensive gift can feel luxurious when it's wrapped beautifully, accompanied by a heartfelt

card, or presented with a handwritten letter explaining why you chose it. Taking the time to write a personal message or share a memory can elevate the emotional value of the gift.

- **Give with Intention:** Think about the message you want your gift to convey. A mindful gift should reflect your appreciation for the recipient and your desire to enhance their happiness, well-being, or quality of life. When you approach gifting with this mindset, even the simplest presents can carry profound meaning.

Conclusion

Mindful gifting on a budget is not about cutting corners; it's about being intentional, creative, and thoughtful in your approach to gift-giving. By focusing on personal meaning, crafting DIY gifts, offering experiences, and shopping smartly, you can create memorable, heartfelt presents that won't strain your finances. In the end, the most cherished gifts are those that come from the heart, and a well-considered, budget-friendly gift can have more impact than the most expensive item in the store. With these strategies, you can embrace the joy of giving while keeping your holiday spending under control.

Chapter 4: DIY Gift Ideas That Save Money and Time

Gift-giving doesn't have to come with a hefty price tag or drain your time during the busy holiday season. DIY gifts offer an opportunity to create something unique and personal while keeping your budget in check. Handmade gifts not only save money but also show thoughtfulness and effort, making them all the more meaningful. In this chapter, we will explore a variety of easy DIY gift ideas that will help you reduce financial stress while still delighting your loved ones. These ideas are designed to be simple, time-efficient, and customizable to suit the preferences of each recipient.

The Appeal of DIY Gifts

DIY gifts have a special charm because they reflect the time, effort, and care put into their creation. Whether you're making something by hand or putting together a creative kit, these gifts stand out for their personal touch. Recipients often value the sentiment behind the gift more than its monetary value, and a homemade present is a tangible expression of love and thoughtfulness.

Beyond the personal connection, DIY gifts allow you to avoid the commercialization of the holidays. You can create something from materials you already have at home or find inexpensive supplies that still result in a beautiful, thoughtful gift. Let's dive into some DIY gift ideas that are sure to impress without causing financial or time-related stress.

1. Homemade Baked Goods

Food gifts are a classic, and for good reason—they are affordable, customizable, and almost universally appreciated. With some basic baking ingredients and a little creativity, you can whip up delicious treats that double as thoughtful gifts.

- **Cookies or Brownies in a Jar:** One popular and visually appealing gift idea is to layer the dry ingredients for cookies or brownies in a mason jar. Include a handwritten recipe tag with instructions for the recipient to add the wet ingredients and bake. You can personalize the jar with festive ribbons or labels, making it an attractive and practical gift.
- **Homemade Jam or Preserves:** If you enjoy making jams or fruit preserves, these can be a wonderful gift. Package your jam in small, decorative jars and add a personalized label with the flavor and date it was made. These are perfect for breakfast lovers and can be paired with homemade bread or scones for an extra thoughtful touch.
- **Festive Treat Boxes:** Bake an assortment of holiday cookies, fudge, or truffles and package them in festive boxes or tins. Arrange the treats neatly, and add a personalized note for the recipient. This is a great option for coworkers, neighbors, or teachers who will appreciate a sweet treat during the holidays.

2. DIY Spa Kits

Everyone loves a little pampering, and DIY spa kits are a great way to offer relaxation without the high cost of commercial products. With a few ingredients, you can create luxurious bath and beauty products that make thoughtful and practical gifts.

- **Homemade Bath Bombs:** Bath bombs are easy to make and can be customized with different colors, scents, and shapes. Basic ingredients like baking soda, citric acid, Epsom salts, and essential oils are inexpensive and can be found at most stores. Mold the bath bombs into festive shapes, wrap them in cellophane, and tie them with a ribbon for a polished look.
- **Sugar Scrubs or Salt Scrubs:** A DIY sugar or salt scrub is a fantastic gift that can be made in just a few minutes. Combine sugar or salt with coconut oil and your choice of essential oils for scent. Package the scrub in a small jar with a label, and include a note on how to use it. Scrubs are perfect for exfoliating and moisturizing skin, making them a thoughtful, spa-like gift.
- **Homemade Candles:** Candle-making kits are affordable and provide everything you need to create custom-scented candles. You can experiment with different essential oils, waxes, and containers to create unique candles tailored to the recipient's preferences. Mason jars, vintage teacups, or small tins make beautiful candle containers.

3. Personalized Photo Gifts

Photos capture special memories, and turning them into a personalized gift can bring joy and nostalgia to the recipient. With just a few supplies, you can transform simple photos into meaningful keepsakes.

- **Framed Photos with a Personal Touch:** Find a frame that suits the recipient's style and insert a meaningful photo, such as a favorite family portrait, vacation snapshot, or sentimental moment. Add a decorative touch by embellishing the frame with paint, glitter, or small charms that reflect the recipient's personality.
- **DIY Photo Calendar:** Create a custom calendar using your favorite photos for each month. You can design this on your computer and print it out, or simply arrange printed photos in a calendar format. Add birthdays, anniversaries, and other important dates for a personalized touch.
- **Photo Coasters:** Transform favorite photos into practical and decorative coasters. Print small photos and use decoupage glue to adhere them to ceramic tiles or wooden coasters. Seal the top with a waterproof varnish to protect the photos. This gift is perfect for someone who loves to host or enjoys home décor.

4. Memory Jars or Keepsake Boxes

A memory jar or keepsake box is a heartfelt gift that captures special moments and memories shared with the recipient. These gifts are simple to create and deeply meaningful.

- **Memory Jar:** Fill a mason jar with small notes, each containing a cherished memory, inspirational quote, or reason why you appreciate the recipient. You can decorate the jar with ribbons, paint, or stickers to make it more festive. The recipient can pull out a note whenever they need a reminder of your love and support, making it a gift that keeps on giving throughout the year.
- **Keepsake Box:** Buy or make a small wooden box and decorate it with paint, decoupage, or other embellishments. Inside, place mementos like ticket stubs, photos, or small trinkets that represent shared experiences or milestones. You can also include a heartfelt letter explaining the significance of each item, making the box a treasured keepsake.

5. DIY Kitchen Gifts

For those who love to cook or entertain, DIY kitchen gifts are both practical and thoughtful. These gifts are easy to make and can be used throughout the year, ensuring that the recipient will think of you every time they cook.

- **Flavored Oils or Vinegars:** Create your own flavored oils or vinegars by infusing olive oil or vinegar with herbs, garlic, or citrus peels. Pour the infused oil or vinegar into decorative bottles and label them with the flavor and suggested uses. These make excellent gifts for food lovers or home chefs.
- **Homemade Spice Blends:** Blend a variety of spices to create custom seasoning mixes, such as taco seasoning, curry powder, or barbecue rub. Package the spice blends in small jars with labels that list the ingredients and suggested recipes. This is a great gift for someone who enjoys experimenting with flavors in the kitchen.
- **Baking Mixes in a Jar:** Similar to cookie mixes, you can create jars of baking mixes for pancakes, muffins, or bread. Layer the dry ingredients in a mason jar, and attach a recipe card with instructions for the recipient to add the wet ingredients and bake. These jars are not only practical but also visually appealing and festive.

6. Handmade Jewelry and Accessories

Handmade jewelry and accessories are thoughtful gifts that can be customized to the recipient's style. With a few basic supplies, you can create beautiful, one-of-a-kind pieces that show your care and attention to detail.

- **Beaded Bracelets or Necklaces:** Purchase beads and string to create custom bracelets or necklaces. You can use colors, patterns, or charms that have special meaning to the recipient, making the jewelry more personal. Package the finished pieces in a small gift box or pouch for a polished presentation.
- **Hand-Knitted or Crocheted Items:** If you enjoy knitting or crocheting, handmade scarves, hats, or mittens are wonderful gifts that will keep your loved ones warm throughout the winter. Choose soft, high-quality yarn in the recipient's favorite colors and create something that is both beautiful and functional.
- **Custom Keychains or Bag Charms:** Using simple materials like leather, beads, or embroidery thread, you can make personalized keychains or bag charms. Add the recipient's initials, favorite colors, or small charms that reflect their interests. These are quick and easy to make, yet highly customizable and meaningful.

7. DIY Kits and Creative Baskets

DIY kits are a fun and interactive gift idea that encourages the recipient to try something new or enjoy a hands-on experience. These kits can be tailored to the recipient's interests and assembled with affordable supplies.

- **Hot Chocolate Kit:** Create a cozy hot chocolate kit by filling a jar or basket with hot cocoa mix, mini marshmallows, candy canes, and a festive mug. You can also include toppings like chocolate chips or caramel sauce for an extra-special touch. This is a great gift for anyone who enjoys a warm drink on a cold winter day.
- **Craft or Art Kit:** For the creative person in your life, assemble a craft kit with supplies like paints, brushes, yarn, or sketchpads. Include instructions for a simple project or leave it open-ended for the recipient to explore their creativity. These kits encourage relaxation and self-expression, making them a thoughtful and engaging gift.
- **DIY S'mores Kit:** Packaged in a cute box or basket, a DIY s'mores kit can include graham crackers, marshmallows, and chocolate bars, along with skewers for roasting. This is a fun and interactive gift that can be enjoyed around a fireplace or campfire.

Conclusion

DIY gifts offer a wonderful way to reduce financial stress while creating thoughtful, heartfelt presents for your loved ones. From homemade treats to personalized crafts, the key to successful DIY gifting is focusing on the recipient's preferences and creating something meaningful with your time and effort. These gifts show that you've put thought into the process, making them all the more special. By embracing the art of DIY gift-making, you can enjoy a holiday season filled with creativity, joy, and connection—without the financial burden that often accompanies traditional gift-giving.

Chapter 5: Avoiding Holiday Debt Traps

The holiday season is a time of joy, family gatherings, and celebration, but it's also a time when many people fall into the trap of overspending. The combination of gift-giving, holiday travel, parties, and year-end sales can push even the most disciplined shoppers into financial trouble. For those who rely heavily on credit cards to fund their holiday activities, this can lead to a financial hangover in the new year, marked by growing debt and the stress of repayment. In this chapter, we will explore strategies to prevent holiday debt, avoid excessive credit card use, and ensure that you start the new year on sound financial footing.

The Allure and Risk of Holiday Spending

The holidays are a perfect storm for overspending. There's the emotional pressure to buy the perfect gifts, attend every holiday party, and make travel plans to see loved ones. On top of that, retailers push hard with sales, promotions, and marketing campaigns designed to get you to spend more. It's easy to fall into the trap of thinking, "I'll just put this on my credit card and pay it off later." However, this kind of thinking often leads to spending beyond your means, resulting in a financial hangover that can last long after the holiday decorations are put away.

Credit card debt, with its high interest rates, can quickly spiral out of control if not managed properly. Even if you have every intention of paying off your balance in January, unexpected expenses or a larger-than-expected bill can leave you carrying debt for months or even years. The key to avoiding this debt trap is to be proactive and intentional with your holiday spending.

Tip 1: Create a Comprehensive Holiday Budget

The best way to avoid holiday debt is to plan ahead by creating a comprehensive budget for all your holiday expenses. A clear budget gives you a roadmap for your spending, helping you stay within your means and avoid impulse purchases.

- **Start by Assessing Your Finances:** Before you set a budget, take a look at your current financial situation. How much disposable income do you have after covering essential expenses like rent, utilities, groceries, and debt payments? Make sure your holiday spending doesn't interfere with your ability to meet these ongoing obligations.
- **List All Potential Holiday Expenses:** Holiday expenses go beyond gifts. Make sure you account for travel costs, decorations, food, holiday cards, party expenses, and charitable donations. Be specific about each category and assign a spending limit to each. This will help you understand where your money is going and identify areas where you might need to cut back.
- **Set Spending Limits for Gifts:** The most significant expense for many people during the holidays is gifts. Make a list of everyone you plan to buy gifts for and set a spending limit for each person. Be realistic about what you can afford and don't feel pressured to spend beyond your means. If you find that your gift list is too long for your budget, consider alternatives such as homemade gifts, experiences, or group gifts.

- **Plan for Unexpected Expenses:** It's easy to forget about small expenses like wrapping paper, postage for holiday cards, or extra ingredients for a holiday meal. Set aside a portion of your budget (5-10%) for unexpected costs so that you're not caught off guard.
- **Stick to Your Budget:** Once your budget is set, the challenge is sticking to it. Use a budgeting app, a spreadsheet, or even an old-fashioned notebook to track your expenses in real time. Review your spending regularly to make sure you're staying on track. If you overspend in one category, look for ways to cut back in another.

Tip 2: Use Cash or Debit Instead of Credit Cards

One of the simplest ways to avoid holiday debt is to limit or completely avoid using credit cards. Paying with cash or debit helps you stay within your budget because you can only spend what you have.

- **Set a Cash Budget for Each Category:** If you're concerned about overspending, withdraw cash for each category of your holiday budget. For example, if you've allocated $200 for gifts, withdraw that amount and only spend from your cash envelope. Once the cash is gone, you know you've hit your limit. Using physical cash makes it harder to overspend compared to swiping a credit card.
- **Use Debit Cards for Online Shopping:** If you prefer the convenience of online shopping, use a debit card instead of a credit card. This way, you're still limited to the money in your account, reducing the risk of accumulating debt. Many banks now offer virtual debit cards, which can also add a layer of security for online transactions.
- **Avoid Store Credit Cards:** Many retailers offer store credit cards with enticing promotions, such as discounts on your first purchase or interest-free periods. However, these cards often come with high interest rates after the promotion ends, and it's easy to lose track of how much you've spent. Avoid the temptation of signing up for new credit cards during the holidays.

Tip 3: Be Cautious with Buy Now, Pay Later Programs

Buy Now, Pay Later (BNPL) programs have become increasingly popular, offering shoppers the ability to spread out payments over several weeks or months without paying interest—at least at first glance. While BNPL options can be helpful for managing cash flow, they can also lead to overspending and debt if used recklessly.

- **Understand the Terms:** Many BNPL programs advertise "no interest" payment plans, but they often come with fees for missed or late payments. Be sure to read the fine print and understand the repayment terms before committing. If you miss a payment, you may be hit with fees or even higher interest rates than a standard credit card.
- **Limit BNPL Use:** While it may be tempting to use BNPL for multiple purchases, doing so can make it difficult to keep track of what you owe. Stick to using BNPL for larger, planned purchases, and make sure you have the funds to cover the installments when they come due.

- **Create a Repayment Plan:** If you use BNPL, treat it as a debt that needs to be repaid immediately. Set aside money from your budget to cover the payments and avoid taking on additional BNPL obligations until your current plan is paid off.

Tip 4: Avoid Impulse Buying and Emotional Spending

The holiday season is filled with opportunities to spend impulsively, whether it's grabbing an extra gift at the checkout line or taking advantage of a last-minute sale. Emotional spending, fueled by the desire to create perfect holiday moments, can also push you to overspend.

- **Make a Shopping List and Stick to It:** Before you start shopping, create a detailed list of the gifts you plan to buy and the maximum amount you're willing to spend on each. Whether you're shopping online or in stores, stick to your list and avoid the temptation to add extra items to your cart.
- **Shop with a Purpose:** To avoid impulse purchases, go shopping only when you know exactly what you're looking for. If you're browsing without a plan, it's easy to get distracted by sales and promotions, leading to overspending.
- **Take Advantage of Sales Thoughtfully:** Sales like Black Friday and Cyber Monday can offer significant discounts, but only if you've planned your purchases in advance. Don't buy something just because it's on sale—ask yourself if it fits within your budget and whether it's truly needed. Use price comparison tools to ensure you're getting the best deal.
- **Delay Gratification:** If you see something you want to buy but it's not on your list, give yourself a cooling-off period. Wait 24 hours before making the purchase to determine whether it's a necessary expense or an impulse buy. More often than not, the initial urge to buy will fade, helping you avoid unnecessary spending.

Tip 5: Focus on Low-Cost, Meaningful Gifts

You don't need to spend a lot of money to give thoughtful and meaningful gifts. By focusing on creativity and personalization, you can give gifts that have a significant emotional impact without a hefty price tag.

- **DIY Gifts:** Handmade gifts, such as baked goods, crafts, or personalized photo albums, can be both meaningful and affordable. In Chapter 4, we explore a variety of easy DIY gift ideas that can save money and time while still delighting recipients.
- **Experiential Gifts:** Instead of physical items, consider giving experiences. For example, you could plan a special outing, offer to cook a meal, or create a homemade coupon for an experience you can share together. These types of gifts create memories that often hold more value than material possessions.
- **Group Gifts:** If you're buying gifts for a family or a couple, consider pooling your resources with other family members to purchase a single, higher-quality gift. This reduces your individual cost while still allowing the recipient to enjoy something special.

- **Set Up Gift Exchanges:** For large families or groups of friends, suggest organizing a Secret Santa or White Elephant gift exchange. This way, each person only needs to buy one gift instead of multiple, making it easier to stay within your budget.

Tip 6: Create a Plan to Pay Off Any Holiday Debt

Even with the best planning, you may still end up using your credit card for some holiday expenses. The key to avoiding long-term financial stress is to create a plan to pay off any holiday debt as quickly as possible.

- **Prioritize High-Interest Debt:** If you have balances on multiple credit cards, focus on paying off the one with the highest interest rate first. This will reduce the amount of interest you pay over time and help you become debt-free faster.
- **Use the Debt Snowball or Debt Avalanche Method:** There are two popular methods for paying down debt—the debt snowball and the debt avalanche. The debt snowball method involves paying off your smallest debt first, which can give you a psychological boost and momentum as you move on to larger debts. The debt avalanche method focuses on paying off high-interest debts first, saving you more money in the long run. Choose the approach that works best for you.
- **Make Extra Payments:** If possible, make extra payments toward your holiday debt to reduce your balance more quickly. Even small amounts, such as putting an extra $50 toward your balance each month, can make a significant difference over time.
- **Set a Repayment Deadline:** Don't let holiday debt linger into the following year. Set a clear deadline for when you plan to have your debt paid off, and stick to it. The sooner you pay off your holiday debt, the less interest you'll owe and the more financially secure you'll feel moving forward.

Conclusion

Avoiding holiday debt traps requires careful planning, discipline, and a shift in mindset. By creating a realistic budget, using cash or debit instead of credit, and focusing on thoughtful, low-cost gifts, you can enjoy the holiday season without the financial hangover. Remember, the spirit of the holidays is about connection, gratitude, and giving—not about going into debt to impress others. By following these tips, you can celebrate the holidays joyfully and start the new year on solid financial footing.

Chapter 6: Holiday Spending Hacks

The holiday season is often synonymous with increased spending on gifts, travel, meals, and festive activities. While it's easy to feel overwhelmed by the costs associated with the holidays, there are plenty of smart ways to reduce expenses without sacrificing the joy and meaning of the season. In this chapter, we'll explore a wide range of clever holiday spending hacks to help you save money on travel, shopping, and meals. By implementing these strategies, you'll be able to enjoy the holiday season while staying financially secure and stress-free.

Travel Hacks: Saving on Holiday Journeys

For many, the holiday season involves traveling to visit friends and family, but holiday travel can be notoriously expensive. The combination of high demand, limited availability, and last-minute planning often leads to elevated airfare, hotel, and rental car prices. Here are some hacks to help you save on holiday travel, whether you're flying, driving, or staying overnight.

1. Book Early or Take Advantage of Last-Minute Deals

Timing is everything when it comes to booking holiday travel. You can save significantly by either booking your flights or accommodations early or keeping an eye out for last-minute deals.

- **Book Early:** Start researching flights and accommodations months in advance, as prices tend to increase as the holidays approach. Set up fare alerts using tools like Google Flights, Hopper, or Skyscanner to track price changes. Booking early not only helps you lock in lower prices but also gives you more options for flight times and accommodations.
- **Last-Minute Deals:** If you have flexible travel dates or are open to spontaneous plans, you can take advantage of last-minute deals. Airlines and hotels often offer deep discounts on unsold seats or rooms as the travel date nears. Websites and apps like LastMinute.com, Hotel-Tonight, and Priceline can help you find these deals.

2. Fly on Off-Peak Days

Flight prices vary significantly depending on the day of the week you travel. Flying on less popular travel days can lead to substantial savings.

- **Avoid Peak Travel Days:** The days immediately before and after major holidays, such as Christmas Eve, Christmas Day, and New Year's Eve, tend to be the most expensive days to fly. If possible, schedule your flights for off-peak days, such as the Tuesday or Wednesday before or after a holiday. Flying early in the morning or late at night can also result in cheaper fares.
- **Extend Your Stay:** Consider flying a few days before or after the peak travel period to save on flights. If your schedule allows, staying longer can not only give you more time with loved ones but also help you avoid the most expensive travel dates.

3. Use Points and Miles

If you've accumulated frequent flyer miles, hotel points, or credit card rewards, the holiday season is the perfect time to cash them in. Many airlines and credit cards offer bonus rewards during the holidays, making it easier to cover travel expenses without dipping into your wallet.

- **Book Flights with Miles:** Use your frequent flyer miles to book holiday flights. Be sure to book early, as award seats tend to fill up quickly during peak travel periods. If you don't have enough miles for a full round-trip ticket, you can often use miles to cover one leg of the journey or reduce the cost of your fare.
- **Use Credit Card Rewards for Travel:** Many credit cards offer travel rewards that can be redeemed for flights, hotels, or rental cars. Check your card's rewards program to see if you can use points to offset your holiday travel expenses.

4. Consider Alternative Airports and Transport

Sometimes a little flexibility can go a long way when it comes to saving on travel. Consider alternative airports or modes of transportation to reduce costs.

- **Fly Into or Out of Alternate Airports:** Larger cities often have multiple airports, and flying into or out of a smaller or less busy airport can lead to cheaper fares. Compare prices across different airports within driving distance, and factor in the cost of transportation to and from the airport.
- **Consider Other Modes of Travel:** Depending on the distance you need to travel, driving or taking a train or bus might be more cost-effective than flying. Look into carpooling options, ridesharing apps, or bus services like Megabus and Greyhound for affordable alternatives to air travel.

5. Save on Accommodation

Accommodations can be one of the most significant travel expenses during the holidays, but there are ways to cut costs without sacrificing comfort.

- **Stay with Friends or Family:** If possible, stay with friends or family during your holiday travels. Not only will this save you the cost of a hotel, but it also allows for more quality time together. If staying with family isn't an option, consider renting an Airbnb or vacation rental with a group to split the cost.
- **Look for Free or Discounted Lodging Options:** Many hotels offer discounts for early bookings or members of loyalty programs. Websites like Hotels.com and Booking.com frequently have special deals, and apps like Couchsurfing allow you to stay with locals for free.

Shopping Hacks: Getting the Best Deals on Holiday Gifts

Holiday gift-giving can quickly add up, but with a few smart shopping strategies, you can find meaningful gifts without blowing your budget.

1. Make a Shopping List and Set a Budget

One of the simplest yet most effective ways to save money on holiday shopping is to create a detailed list of the gifts you need to buy and set a budget for each.

- **Prioritize Your Gift List:** Start by listing everyone you plan to buy gifts for and assigning a spending limit for each person. If your list feels too long, consider trimming it down by opting for group gifts or focusing on your closest friends and family members.
- **Stick to Your Budget:** Once you've set your gift budget, it's essential to stick to it. Avoid impulse purchases by keeping your shopping list on hand and crossing off items as you buy them.

2. Take Advantage of Black Friday, Cyber Monday, and Holiday Sales

The holiday season is full of sales, from Black Friday and Cyber Monday to ongoing deals throughout December. Shopping during these sales can help you score significant discounts.

- **Plan Your Purchases Around Sales:** Start by researching the items on your gift list to see when and where they're likely to go on sale. Use price tracking tools like Honey, Camel-CamelCamel, or RetailMeNot to monitor price drops and ensure you're getting the best deal.
- **Shop Early:** While Black Friday and Cyber Monday are traditionally the biggest sale days, many retailers now offer early access to discounts or extend their sales throughout the holiday season. Shopping early can help you avoid price hikes closer to the holidays and ensure that items don't sell out.
- **Use Coupons and Cashback Offers:** Take advantage of coupons and cashback offers to save even more. Websites and browser extensions like Rakuten, Ibotta, and Swagbucks offer cashback on purchases from major retailers. You can also search for online coupon codes on sites like RetailMeNot and Honey.

3. Buy in Bulk

Buying in bulk can be a cost-effective way to save on gifts, especially if you need to purchase multiple presents for coworkers, neighbors, or extended family.

- **Buy Gift Sets or Multipacks:** Many retailers offer holiday gift sets or multipacks at discounted prices. You can buy a set and divide it into individual gifts, or use the items to create custom gift baskets for multiple recipients.
- **Purchase Everyday Items in Bulk:** Stocking up on holiday essentials like wrapping paper, greeting cards, or decorations at warehouse stores like Costco or Sam's Club can save you

money in the long run. Consider buying these items in bulk and using them throughout the holiday season or even saving them for next year.

4. Consider Secondhand or Thrifted Gifts

Secondhand or thrifted gifts are an excellent option for both your wallet and the environment. You can find unique, high-quality items at a fraction of the cost of buying new.

- **Shop at Thrift Stores and Consignment Shops:** Many thrift stores and consignment shops have an abundance of gently used or even new items that make perfect gifts. Look for unique clothing, home décor, or vintage items that the recipient would love.
- **Buy Refurbished or Pre-Owned Electronics:** If you're shopping for electronics, consider buying refurbished or pre-owned items. Many retailers, including Apple, Amazon, and Best Buy, offer certified refurbished products that are significantly discounted and come with warranties.

5. Opt for DIY Gifts

DIY gifts can be a thoughtful and budget-friendly way to show someone you care. These gifts often carry more sentimental value because they're handmade, personalized, and show that you put effort into the creation.

- **Make Baked Goods or Treats:** Holiday cookies, homemade jams, or festive bread loaves are always appreciated. Package your homemade treats in decorative boxes or tins for a personal touch.
- **Create Personalized Gift Baskets:** You can put together a thoughtful and inexpensive gift basket by filling it with small, themed items like snacks, candles, or DIY beauty products. Tailor the contents to the recipient's interests, such as a "movie night" basket with popcorn, candy, and a DVD, or a "spa day" basket with homemade bath bombs and scrubs.

Meal Hacks: Budget-Friendly Holiday Feasts

Holiday meals are often a big part of the celebration, but feeding a large group can quickly become expensive. With a few smart strategies, you can host a delicious and memorable meal without overspending.

1. Plan Your Menu Around Sales and Seasonal Ingredients

When planning your holiday menu, focus on ingredients that are in season or on sale. Seasonal produce is often fresher and cheaper, while sale items can help you save on expensive cuts of meat or specialty ingredients.

- **Shop for Sales and Stock Up Early:** Many grocery stores offer discounts on holiday staples like turkey, ham, or canned goods in the weeks leading up to the holidays. Start buying non-perishable items early, and keep an eye out for sales on meat or other expensive ingredients that you can freeze and store until the holiday meal.
- **Use Seasonal and Affordable Ingredients:** Base your menu on seasonal produce like root vegetables, squash, and citrus fruits, which are often cheaper in the winter months. These ingredients can be used to create hearty side dishes and desserts without breaking the bank.

2. Host a Potluck

If you're hosting a holiday meal, consider making it a potluck to share the cost and effort with your guests.

- **Assign Dishes to Guests:** Coordinate with your guests to determine who will bring appetizers, side dishes, desserts, or drinks. This allows everyone to contribute, reduces your overall cost, and creates a diverse, communal meal.
- **Provide the Main Dish:** As the host, you can focus on preparing the main dish, such as a roast or turkey, while your guests bring the sides and desserts. This spreads out the cost and work, making the meal more affordable for everyone.

3. Limit Alcohol or Offer BYOB

Alcohol can be one of the most expensive parts of a holiday meal, but there are ways to manage costs without eliminating it entirely.

- **Opt for Affordable Wine or Spirits:** You don't need to splurge on expensive wine or spirits for your holiday meal. Many affordable options taste just as good and can be purchased in bulk for a discount.
- **Offer a Signature Drink:** Instead of providing a full bar, offer a signature holiday cocktail or punch. This limits the amount of alcohol you need to buy while still adding a festive touch to your meal.
- **Make It BYOB:** If you know your guests enjoy wine or cocktails, encourage them to bring a bottle to share. This can help reduce the overall cost of alcohol while ensuring there's a variety of drinks to enjoy.

4. Make Use of Leftovers

Holiday leftovers can be a valuable resource, allowing you to stretch your food budget further into the week.

- **Plan for Leftovers:** When cooking your holiday meal, plan for leftovers by making slightly larger portions of dishes that can be easily reheated or repurposed. For example, leftover turkey can be used in soups, sandwiches, or casseroles.
- **Send Guests Home with Leftovers:** If you have more food than you can reasonably consume, send your guests home with leftover containers. This not only reduces food waste but also ensures that everyone enjoys the meal for days to come.

Conclusion

The holiday season doesn't have to be a financial burden. By implementing these clever holiday spending hacks, you can enjoy festive meals, thoughtful gifts, and memorable travels without breaking the bank. Whether it's taking advantage of travel deals, shopping smart during sales, or hosting a budget-friendly holiday meal, these strategies will help you make the most of your holiday celebrations while staying financially secure. Remember, the true spirit of the holidays lies in connection, gratitude, and generosity—not in how much money you spend.

Part 2: Family and Relationship Dynamics

Chapter 7: Navigating Family Conflicts

The holiday season is a time for togetherness, but for many families, it can also be a time when tensions run high. As family members gather, unresolved conflicts, differing opinions, and clashing personalities can turn what should be joyful reunions into stressful experiences. Navigating family conflicts during the holidays requires patience, diplomacy, and intentional strategies to avoid holiday arguments and maintain harmony.

This chapter will explore effective techniques for managing difficult family members, defusing tension, and fostering a more peaceful, enjoyable holiday experience. By understanding how to handle challenging situations with grace, you can minimize conflict and focus on the positive aspects of your family gatherings.

Why Family Conflicts Arise During the Holidays

Family conflicts can be triggered by a variety of factors, and the holidays tend to amplify these tensions. Understanding why conflicts arise can help you prepare for and prevent them.

1. Heightened Expectations

The holidays come with an expectation of harmony, joy, and perfection. Many people put pressure on themselves and others to create the "perfect" holiday experience, which can lead to frustration when things don't go as planned. Unrealistic expectations of how family members should behave, participate, or contribute can result in disappointment and conflict.

2. Unresolved Past Issues

For many families, unresolved emotional baggage and old grievances resurface during holiday gatherings. Whether it's sibling rivalry, parent-child tensions, or long-standing disagreements, these underlying issues can lead to arguments when family members are together for an extended period.

3. Clashing Personalities and Values

Families are made up of diverse individuals with different personalities, political views, life choices, and communication styles. These differences can be a source of conflict, especially when family members feel misunderstood or disrespected by others.

4. Stress and Fatigue

The holiday season is inherently stressful. Financial pressures, busy schedules, and travel can leave people feeling exhausted and irritable, making them more susceptible to arguments. Additionally, the expectation to spend extended periods of time with family members can increase tension, especially when personalities clash.

5. Alcohol Consumption

Holiday celebrations often include alcohol, which can lower inhibitions and escalate tensions. While a glass of wine might help relax the atmosphere, excessive alcohol consumption can impair judgment, leading to confrontations and emotional outbursts.

Strategies for Preventing and Managing Family Conflicts

To navigate family conflicts during the holidays, it's essential to approach family gatherings with intentionality and a plan. These techniques will help you manage difficult family members, defuse tension, and avoid holiday arguments.

1. Set Realistic Expectations

The holidays are rarely perfect, and expecting everything to go smoothly can set you up for disappointment. Instead of aiming for a flawless family gathering, set realistic expectations for the event and your family members.

- **Let Go of Perfection:** Accept that there may be moments of tension or disagreement, and that's okay. Focus on enjoying the positive aspects of the gathering rather than getting caught up in making everything perfect.
- **Manage Your Emotional Expectations:** If you know certain family members tend to trigger you or behave in ways that irritate you, manage your emotional expectations before the event. Acknowledge that their behavior is unlikely to change overnight and prepare yourself to respond calmly.
- **Be Kind to Yourself:** Family gatherings can be emotionally exhausting, and it's important to give yourself permission to step away when you need a break. Don't feel obligated to meet everyone's expectations or engage in every conversation.

2. Establish Boundaries

Setting healthy boundaries with family members is crucial for maintaining peace and protecting your emotional well-being during the holidays. Boundaries can help you avoid being pulled into conflicts or situations that make you uncomfortable.

- **Define Your Limits:** Before the holiday gathering, identify your personal boundaries. This might include limits on the types of conversations you're willing to engage in (such as avoiding politics or family drama) or how much time you're willing to spend at the event.
- **Communicate Boundaries Clearly:** It's important to communicate your boundaries to family members respectfully. For example, if you want to avoid a sensitive topic, you could say, "I'd prefer not to talk about politics today. Let's focus on enjoying the holiday."
- **Exit Strategies:** If a conversation becomes too heated or uncomfortable, have an exit strategy in place. Excuse yourself to go to the bathroom, help in the kitchen, or step outside for some fresh air. Taking a break from a tense situation can help you regain your composure and avoid saying something in the heat of the moment.

3. Practice Active Listening and Empathy

One of the most effective ways to navigate family conflicts is by practicing active listening and empathy. When people feel heard and understood, they are less likely to become defensive or argumentative.

- **Listen Without Interrupting:** If a family member is expressing their feelings or opinions, let them speak without interrupting. Even if you disagree, showing that you're listening and taking their perspective seriously can defuse potential conflict.
- **Validate Their Feelings:** Empathy doesn't mean you have to agree with everything a family member says, but it does mean acknowledging their feelings. You can say something like, "I understand you're upset," or "I see how this situation is frustrating for you." This can go a long way in reducing defensiveness and making the conversation more constructive.
- **Keep Calm in Heated Conversations:** If a conversation starts to get heated, focus on staying calm. Take deep breaths and speak in a measured tone. If you remain calm, you can help de-escalate the situation and prevent it from turning into a full-blown argument.

4. Agree to Disagree

One of the most common sources of conflict during the holidays is differing opinions, whether they're about politics, religion, or lifestyle choices. Trying to convince a family member to change their views or forcing them to see your perspective often leads to frustration and arguments. In these situations, it's better to agree to disagree.

- **Respect Differences:** Accept that not everyone in your family will share your opinions or values, and that's okay. Instead of trying to win an argument, focus on respecting each other's differences and moving on from contentious topics.
- **Change the Subject:** If a conversation is heading into dangerous territory, politely change the subject to something more neutral. You could steer the conversation toward shared interests, holiday traditions, or lighthearted topics like movies or travel plans.
- **Know When to Walk Away:** If a disagreement is becoming unproductive or overly emotional, it's okay to walk away from the conversation. You can say something like, "Let's agree to disagree," or, "I don't think this is the best time to discuss this," and move on to another topic or activity.

5. Use Humor to Diffuse Tension

Humor can be a powerful tool for diffusing tension and lightening the mood during difficult family interactions. By introducing a bit of lightheartedness, you can break the cycle of escalating conflict.

- **Make a Joke or Laugh It Off:** If a conversation starts to get tense, a well-placed joke or a bit of self-deprecating humor can help ease the tension. For example, if a family member criticizes your life choices, you could respond with something like, "Well, at least I didn't become a lion tamer!" The goal is to inject levity, not mock or belittle anyone.
- **Steer the Conversation Toward Shared Joys:** If things are getting heated, use humor to steer the conversation toward happy memories or family traditions. For example, "Remember when Uncle Joe tried to deep-fry the turkey and almost burned down the garage?" can be a way to shift the focus back to shared family experiences.

6. Manage Alcohol Consumption

Alcohol can exacerbate family conflicts by lowering inhibitions and making people more prone to emotional outbursts. If alcohol is part of your family's holiday celebration, managing consumption can help prevent conflicts from escalating.

- **Drink in Moderation:** If you choose to drink, pace yourself and keep your consumption moderate. Drinking slowly and alternating between alcoholic and non-alcoholic beverages can help you stay clear-headed throughout the gathering.
- **Encourage Non-Alcoholic Options:** Provide plenty of non-alcoholic beverages for guests, and encourage everyone to take it easy with the alcohol. You could offer festive mocktails or sparkling water as an alternative to alcoholic drinks.
- **Avoid Sensitive Topics When Drinking:** Alcohol can make it more difficult to keep emotions in check, so if alcohol is involved, be especially mindful of avoiding sensitive or controversial topics that could lead to arguments.

7. Focus on Gratitude and Positivity

During the holidays, it's easy to get caught up in the stress of family gatherings and lose sight of what the season is all about—gratitude, connection, and joy. Focusing on the positive aspects of the holiday can help you navigate difficult family dynamics and avoid conflict.

- **Practice Gratitude:** Take time to reflect on the things you're grateful for during the holiday season, whether it's your health, your family, or the simple joy of being together. Expressing gratitude can help shift your mindset from focusing on what's wrong to appreciating what's right.
- **Lead by Example:** If you want to avoid conflict, set a positive tone by being kind, patient, and understanding with your family members. Your behavior can influence others, and by remaining calm and positive, you can encourage a more peaceful environment.

- **Plan Activities that Foster Togetherness:** Organize holiday activities that focus on fun and connection rather than conversation. Playing a board game, watching a holiday movie, or going for a family walk can create shared experiences that help reduce tension and promote bonding.

8. Prepare for Post-Gathering Self-Care

Even if you successfully navigate family conflicts during the holidays, spending extended time with family can be emotionally draining. It's important to prioritize self-care once the gathering is over.

- **Schedule Alone Time:** After the holiday event, give yourself some time to recharge. Whether it's taking a quiet walk, reading a book, or simply resting, having some alone time will help you decompress and reflect on the positive aspects of the gathering.
- **Talk It Out:** If family tensions linger, consider talking things over with a trusted friend or therapist. Sometimes, simply expressing your feelings can help you process the experience and move on.
- **Release Resentments:** The holidays are an opportunity to practice forgiveness and release resentments that may have built up over time. While this doesn't mean tolerating harmful behavior, it does mean letting go of minor annoyances and focusing on maintaining inner peace.

Conclusion

Navigating family conflicts during the holidays can be challenging, but with the right mindset and strategies, it's possible to manage difficult situations and maintain harmony. By setting realistic expectations, establishing boundaries, practicing active listening, and focusing on gratitude, you can reduce tension and avoid unnecessary arguments. Remember that the true spirit of the holidays lies in connection, love, and understanding, and with a little patience and effort, you can create a more peaceful, enjoyable holiday experience for yourself and your family.

Chapter 8: Setting Boundaries with Family and Friends

The holiday season is often seen as a time to come together with loved ones, celebrate traditions, and create lasting memories. However, the demands and expectations of family and friends during this time can sometimes feel overwhelming. From attending multiple holiday gatherings to buying gifts for an extended network of people, the holiday season can strain your mental well-being if you don't set clear boundaries. Learning how to say "no" politely and assertively is essential for protecting your mental health, maintaining balance, and avoiding burnout.

In this chapter, we will explore how to establish and communicate healthy boundaries with family and friends during the holiday season. You'll discover strategies for gracefully declining invitations, managing gift-giving expectations, and navigating tricky emotional dynamics so that you can enjoy the holidays without sacrificing your peace of mind.

The Importance of Setting Boundaries During the Holidays

The holiday season often brings increased pressure to say "yes" to every invitation, request, and tradition. While it's natural to want to make the people around you happy, trying to please everyone can leave you feeling exhausted, stressed, and resentful. Setting boundaries is not about being selfish or unkind—it's about protecting your emotional and mental well-being so that you can fully engage with the holiday spirit in a way that feels healthy and sustainable.

1. Avoiding Overcommitment

One of the most common challenges during the holidays is the sheer number of events, gatherings, and obligations that arise. From office parties to family dinners and gift exchanges, it's easy to overcommit, leaving little time for yourself. By setting boundaries, you can avoid spreading yourself too thin and ensure that you're fully present at the events that truly matter.

2. Preserving Mental and Emotional Health

Holidays can be emotionally charged, especially when dealing with difficult family dynamics, financial pressures, or personal grief. Setting boundaries allows you to create space for self-care, reflection, and emotional recovery during a season that can otherwise be overwhelming.

3. Fostering Healthy Relationships

When you communicate your boundaries clearly and respectfully, you foster healthier relationships with family and friends. Boundaries create mutual respect and understanding, helping to prevent misunderstandings, resentment, and emotional burnout. By being honest about your limits, you're ensuring that your relationships are based on authenticity and mutual respect.

Common Holiday Boundary Challenges

Before diving into specific strategies, it's helpful to understand some of the common challenges people face when it comes to setting boundaries during the holidays. These situations often require careful thought and tact to navigate successfully.

- **Multiple Holiday Invitations:** The holidays can bring a flood of invitations from friends, family, coworkers, and acquaintances. While it may be tempting to attend every gathering, trying to do so can leave you feeling drained and resentful.
- **Gift-Giving Expectations:** Gift-giving can become a financial and emotional burden, especially when expectations are high or when you're part of large groups, such as extended families or workplace gift exchanges.
- **Family Traditions and Obligations:** Many families have long-standing holiday traditions that may no longer feel aligned with your needs or values. Breaking from these traditions or introducing new ones can be challenging, especially if family members resist change.
- **Emotional and Time-Consuming Conversations:** Holiday gatherings often bring together people with different viewpoints, values, and emotional dynamics. Navigating these interactions without sacrificing your emotional well-being requires setting boundaries around the topics you're willing to discuss and how much time you're willing to spend in potentially draining conversations.

How to Say No Politely: Strategies for Boundary-Setting

Saying no can be difficult, especially during the holidays when people expect participation and enthusiasm. However, there are ways to say no politely and assertively that respect both your needs and the feelings of others.

1. Know Your Limits

The first step in setting boundaries is understanding your own limits. Take time before the holiday season begins to reflect on what you are realistically able and willing to commit to, both emotionally and practically.

- **Assess Your Priorities:** Consider which events, traditions, and commitments are most important to you. Prioritize the gatherings and activities that align with your values and bring you the most joy. Let go of the pressure to attend every event or buy gifts for everyone.
- **Understand Your Emotional Triggers:** Reflect on past holiday experiences to identify situations or people that may cause you stress or anxiety. By knowing what drains your energy, you can proactively set boundaries to protect yourself from unnecessary discomfort.
- **Balance Giving and Receiving:** The holiday season is a time for giving, but it's equally important to ensure you're receiving what you need—whether that's time to rest, space for reflection, or emotional support. Don't feel guilty for prioritizing your own well-being.

2. Use Polite but Firm Language

When saying no to an invitation or request, it's important to be both polite and firm. This ensures that your message is clear and reduces the likelihood of guilt or pushback from others.

- **Acknowledge the Invitation with Gratitude:** Start by expressing appreciation for the invitation or request. This demonstrates respect for the person's intentions and helps soften the impact of your "no." For example, "Thank you so much for inviting me to the holiday party."
- **Be Clear and Direct in Your Response:** Avoid vague or ambiguous language that could lead to confusion or pressure to reconsider. Be straightforward about your decision, and don't feel obligated to offer lengthy explanations. For example, "Unfortunately, I won't be able to attend this year" or "I've decided to keep things low-key this holiday season, so I won't be able to join."
- **Offer an Alternative (If Appropriate):** If you feel comfortable, offer an alternative that respects both your boundaries and the other person's needs. For example, "I won't be able to attend the big family gathering, but I'd love to meet for coffee before the holidays" or "I won't be participating in the gift exchange this year, but I'm happy to help with organizing the event."

3. Set Boundaries Around Gift-Giving

Gift-giving can be a source of financial and emotional stress during the holidays, especially if there are expectations to give to a large number of people. Establishing clear boundaries around gift-giving will help you manage these expectations and avoid overspending.

- **Suggest a Secret Santa or Gift Exchange:** If you're part of a large family or group of friends, suggest organizing a Secret Santa or gift exchange. This limits the number of gifts you need to buy while still participating in the tradition. For example, "This year, I'd love to simplify gift-giving. How about we do a Secret Santa instead of buying for everyone?"
- **Set a Spending Limit:** If your group is open to it, propose setting a reasonable spending limit for gifts. This ensures that everyone stays within a budget and reduces financial pressure. You might say, "Let's agree on a budget of $25 per gift so it's fair and affordable for everyone."
- **Opt Out of Gift-Giving:** If you're not in a position to give gifts this year, it's okay to set that boundary clearly and respectfully. For example, "I've decided not to exchange gifts this year, but I'm looking forward to spending time together during the holidays." This shifts the focus from material gifts to quality time and shared experiences.

4. Communicate Boundaries Around Holiday Gatherings

Attending holiday gatherings can be emotionally draining, especially if you're dealing with family dynamics that are stressful or complex. Setting boundaries around how much time you're willing to spend at these events, or even deciding not to attend at all, can protect your emotional well-being.

- **Limit Your Time at Events:** If you want to attend a gathering but don't feel comfortable staying for an extended period, set a clear time limit for yourself. Let the host know in advance so they aren't caught off guard by your early departure. For example, "I'd love to stop by, but I can only stay for an hour. I have another commitment later in the evening."
- **Decline Invitations Without Guilt:** If a holiday gathering feels too overwhelming or conflicts with your emotional needs, it's okay to decline the invitation altogether. Be respectful but firm in your response. For example, "I'm going to have to pass on the gathering this year, but I appreciate the invite."
- **Suggest Alternative Ways to Connect:** If you don't want to attend a large or stressful event but still want to connect with family or friends, offer a more intimate or manageable alternative. For example, "The big family dinner feels like a lot for me this year, but I'd love to meet up for coffee or a small lunch before the holidays."

5. Navigate Difficult Conversations and Emotional Dynamics

Family gatherings often bring together people with different values, beliefs, and emotional histories. These differences can sometimes lead to uncomfortable or heated conversations. Setting conversational boundaries can help you avoid getting drawn into stressful or emotionally charged discussions.

- **Avoid Sensitive Topics:** If certain topics—such as politics, religion, or family grievances—tend to lead to conflict, it's perfectly acceptable to set a boundary around those discussions. You might say, "I'd prefer not to talk about politics today. Let's focus on enjoying the holiday instead."
- **Use Deflection or Humor:** If someone brings up a sensitive topic, you can gently deflect or use humor to change the subject. For example, "Let's save that conversation for another time. Have you tried the pie yet? It's amazing!"
- **Know When to Walk Away:** If a conversation is becoming too heated or emotionally draining, give yourself permission to step away. You don't need to stay in a conversation that feels uncomfortable or harmful. Politely excuse yourself with something like, "I'm going to step outside for a breath of fresh air" or "I need to take a break from this conversation."

Protecting Your Mental Well-Being During the Holidays

Setting boundaries isn't just about managing external expectations—it's also about protecting your mental health and well-being during a busy and often stressful season. Here are additional strategies for staying balanced and emotionally healthy during the holidays.

1. Prioritize Self-Care

Self-care is essential during the holidays, especially when you're navigating multiple demands from family and friends. Make time for activities that recharge you, whether it's reading, meditating, going for a walk, or simply resting.

- **Schedule Downtime:** Block off time in your schedule for relaxation and recovery. Don't feel obligated to fill every moment with social events. Having dedicated downtime will help you stay grounded and avoid burnout.
- **Practice Mindfulness and Stress-Reduction Techniques:** Incorporate mindfulness practices such as deep breathing, meditation, or journaling into your holiday routine. These practices can help you stay centered and manage stress more effectively.

2. Seek Support When Needed

If family dynamics or holiday pressures are affecting your mental health, don't hesitate to seek support from friends, a therapist, or a support group. Talking through your feelings with a trusted person can help you gain perspective and emotional clarity.

- **Build a Support Network:** Surround yourself with people who understand your boundaries and respect your emotional needs. Whether it's a close friend, partner, or mental health professional, having someone to talk to can make a world of difference during stressful times.
- **Don't Be Afraid to Ask for Help:** If holiday responsibilities are piling up, such as preparing meals, hosting events, or shopping for gifts, don't be afraid to ask for help. Delegating tasks to family members or friends can relieve some of the pressure and allow you to enjoy the holiday season more fully.

Conclusion

Setting boundaries with family and friends during the holidays is crucial for protecting your mental well-being and maintaining a healthy balance between giving and receiving. By learning how to say no politely and assertively, you can avoid overcommitting, reduce holiday stress, and ensure that your holiday season is filled with joy, connection, and self-care. Remember that boundaries are an act of self-respect and that saying no when needed allows you to say yes to the things that truly matter. With clear, thoughtful communication, you can navigate the holiday season with confidence and peace of mind.

Chapter 9: Coping with Grief and Loss During the Holidays

The holiday season is often portrayed as a time of joy, togetherness, and celebration. However, for those who have experienced the loss of a loved one, this time of year can be particularly painful. The sights, sounds, and traditions associated with the holidays can serve as constant reminders of the person who is no longer there, intensifying feelings of grief and loneliness. Navigating grief during a period when others are celebrating can feel isolating, overwhelming, and emotionally draining.

In this chapter, we will explore strategies for coping with grief and loss during the holidays. Whether you've lost a loved one recently or are dealing with grief from a loss in the past, these techniques will help you manage your emotional pain and find ways to honor your loved one while taking care of your own well-being.

The Unique Challenges of Grieving During the Holidays

Grief is a deeply personal experience, and it doesn't follow a linear timeline. The holidays, with their emphasis on family, traditions, and togetherness, can amplify the pain of loss in several ways.

1. Heightened Feelings of Loneliness

For many people, the holidays are a time to gather with family and friends. If you've lost a loved one, their absence can be especially noticeable during these gatherings, leaving you feeling isolated or out of place. Even in a room full of people, you may feel an acute sense of loneliness as you miss the person who is no longer there.

2. Memories and Traditions

Holiday traditions can be both a source of comfort and a trigger for grief. The rituals, songs, foods, and decorations associated with the holidays may remind you of special moments shared with the person you've lost. What once brought joy may now bring sadness, and navigating these emotional triggers can be challenging.

3. Pressure to Be Happy

There is often societal pressure to feel cheerful and "in the holiday spirit," even when you're grieving. This pressure can lead to feelings of guilt or frustration if you're unable to summon happiness. You may feel disconnected from the festive atmosphere around you, further intensifying your grief.

4. Loss of Support Networks

For some, the loss of a loved one can also mean the loss of a key support system during the holidays. If the person you've lost was a central figure in your family or social circle, their absence may create a void that affects how you and others connect and support each other.

Strategies for Coping with Grief During the Holidays

Grieving during the holidays requires a delicate balance between honoring your emotions and finding ways to navigate the season in a way that feels manageable. Below are strategies to help you cope with grief and loss during this time.

1. Acknowledge Your Feelings

One of the most important things you can do when coping with grief during the holidays is to acknowledge your emotions without judgment. Grief is complex, and it's normal to experience a wide range of feelings, including sadness, anger, guilt, and even moments of happiness or relief.

- **Give Yourself Permission to Grieve:** It's okay to feel sad, angry, or lonely during the holidays. You don't need to "fake" happiness or push yourself to meet others' expectations. Allow yourself to grieve in whatever way feels natural to you, and don't feel pressured to suppress your emotions to fit the festive atmosphere.
- **Recognize That Grief Is Cyclical:** Grief doesn't have a set timeline, and it often comes in waves. Some moments may be more painful than others, especially when you encounter reminders of your loved one. Acknowledging that these emotional ups and downs are a normal part of the grieving process can help you navigate them with more self-compassion.

2. Create Space for Your Grief

While the holidays are typically filled with activities, gatherings, and obligations, it's important to create space in your schedule for your grief. This may mean setting aside time for reflection, processing your emotions, or participating in rituals that help you honor your loved one.

- **Set Boundaries Around Holiday Events:** If attending large holiday gatherings feels too overwhelming, give yourself permission to decline invitations or leave early. You don't need to participate in every event, especially if it feels emotionally draining. Prioritize the gatherings that feel most meaningful or supportive, and set boundaries around how much time you spend at social functions.
- **Find Quiet Moments for Reflection:** Whether it's lighting a candle, taking a walk, or sitting quietly with your thoughts, finding moments of solitude during the holiday season can provide a much-needed opportunity to process your grief. These moments can serve as a time to remember your loved one and connect with your emotions in a safe, private space.

3. Honor Your Loved One's Memory

Finding ways to honor the memory of your loved one during the holidays can provide a sense of connection and comfort. Incorporating their memory into holiday traditions or creating new rituals can help you feel closer to them while also acknowledging their absence.

- **Create a Special Tribute:** Consider creating a tribute to your loved one that is meaningful to you. This could involve lighting a candle in their honor, displaying a photo of them, or setting aside a special place at the holiday table for them. These small acts of remembrance can offer comfort and keep their memory alive during the holiday season.
- **Continue or Modify Traditions:** If certain holiday traditions were shared with your loved one, you might choose to continue them as a way of honoring their memory. Alternatively, you may decide to modify or create new traditions that reflect how your life has changed since their passing. For example, if you used to bake a specific dessert together, you might continue the tradition or invite others to participate in their honor.
- **Share Memories with Others:** Talking about your loved one and sharing memories with family and friends can be a comforting way to keep their spirit alive during the holidays. Don't hesitate to bring up their name or reminisce about shared experiences. These conversations can provide a sense of connection and support, reminding you that your loved one's memory lives on in the hearts of those who knew them.

4. Be Selective About Holiday Involvement

Navigating holiday gatherings and traditions while grieving can feel overwhelming, especially if you're expected to participate in multiple events. Being selective about how you spend your time and energy can help you protect your emotional well-being.

- **Say No When You Need To:** It's okay to say no to events, parties, or obligations that feel too emotionally or physically taxing. Don't feel obligated to attend every gathering, especially if you're struggling to manage your grief. Politely declining invitations and setting boundaries around your availability can give you the space you need to cope.
- **Plan Ahead for Triggers:** If you anticipate certain events, traditions, or people will trigger strong emotions, plan ahead for how you'll handle those situations. For example, if decorating the holiday tree reminds you of your loved one, you might decide to approach it with a new mindset—perhaps inviting someone to help, listening to music, or modifying the tradition to make it feel more manageable.
- **Give Yourself an "Out" at Gatherings:** If you do choose to attend holiday events, give yourself permission to leave early if you're feeling overwhelmed. Let the host know in advance that you may need to leave after a certain time, or find a quiet space during the event where you can step away if needed. This gives you control over how much time you spend in social situations without feeling trapped.

5. Lean on Your Support System

Grief can be isolating, but it's important to remember that you don't have to go through it alone. Leaning on your support system—whether that's family, friends, or a grief counselor—can provide comfort and help you navigate the emotional challenges of the holiday season.

- **Communicate Your Needs:** Let your loved ones know how they can support you during the holidays. Whether it's listening to you talk about your grief, offering practical help, or simply spending time with you, clear communication can ensure that you're receiving the support you need.
- **Join a Support Group:** If you're feeling isolated in your grief, consider joining a grief support group, either in person or online. Support groups provide a safe space to share your feelings with others who are going through similar experiences. Connecting with people who understand your pain can offer validation and reduce feelings of loneliness.
- **Don't Hesitate to Seek Professional Help:** If you're finding it difficult to cope with your grief during the holidays, seeking the help of a therapist or grief counselor can be invaluable. Professional support can provide you with coping strategies, emotional guidance, and a safe space to express your feelings without judgment.

6. Practice Self-Compassion

Grieving during the holidays can be emotionally exhausting, so it's essential to treat yourself with kindness and compassion. Allow yourself to feel whatever emotions arise and be gentle with yourself if you're struggling.

- **Let Go of Expectations:** It's common to feel pressured to meet the expectations of others—or even your own—during the holiday season. Whether it's participating in traditions or feeling "cheerful," let go of any pressure to conform to societal norms or what you think the holidays "should" look like. Focus on what feels right for you in your grieving process.
- **Engage in Self-Care Activities:** Take time for self-care during the holidays, especially when emotions feel overwhelming. This could include physical activities like exercise, yoga, or walks in nature, as well as relaxing activities like reading, taking a bath, or practicing mindfulness. Caring for your body and mind can help you manage the emotional toll of grief.
- **Embrace Moments of Joy Without Guilt:** If you find moments of happiness or laughter during the holiday season, don't feel guilty about experiencing joy. It's possible to grieve while still finding joy in the present moment, and allowing yourself to feel both emotions is a natural part of healing.

7. Create a New Narrative for the Holidays

After the loss of a loved one, the holidays may never feel the same as they once did. However, that doesn't mean the holidays can't still hold meaning and comfort. By creating new traditions and redefining what the holidays represent for you, you can begin to craft a new narrative that honors both your grief and the possibility of healing.

- **Incorporate Meaningful Rituals:** Introduce new rituals that feel significant to your grief journey. This could be lighting a candle each night in honor of your loved one, writing a letter to them, or dedicating a day during the holiday season to reflect on their life. These rituals can help create a sense of continuity and connection, even as you move forward.
- **Focus on What Matters Most to You:** Take time to reflect on what the holidays mean to you now. Perhaps it's spending quality time with a few close family members or volunteering for a cause that's meaningful to you. Focusing on what brings you a sense of purpose or comfort can help you navigate the holidays with more intention and less pressure to meet traditional expectations.
- **Be Open to Evolving Traditions:** Grief changes over time, and so too can your relationship with the holidays. As you move through different stages of your grieving process, be open to evolving your holiday traditions to reflect where you are emotionally. What feels overwhelming this year might feel comforting next year, and vice versa. Give yourself the freedom to adapt as needed.

Conclusion

Coping with grief and loss during the holidays is undeniably challenging, but with the right strategies, it's possible to navigate this difficult time with compassion and resilience. By acknowledging your feelings, setting boundaries, honoring your loved one's memory, and leaning on your support system, you can find ways to move through the season while caring for your emotional well-being. Remember that there is no "right" way to grieve, and it's okay to redefine the holidays in a way that feels meaningful to you. Through self-compassion and intentionality, you can honor both your grief and the memory of your loved one while finding moments of peace and healing.

Chapter 10: Strengthening Relationships During Stressful Times

The holiday season is often thought of as a time of connection and celebration with loved ones, but it can also be a period of heightened stress and tension. From managing family dynamics to dealing with financial pressures and packed schedules, the holidays can strain even the closest relationships. Despite the stress, the festive season also offers a unique opportunity to strengthen relationships through intentional communication, empathy, and emotional connection.

In this chapter, we'll explore practical tips for improving communication and deepening emotional bonds with your partner, family members, and friends during stressful times. Whether you're navigating the pressures of holiday planning or managing conflict, these strategies will help you cultivate stronger, more resilient relationships.

The Impact of Holiday Stress on Relationships

Holiday stress can take a toll on relationships in several ways. The pressures to meet expectations, maintain traditions, and juggle multiple commitments can lead to irritability, miscommunication, and emotional disconnection. Understanding how stress manifests in your relationships can help you address issues before they escalate.

1. Increased Tension and Misunderstandings

When people are stressed, they tend to be more irritable, reactive, and prone to misunderstandings. The holidays can amplify these tensions, as families come together with differing expectations and perspectives. Misunderstandings may arise over seemingly small things, such as how to decorate the house, plan a meal, or allocate time among different family members.

2. Emotional Overload

Holiday stress can cause emotional overload, where individuals feel overwhelmed by the demands placed on them—whether it's financial strain, family obligations, or the pressure to create a perfect holiday experience. Emotional overload can lead to withdrawal or outbursts, making it difficult to maintain meaningful connections with loved ones.

3. Disconnection in Relationships

During times of stress, it's easy to become disconnected from loved ones as you focus on managing external pressures. The result can be emotional distance, where communication breaks down, and partners or family members feel neglected or misunderstood.

The good news is that stress doesn't have to weaken your relationships. By improving communication, practicing empathy, and intentionally fostering connection, you can navigate the holiday season in a way that strengthens your relationships and brings you closer to the people who matter most.

Tips for Strengthening Relationships During the Holidays
1. Prioritize Open and Honest Communication
Effective communication is the foundation of any strong relationship, especially during stressful times. When you and your loved ones are clear about your needs, expectations, and boundaries, it's easier to work together harmoniously.

- **Express Your Needs and Expectations Clearly:** Whether it's with your partner, family, or friends, be upfront about what you need and expect during the holidays. If you're feeling overwhelmed by the demands of the season, let your loved ones know. For example, you might say, "I'm feeling a bit stressed about our schedule this week. Can we simplify some of our plans?"
- **Be Open About Your Emotions:** The holidays can bring up a range of emotions, from joy to anxiety to sadness. Sharing your feelings with your partner or family members can create space for understanding and empathy. For instance, if you're grieving a loved one during the holidays, let your family know how you're feeling, so they can support you emotionally.
- **Listen Actively:** Communication is a two-way street, and it's essential to listen as much as you speak. When your partner or family member shares their thoughts or concerns, listen without interrupting or jumping to conclusions. Show that you're engaged by asking questions or reflecting back what they've said, such as, "It sounds like you're worried about how we'll manage everything. How can I help?"
- **Avoid Assumptions:** It's easy to assume you know what your partner or family member is thinking or feeling, especially if you've been together for a long time. However, assumptions can lead to misunderstandings and conflict. Instead of assuming, ask questions to clarify their perspective. For example, "I noticed you seemed quiet at dinner. Is something on your mind?"

2. Practice Empathy and Understanding
Empathy is the ability to put yourself in someone else's shoes and understand their emotions and experiences. During stressful times, practicing empathy can help you strengthen emotional connections and avoid conflict.

- **Acknowledge the Other Person's Perspective:** Even if you don't fully agree with your partner's or family member's point of view, acknowledging their feelings and experiences can go a long way in fostering understanding. You might say, "I see that you're feeling frustrated with how things are going. I understand this is important to you, and I want to find a solution together."
- **Show Patience and Compassion:** Stress often makes people more reactive or short-tempered. If your partner or family member is irritable, try to respond with patience and com-

passion rather than taking it personally. Remind yourself that their stress may be influencing their behavior, and they may not be intentionally lashing out.

- **Offer Emotional Support:** Sometimes, what your loved ones need most during stressful times is simply emotional support. Offer a listening ear, a comforting hug, or words of reassurance. For example, "I know you've been under a lot of pressure lately, but I'm here for you, and we'll get through this together."

3. Set Realistic Expectations for the Holidays

One of the biggest sources of holiday stress is the pressure to meet unrealistic expectations—whether it's creating the perfect holiday meal, buying the best gifts, or attending every gathering. Setting realistic expectations for yourself and your relationships can help reduce stress and prevent conflict.

- **Let Go of Perfectionism:** It's easy to get caught up in the idea that the holidays need to be "perfect," but perfectionism can lead to frustration and disappointment. Instead of striving for perfection, focus on what really matters—spending quality time with loved ones and creating meaningful memories. For example, if the holiday dinner doesn't go exactly as planned, remind yourself that what's most important is the time spent together, not the flawless execution of the meal.
- **Be Flexible with Plans:** During the holidays, plans may change, and things may not always go as expected. Being flexible and adaptable can help you navigate changes without becoming overly stressed. For example, if a family member cancels plans last minute, instead of feeling upset, consider alternative ways to connect, such as scheduling a phone call or virtual get-together.
- **Manage Financial Expectations:** Financial stress can strain relationships, especially if there are differing opinions on how much to spend during the holidays. Have open conversations with your partner or family members about holiday spending and set a budget that works for everyone. If necessary, suggest alternative ways to celebrate that don't involve expensive gifts or outings.

4. Make Time for Emotional Connection

The holiday season is often busy, but carving out time for emotional connection with your loved ones is essential for strengthening your relationships. Whether it's with your partner, family members, or friends, prioritizing connection can help counteract the stress and busyness of the season.

- **Plan One-on-One Time:** Amidst the hustle and bustle of the holidays, it's important to make time for one-on-one connection with the people who matter most to you. Whether it's a quiet evening with your partner, a coffee date with a friend, or a walk with a family member, these moments of connection can help you stay grounded and emotionally connected.
- **Engage in Shared Activities:** One of the best ways to strengthen emotional bonds is by engaging in activities that you enjoy together. This could be something as simple as baking cook-

ies, watching a holiday movie, or taking a family walk through a decorated neighborhood. Shared experiences create opportunities for connection and joy, even during stressful times.

- **Show Appreciation and Gratitude:** Expressing gratitude and appreciation for your loved ones can strengthen emotional connections and foster a positive atmosphere. Make a point to thank your partner, family, or friends for their support, kindness, and presence. You could write a heartfelt note, give a small gift, or simply say, "I appreciate everything you do, and I'm grateful to have you in my life."

5. Resolve Conflicts Constructively

Conflicts are inevitable in any relationship, but how you handle them during stressful times can either strengthen or weaken your connection. Learning how to resolve conflicts constructively is key to maintaining a healthy, respectful relationship during the holidays.

- **Address Issues Calmly and Respectfully:** If a conflict arises, approach it calmly and respectfully. Avoid raising your voice, using hurtful language, or blaming the other person. Instead, focus on explaining your feelings and concerns in a constructive way. For example, "I felt hurt when you made that comment earlier, and I'd like to talk about it so we can resolve the issue."
- **Take Responsibility for Your Actions:** If you've said or done something that contributed to the conflict, take responsibility for your actions. Apologize if necessary, and focus on finding a solution together. For instance, "I'm sorry I snapped at you earlier. I've been feeling stressed, but that's no excuse for my behavior. Let's talk about how we can avoid this happening again."
- **Find Common Ground:** During disagreements, look for areas of common ground where you and the other person can compromise. Even if you don't agree on everything, finding shared goals or values can help bridge the gap and create a path toward resolution. For example, "We may not agree on how to handle this situation, but we both want the holidays to be a positive experience for everyone."

6. Take Care of Your Mental and Emotional Health

During stressful times, it's easy to neglect your own mental and emotional well-being, which can negatively impact your relationships. Prioritizing self-care will help you stay emotionally balanced and better equipped to support your loved ones.

- **Practice Stress-Reduction Techniques:** Incorporate stress-reducing activities into your daily routine, such as meditation, deep breathing, or yoga. Taking time to unwind and relax can help you stay centered and calm when interacting with loved ones.
- **Set Boundaries for Your Well-Being:** It's important to set personal boundaries around your time and energy to protect your mental health. For example, if you're feeling overwhelmed, let your family know that you need some time to recharge before joining the festivities.

- **Seek Support When Needed:** If holiday stress is affecting your mental health or relationships, don't hesitate to seek support from a therapist, counselor, or support group. Professional guidance can help you navigate stress, manage emotions, and strengthen your relationships during challenging times.

Conclusion

The holiday season may come with its share of stress, but it also offers a unique opportunity to strengthen your relationships through improved communication, empathy, and emotional connection. By being intentional about how you engage with your loved ones, setting realistic expectations, and prioritizing emotional connection, you can deepen your bonds and create a more harmonious holiday experience. Remember that the key to strong relationships during stressful times is not perfection, but rather a commitment to understanding, supporting, and caring for one another amidst the challenges. Through these strategies, you can build stronger, more resilient relationships that last well beyond the holiday season.

Chapter 11: Managing Family Gatherings Without Burnout

The holiday season is synonymous with family gatherings, festive meals, and time spent with loved ones. While these events can be joyous and heartwarming, they can also be overwhelming and exhausting—especially if you're responsible for organizing or attending multiple events in a short period of time. Managing family gatherings without succumbing to burnout requires careful planning, setting realistic expectations, and prioritizing self-care.

This chapter provides practical advice for both hosting and attending holiday gatherings in a way that helps you stay present and engaged while protecting your mental and physical well-being. By learning how to balance the demands of the season with your personal limits, you can enjoy the holidays without feeling depleted.

Understanding the Causes of Holiday Burnout

Holiday burnout often stems from a combination of physical exhaustion, emotional stress, and overcommitment. Hosting or attending family gatherings can add to this stress, particularly if you feel obligated to meet everyone's expectations, prepare elaborate meals, or navigate complicated family dynamics.

1. Overcommitment

The desire to make everyone happy and attend every family event can lead to overcommitment. Juggling multiple holiday gatherings, managing travel plans, and trying to meet various social obligations can quickly become overwhelming, leaving you feeling stretched too thin.

2. Perfectionism

Many people feel pressured to create the "perfect" holiday experience, whether that means hosting a flawless dinner, buying the best gifts, or ensuring that everyone is happy and comfortable. This pressure can lead to perfectionism, which adds to stress and often results in burnout when things don't go as planned.

3. Emotional Stress

Family gatherings often bring together people with different personalities, values, and emotional dynamics. This can lead to emotional stress, particularly if you're dealing with unresolved family conflicts, difficult personalities, or feelings of grief or loss during the holidays.

4. Physical Exhaustion

The physical demands of organizing and hosting a family gathering—cooking, cleaning, decorating, and preparing—can lead to burnout if you don't take time to rest and recharge. Additionally, attending multiple events with little downtime can leave you feeling physically drained.

Tips for Organizing Family Gatherings Without Burnout

Hosting a family gathering can be a rewarding experience, but it also comes with a lot of responsibility. By planning ahead, setting boundaries, and simplifying your approach, you can create a joyful event without exhausting yourself in the process.

1. Plan and Delegate Early

One of the most effective ways to avoid burnout as a host is to plan your gathering well in advance and delegate tasks to others. Trying to do everything yourself is a recipe for exhaustion, but with proper planning and shared responsibilities, you can lighten the load and enjoy the event without stress.

- **Start Planning Early:** Begin planning your gathering several weeks (or even months) ahead of time. Create a checklist of everything that needs to be done, from preparing the guest list and menu to shopping and cleaning. Early planning allows you to spread out tasks, reducing the last-minute rush.
- **Delegate Tasks:** Don't hesitate to ask for help from family members or guests. Whether it's assigning dishes for a potluck, asking someone to help with decorations, or having someone else manage the entertainment, delegating tasks ensures that you're not shouldering the entire burden yourself. Most people are happy to contribute and appreciate being included in the preparations.
- **Set Realistic Expectations:** Be realistic about what you can accomplish within your time, budget, and energy limits. You don't need to prepare a gourmet meal or decorate your home to perfection to host a memorable gathering. Focus on what's most important to you—whether that's spending quality time with loved ones or sharing a simple, delicious meal.

2. Simplify the Menu

Preparing a holiday feast can be one of the most stressful parts of hosting, but it doesn't have to be. Simplifying the menu and incorporating easy, crowd-pleasing dishes can help reduce the time and effort spent in the kitchen.

- **Opt for Potluck-Style Meals:** One of the best ways to reduce the workload is by hosting a potluck-style meal where each guest brings a dish to share. This not only lightens the cooking load but also adds variety to the meal. Assign categories like appetizers, side dishes, and desserts to ensure a balanced spread.
- **Choose Make-Ahead Dishes:** Whenever possible, choose recipes that can be made in advance, allowing you to spend less time in the kitchen on the day of the gathering. Casseroles, soups, and baked goods are excellent options that can be prepared ahead and reheated just before serving.
- **Simplify the Menu:** Rather than trying to create an elaborate, multi-course meal, opt for a simple, yet satisfying menu. Focus on a few key dishes that you know your guests will enjoy,

and skip the extras. For example, a roasted turkey or ham, a couple of side dishes, and a festive dessert can create a wonderful meal without overwhelming you.

3. Set Boundaries Around Time and Energy

As a host, it's easy to feel like you need to be "on" for the entire event, but this can quickly lead to burnout. Setting boundaries around your time and energy will help you stay balanced and present throughout the gathering.

- **Establish a Time Frame for the Event:** Set clear start and end times for the gathering. Let guests know when you expect them to arrive and when the event will wind down. This prevents the event from dragging on and gives you a set time to relax afterward. You might say, "We're starting dinner at 6:00 p.m. and wrapping up around 9:00 p.m. so we can all get some rest."
- **Take Breaks When Needed:** During the gathering, give yourself permission to step away for a few moments to recharge. Whether it's taking a short walk, retreating to a quiet room, or simply sitting down for a breather, these small breaks can help you reset and avoid feeling overwhelmed.
- **Don't Be Afraid to Ask for Help:** If you're feeling tired or overwhelmed during the event, don't hesitate to ask for help from your guests. Whether it's clearing the table, serving drinks, or helping with cleanup, many guests are happy to pitch in, and sharing the workload can make the event more enjoyable for everyone.

4. Focus on Connection Over Perfection

The true spirit of family gatherings lies in connection, not perfection. Shifting your focus away from creating a flawless event and toward meaningful interactions with your loved ones will help reduce stress and enhance your experience.

- **Embrace Imperfection:** It's inevitable that something will go wrong—a dish might burn, the table might be a little messy, or someone might spill a drink. Instead of worrying about every detail, embrace these imperfections as part of the experience. What matters most is the time spent together, not whether everything is perfect.
- **Prioritize Time with Guests:** During the gathering, make an effort to spend quality time with your guests rather than getting caught up in hosting duties. Sit down and enjoy the meal with everyone, engage in conversations, and be fully present. Your guests will appreciate your company more than an impeccably decorated table or a perfectly cooked dish.

Tips for Attending Family Gatherings Without Burnout

Attending multiple family gatherings during the holiday season can also lead to burnout, especially if you're juggling numerous events, managing travel, or navigating complex family dynamics. By setting boundaries, managing your energy, and practicing self-care, you can attend these gatherings without becoming overwhelmed.

1. Be Selective About Which Events to Attend

It's common to receive multiple invitations during the holiday season—from extended family dinners to friends' parties and workplace events. While it's tempting to say yes to everything, over-committing can quickly lead to exhaustion. Being selective about which gatherings to attend will help you preserve your energy and focus on what matters most.

- **Prioritize Meaningful Events:** Reflect on which gatherings are most meaningful to you and your family. If certain events hold sentimental value or involve close loved ones, prioritize those. Don't feel obligated to attend every event, especially if it's causing unnecessary stress. For example, you might choose to attend your immediate family's Christmas dinner but skip a large extended family gathering that feels overwhelming.
- **Politely Decline When Necessary:** It's okay to say no to invitations, especially if attending multiple events will leave you feeling drained. Be polite but firm when declining. For example, "Thank you so much for inviting me, but I won't be able to make it this year. I hope you have a wonderful celebration!"

2. Set Time Limits for Gatherings

Family gatherings can be enjoyable, but they can also be emotionally and physically draining, especially if they last for hours on end. Setting time limits for how long you'll stay at an event can help prevent burnout and ensure you have enough time to rest.

- **Arrive Late or Leave Early:** If you know a gathering will be long, consider arriving later or leaving earlier to manage your energy levels. Let the host know in advance if you'll only be able to stay for part of the event. For example, "I'm so excited to see everyone, but I'll need to leave by 8:00 p.m. because I have an early morning."
- **Plan for Breaks:** If you're attending a large family event that's likely to be emotionally intense, plan for breaks during the gathering. Take a walk, step outside for fresh air, or retreat to a quiet space to recharge. These small breaks can help you manage stress and stay present without becoming overwhelmed.

3. Manage Family Dynamics with Care

Family gatherings can sometimes be emotionally charged, especially if there are unresolved conflicts, difficult personalities, or differing opinions among family members. Learning how to navigate these dynamics with care can help you avoid emotional burnout and maintain your peace of mind.

- **Set Boundaries Around Sensitive Topics:** If certain topics—such as politics, religion, or personal issues—tend to cause conflict, it's okay to set boundaries around them. You might say, "I'd rather not talk about that today. Let's focus on enjoying the holidays."
- **Choose Your Battles Wisely:** Not every disagreement needs to turn into a conflict. If a family member says something that bothers you, consider whether it's worth addressing in the moment or if it's better to let it go for the sake of peace. You can always address issues at a later time if necessary.
- **Stay Calm and Grounded:** Family gatherings can sometimes bring out strong emotions, but it's important to stay calm and grounded. Practice deep breathing or mindfulness techniques to manage stress in the moment, and remind yourself that you're in control of your reactions. If a conversation becomes heated, politely excuse yourself and take a break.

4. Take Care of Yourself Before and After the Gathering

Attending a family gathering can be emotionally and physically draining, so it's important to prioritize self-care before and after the event to prevent burnout.

- **Rest and Recharge Before the Event:** Make sure you're well-rested and emotionally prepared before attending a family gathering. If you know the event may be stressful, practice relaxation techniques, meditate, or engage in activities that calm and center you.
- **Schedule Downtime After the Event:** After the gathering, give yourself time to unwind and recharge. Whether it's spending a quiet evening at home, going for a walk, or taking a bath, allow yourself the space to recover from the emotional and physical demands of the event.

Conclusion

Managing family gatherings without burnout during the holiday season is possible with careful planning, setting boundaries, and prioritizing self-care. Whether you're hosting or attending, it's important to recognize your limits and make decisions that protect your mental and physical well-being. By simplifying your approach, delegating tasks, and focusing on meaningful connections rather than perfection, you can create and enjoy memorable holiday gatherings without feeling overwhelmed. Ultimately, the holiday season should be a time of joy and connection, and with the right strategies, you can navigate family gatherings with confidence and ease.

Part 3: Time Management and Organization

Chapter 12: Planning a Stress-Free Holiday Calendar

The holiday season is often a whirlwind of activities, from shopping and decorating to attending gatherings and preparing meals. While it can be a time of joy and celebration, the sheer number of tasks and events can also lead to overwhelming stress and burnout. One of the most effective ways to manage the holiday chaos is by creating an organized and realistic holiday calendar. Planning ahead allows you to break down tasks into manageable steps, prioritize what matters most, and ensure that you have enough time to enjoy the season without feeling rushed or overwhelmed.

In this chapter, we'll explore how to create a stress-free holiday calendar that helps you stay on top of your to-do list, avoid last-minute stress, and balance your commitments with time for rest and self-care. By developing a clear timeline and setting realistic goals, you can ensure a more organized, enjoyable holiday season.

Why a Holiday Calendar Is Essential

With so many demands on your time during the holidays—shopping, gift-wrapping, cooking, decorating, and attending events—it's easy to feel like you're constantly racing against the clock. Without a clear plan in place, tasks can pile up, leading to last-minute scrambling and unnecessary stress. A well-structured holiday calendar helps you:

- **Stay Organized:** A calendar provides a visual overview of your commitments and tasks, making it easier to manage your time effectively. By seeing everything laid out, you can prioritize your most important activities and ensure that nothing falls through the cracks.
- **Avoid Overcommitment:** It's common to overcommit during the holiday season, saying yes to every event or task without realizing how quickly your schedule fills up. A calendar helps you set boundaries and make informed decisions about how much you can realistically handle.
- **Prevent Last-Minute Stress:** By breaking down holiday preparations into manageable chunks, a calendar helps you avoid the last-minute rush to finish shopping, wrapping, or cooking. Spreading tasks out over several weeks allows you to stay on top of your to-do list without feeling overwhelmed.
- **Ensure Time for Self-Care:** A well-planned calendar includes time for relaxation and self-care, ensuring that you don't neglect your own well-being in the midst of holiday activities.

Step-by-Step Guide to Creating a Stress-Free Holiday Calendar

Creating a stress-free holiday calendar involves setting clear priorities, breaking tasks into manageable steps, and allowing for flexibility. Follow these steps to develop an organized and realistic timeline for the holiday season.

1. Assess Your Holiday Priorities

Before you start filling in your calendar, take a moment to assess your priorities for the holiday season. This will help you focus on what matters most to you and avoid getting caught up in unnecessary tasks or obligations.

- **Reflect on Past Holiday Seasons:** Think back to previous holiday seasons and reflect on what worked well and what caused stress. Were there events or traditions that felt overwhelming or unimportant? Are there certain activities or gatherings that you truly enjoyed and want to prioritize this year?
- **Define Your Priorities:** Make a list of the most important aspects of the holiday season for you. This might include spending quality time with family, attending specific gatherings, participating in religious or cultural traditions, or simply taking time to rest and recharge. Use this list to guide your decisions about how you'll spend your time.
- **Set Realistic Expectations:** It's important to set realistic expectations for what you can accomplish during the holiday season. You don't need to do everything, and it's okay to let go of tasks or traditions that no longer serve you. Focus on what brings you joy and fulfillment rather than trying to meet external expectations.

2. Create a Master To-Do List

Once you've identified your priorities, the next step is to create a master to-do list that includes all the tasks you need to complete before the holiday season. Breaking down your tasks into smaller, manageable steps will make it easier to organize them on your calendar.

- **Include All Major Tasks:** Your to-do list should include all the major tasks you need to complete, such as shopping for gifts, wrapping presents, decorating the house, sending holiday cards, planning meals, and attending events. Be as specific as possible so that you have a clear sense of what needs to be done.
- **Break Down Large Tasks:** For larger tasks like holiday shopping, break them down into smaller steps. For example, instead of simply writing "buy gifts," break it down into categories such as "buy gifts for family," "buy gifts for coworkers," and "buy stocking stuffers." This will make the tasks feel more manageable and allow you to spread them out over time.
- **Don't Forget Self-Care:** Include self-care activities on your to-do list, such as scheduling downtime, planning moments of relaxation, or enjoying activities that help you unwind. These tasks are just as important as your holiday preparations and should be given equal priority.

3. Organize Your Calendar by Weeks

Now that you have a master to-do list, it's time to organize your tasks on a weekly basis. Spreading tasks out over several weeks helps prevent last-minute stress and ensures that you have enough time to complete everything without feeling rushed.

- **Start Early:** The earlier you start planning, the less stressful the holiday season will be. Ideally, you should begin organizing your calendar at least 6-8 weeks before the holidays. This gives you plenty of time to complete tasks gradually and avoid the last-minute rush.
- **Assign Tasks to Specific Weeks:** Review your master to-do list and assign tasks to specific weeks leading up to the holidays. For example, you might dedicate one week to gift shopping, another week to holiday cards, and another week to decorating. Be realistic about how much you can accomplish each week and avoid overloading any single week with too many tasks.
- **Plan for Flexibility:** Leave some buffer time in your schedule for unexpected tasks or last-minute changes. Flexibility is key to reducing stress, so don't pack your calendar too tightly. If something takes longer than expected, having extra time built into your schedule will allow you to adjust without feeling overwhelmed.

4. Set Deadlines for Major Tasks

Setting specific deadlines for major tasks will help you stay on track and prevent procrastination. By giving yourself clear deadlines, you can avoid the panic of trying to complete everything at the last minute.

- **Gift Shopping:** Set a deadline for completing your holiday shopping at least one to two weeks before the holidays. This gives you time to wrap gifts and avoid the stress of last-minute shopping in crowded stores. If you're ordering gifts online, factor in shipping times and set an earlier deadline.
- **Holiday Cards:** If you plan to send holiday cards, set a deadline for addressing and mailing them. Aim to have your cards mailed by early to mid-December to ensure they arrive in time. If possible, start addressing your cards in batches a few weeks in advance so you're not rushing to complete them all at once.
- **Meal Planning:** If you're hosting a holiday meal, set a deadline for finalizing your menu and creating a shopping list. Plan to do your grocery shopping a few days before the event to avoid the last-minute rush at the store. If any dishes can be prepared in advance, schedule time for meal prep earlier in the week.

5. Incorporate Social Events and Gatherings

Social events, family gatherings, and holiday parties can quickly fill up your calendar, so it's important to plan for them early. By incorporating these events into your calendar, you can manage your time more effectively and avoid overcommitting.

- **Add Events to Your Calendar Early:** As soon as you receive invitations or confirm plans for gatherings, add them to your calendar. This gives you a clear overview of your commitments and helps you avoid scheduling conflicts.
- **Be Selective About Which Events to Attend:** It's easy to overcommit during the holidays, especially if you're invited to multiple gatherings. Be selective about which events you attend and prioritize those that are most meaningful to you. Don't feel obligated to say yes to every invitation—declining a few events will give you more time to focus on what matters most.
- **Plan for Travel Time:** If you're traveling to attend family gatherings or holiday parties, make sure to account for travel time in your calendar. Give yourself plenty of time to get to and from events, especially if you're traveling long distances or dealing with holiday traffic.

6. Schedule Time for Relaxation and Self-Care

Amidst all the holiday planning and social events, it's essential to carve out time for relaxation and self-care. This will help you recharge and prevent burnout during the busy season.

- **Block Off Downtime on Your Calendar:** Just as you schedule tasks and events, block off dedicated downtime on your calendar. This could be a few hours in the evening to unwind with a book, a morning walk, or a relaxing bath. Scheduling downtime ensures that you prioritize self-care and don't overbook yourself.
- **Practice Mindfulness and Stress Reduction:** Incorporate mindfulness practices, such as meditation, deep breathing, or yoga, into your holiday routine. These activities can help you manage stress and stay centered, even when your schedule gets busy.
- **Say No When Necessary:** If your calendar starts to feel too full, give yourself permission to say no to additional commitments. Setting boundaries around your time is essential for maintaining balance and protecting your mental and physical well-being.

7. Review and Adjust Your Calendar Weekly

Your holiday calendar should be flexible and adaptable to changing circumstances. As the holiday season progresses, review your calendar regularly and make adjustments as needed.

- **Review Your Calendar Weekly:** At the beginning of each week, review your calendar to see what tasks and events are coming up. This allows you to prepare for the week ahead and make any necessary adjustments. If you didn't complete certain tasks the previous week, reschedule them for a later date.

- **Stay Flexible:** Unexpected events or changes in plans are inevitable during the holiday season. Stay flexible and be willing to adjust your calendar as needed. If something doesn't go as planned, don't be afraid to let go of less important tasks or rearrange your schedule to accommodate changes.

Sample Holiday Calendar Timeline

To help you get started, here's a sample holiday calendar timeline that spreads out tasks and events over several weeks. Feel free to adapt this timeline to your specific needs and preferences.

6-8 Weeks Before the Holidays:

- Create your master to-do list and holiday budget.
- Start shopping for non-perishable gifts or decorations.
- Send out invitations for any holiday gatherings you're hosting.
- Begin addressing holiday cards (if sending).

4-5 Weeks Before the Holidays:

- Finalize your gift list and continue shopping for gifts.
- Plan any travel arrangements and book accommodations if needed.
- Finalize your holiday meal menu.
- Begin decorating your home.

3 Weeks Before the Holidays:

- Wrap and label gifts as you purchase them.
- Send out holiday cards to ensure timely delivery.
- Start shopping for any non-perishable ingredients for holiday meals.

2 Weeks Before the Holidays:

- Complete any remaining gift shopping and wrapping.
- Finalize plans for attending holiday gatherings or parties.
- Continue meal prep, focusing on dishes that can be made ahead.

1 Week Before the Holidays:

- Shop for perishable ingredients and finalize your holiday meal plans.
- Double-check your calendar for any last-minute events or tasks.
- Make time for relaxation and self-care leading up to the holidays.

Holiday Week:

- Enjoy the holiday gatherings and celebrations you've planned for!
- Take time to relax and reflect on the season.
- Focus on being present with loved ones and celebrating in a way that brings you joy.

Conclusion

Planning a stress-free holiday calendar is all about creating a realistic, organized timeline that balances holiday preparations with time for rest and self-care. By setting priorities, breaking down tasks, and spreading them out over several weeks, you can avoid the last-minute rush and enjoy a more peaceful, meaningful holiday season. Remember to stay flexible, review your calendar regularly, and don't be afraid to say no to additional commitments. With a well-structured calendar in place, you'll be able to fully embrace the joy of the season without feeling overwhelmed.

Chapter 13: Prioritizing What Really Matters

The holiday season is a time that many people look forward to each year, filled with traditions, celebrations, and time spent with loved ones. However, it can also become overwhelming, with a seemingly endless list of obligations and expectations that pull you in different directions. From gift shopping and attending parties to preparing elaborate meals and decorating your home, it's easy to get caught up in the hustle and bustle of the season. Often, in the quest to do it all, the true meaning and joy of the holidays can get lost.

This chapter will explore how to prioritize what truly matters during the holidays and let go of unnecessary obligations that create stress or detract from the season's core values. By identifying what is most meaningful to you and your loved ones, you can focus on creating a more intentional, fulfilling holiday experience that brings joy rather than exhaustion.

The Pressure of Holiday Expectations

The holidays often come with high expectations, both from ourselves and from others. The desire to create perfect holiday experiences can be fueled by societal pressure, family traditions, or even social media, where carefully curated images of holiday cheer set unrealistic standards. These expectations can lead to:

- **Overcommitting to Activities:** Feeling obligated to attend every event, host gatherings, or participate in every tradition, even when it becomes overwhelming.
- **Financial Strain:** Pressure to buy expensive gifts, decorations, or meals, leading to overspending and financial stress.
- **Emotional Burnout:** The emotional toll of trying to make everyone happy while neglecting your own well-being.
- **Disconnect from Meaning:** Losing sight of the true meaning of the holidays—whether that's spending quality time with family, practicing gratitude, or embracing spiritual or cultural traditions—in the rush to meet external expectations.

By focusing on what truly matters, you can take control of your holiday season, avoid burnout, and make room for joy, connection, and reflection.

Identifying What Matters Most to You

The first step in creating a more meaningful holiday experience is identifying what is most important to you. This involves reflecting on your personal values, your favorite holiday traditions, and what brings you joy during the season.

1. Reflect on Past Holidays

Take a moment to reflect on your past holiday experiences. What moments stand out to you as the most meaningful or fulfilling? Conversely, what aspects of the holidays have caused stress, frustration, or disappointment?

- **Positive Memories:** Think about the moments that brought you the most happiness or connection in past holidays. Was it spending time with family, a particular tradition, or quiet moments of reflection? Identifying these positive experiences can help you focus on what you want to prioritize going forward.
- **Sources of Stress:** Consider the things that have caused unnecessary stress in previous holiday seasons. Were there events, tasks, or obligations that felt overwhelming or unimportant? Understanding what didn't work well in the past can guide you in letting go of obligations that aren't meaningful to you.

2. Clarify Your Values

Your values are the foundation of how you approach the holidays. Clarifying what matters most to you—whether it's family, gratitude, generosity, or spirituality—can help you make decisions that align with those values.

- **What Do You Value Most About the Holidays?** Ask yourself what you hope to experience or cultivate during the holiday season. For some, it may be about spending quality time with loved ones, while for others, it might be about practicing gratitude, giving back to the community, or honoring spiritual traditions. Defining your core values will help you focus on the aspects of the holidays that truly resonate with you.
- **Discuss Values with Your Loved Ones:** It's also important to have conversations with your family or partner about what they value most during the holidays. Understanding each other's priorities will help you create a holiday experience that feels meaningful to everyone involved.

3. Set Intentions for the Holiday Season

Once you've clarified your values, set specific intentions for the holiday season. These intentions can serve as a guiding principle for how you approach your time, energy, and commitments.

- **What Do You Want to Feel During the Holidays?** Think about the emotional experience you want to have during the holidays. Do you want to feel calm and peaceful? Connected to your family? Spiritually renewed? Setting intentions around your emotional experience will help you prioritize activities that align with those feelings.

- **What Memories Do You Want to Create?** Consider the memories you want to create for yourself and your loved ones. Whether it's a quiet night decorating the tree together, a meaningful conversation over dinner, or a day spent volunteering, focus on the moments that will leave a lasting impact.

Letting Go of Unnecessary Obligations

Once you've identified what truly matters to you, the next step is learning to let go of obligations, tasks, and expectations that don't align with your values. This can be challenging, especially if you've grown accustomed to saying "yes" to every holiday invitation or feel pressure to meet societal expectations. However, letting go of what isn't necessary is essential for reducing stress and creating space for the things that bring you joy.

1. Examine Holiday Traditions

Holiday traditions can bring comfort and continuity, but they can also become burdensome if they no longer resonate with you or your family. It's important to evaluate which traditions are meaningful and which have become more of a chore.

- **Keep, Modify, or Let Go:** Make a list of your holiday traditions and decide which ones are worth keeping, which ones could be modified to better fit your current life, and which ones you're ready to let go of. For example, if hosting a large holiday dinner is too overwhelming, consider downsizing the event or turning it into a potluck.
- **Create New Traditions:** If certain traditions no longer feel meaningful, use this opportunity to create new ones that align with your values. For example, you might start a tradition of volunteering as a family, writing gratitude letters to each other, or having a tech-free holiday evening where you focus on conversation and connection.

2. Learn to Say No

One of the most effective ways to reduce holiday stress is by learning to say no to obligations that don't align with your priorities. Whether it's declining an invitation to a holiday party, opting out of a gift exchange, or setting boundaries around your time, saying no allows you to protect your energy and focus on what matters most.

- **Be Honest and Direct:** When declining an invitation or obligation, be honest and direct about your reasons. You don't need to provide lengthy explanations—simply stating that you're focusing on a more relaxed holiday season or prioritizing time with family is enough. For example, "Thank you for the invitation, but I'm keeping my holiday commitments light this year so I can spend more time with family."
- **Offer Alternatives:** If you still want to maintain a connection with someone but can't commit to their event, offer an alternative that fits your schedule or energy level. For example, "I won't be able to make the holiday party, but I'd love to meet for coffee after the holidays."
- **Release the Guilt:** Saying no can sometimes come with feelings of guilt, especially if you're worried about disappointing others. Remind yourself that prioritizing your well-being and

focusing on what matters most is not selfish—it's essential for enjoying the holidays in a meaningful way.

3. Simplify Gift-Giving

Gift-giving is often one of the most stressful and time-consuming aspects of the holidays, particularly if you feel obligated to buy gifts for a large number of people or spend more than you can afford. Simplifying your approach to gift-giving can reduce financial strain and allow you to focus on more meaningful expressions of love and appreciation.

- **Set Clear Limits:** Decide in advance how much you're willing to spend on gifts, both in terms of time and money. Set a budget that feels comfortable for you and stick to it. If you have a large family or group of friends, consider suggesting a Secret Santa exchange or setting a spending limit to keep things manageable.
- **Focus on Thoughtful, Low-Cost Gifts:** The most meaningful gifts are often those that come from the heart rather than those with the highest price tag. Consider giving homemade gifts, personalized items, or experience-based gifts such as spending time together or creating new memories.
- **Give the Gift of Time or Service:** If you're trying to reduce material consumption during the holidays, consider giving the gift of your time or service. This could involve offering to babysit for a friend, helping with household tasks, or organizing a fun day out with a loved one. These types of gifts are often more valuable than anything you can buy in a store.

4. Streamline Holiday Preparations

Holiday preparations, from decorating to meal planning, can quickly become overwhelming if you try to do everything perfectly. Streamlining your approach will help you enjoy the process rather than becoming stressed by it.

- **Simplify Decorations:** If decorating your home feels like a major source of stress, simplify your holiday décor. Focus on a few key areas that bring you joy, such as the tree or the dining table, and let go of the pressure to decorate every room. You can also involve your family in the decorating process, turning it into a fun, shared activity rather than a solo task.
- **Streamline Holiday Meals:** Hosting a holiday meal doesn't have to mean preparing a multi-course feast. Simplify your menu by focusing on a few favorite dishes and asking guests to contribute by bringing sides or desserts. A potluck-style meal allows everyone to participate and takes the pressure off of you to do everything.

Staying Focused on What Matters Throughout the Season

As the holiday season unfolds, it's important to regularly check in with yourself and make sure you're staying aligned with your priorities. Here are some strategies to help you stay focused on what truly matters:

1. Practice Mindfulness

Mindfulness is a powerful tool for staying present and connected to what's most meaningful during the holidays. By practicing mindfulness, you can slow down, savor the moment, and avoid getting caught up in the rush of the season.

- **Be Present in Each Moment:** Whether you're spending time with loved ones, decorating your home, or preparing a meal, focus on being fully present in the moment. Avoid multitasking and resist the urge to rush through tasks. Instead, take a deep breath and appreciate the experience.
- **Notice When You're Feeling Overwhelmed:** Pay attention to your body and emotions. If you start to feel overwhelmed or stressed, take a step back and give yourself permission to rest. Mindfulness helps you recognize when you need a break and allows you to respond to your needs with self-compassion.

2. Check In with Your Values Regularly

As the season progresses, it's easy to get swept up in the demands of the holidays and lose sight of your priorities. Make it a habit to check in with your values regularly and adjust your plans as needed.

- **Revisit Your Intentions:** Periodically revisit the intentions you set at the beginning of the season. Are you staying true to your values? Are you focusing on what matters most, or have you become distracted by external pressures? Use these check-ins as an opportunity to realign your actions with your priorities.
- **Adjust Your Plans if Needed:** If you find that your holiday plans have become too hectic or stressful, don't be afraid to make adjustments. You might decide to scale back on certain activities, decline a few more invitations, or simplify your remaining tasks. Flexibility is key to maintaining balance and preventing burnout.

3. Celebrate Meaningful Moments

Finally, make time to celebrate the moments that are most meaningful to you. Whether it's sharing a meal with family, reflecting on the year's blessings, or giving back to others, find joy in the experiences that align with your values.

- **Create Meaningful Traditions:** Consider creating new traditions that reflect what matters most to you and your family. This could involve volunteering together, setting aside time for quiet reflection, or hosting a gratitude circle where everyone shares what they're thankful for.
- **Focus on Connection Over Perfection:** Remember that the true joy of the holidays comes from connection, not perfection. Focus on creating meaningful memories with your loved ones rather than striving for an idealized version of the holidays. Whether things go exactly as planned or not, what matters most is the time spent together and the love shared.

Conclusion

Prioritizing what really matters during the holidays is about letting go of the unnecessary obligations and expectations that create stress and focusing on the aspects of the season that bring you joy, fulfillment, and connection. By clarifying your values, setting intentions, and simplifying your approach to holiday preparations, you can create a more meaningful and enjoyable holiday experience. Remember, the holidays are an opportunity to celebrate what is most important to you—whether that's spending time with loved ones, practicing gratitude, or finding moments of peace and reflection. Through thoughtful planning and mindful decision-making, you can embrace the true spirit of the season and let go of anything that no longer serves you.

Chapter 14: Creating To-Do Lists That Work

The holiday season often brings with it an overwhelming number of tasks—shopping for gifts, decorating the house, attending events, cooking meals, sending out holiday cards, and much more. With so many responsibilities, it's easy to feel scattered and stressed. That's where a well-organized to-do list can make a world of difference. A well-crafted to-do list not only helps you keep track of your tasks but also allows you to break them down into manageable chunks, ensuring that you stay focused, productive, and in control of your time.

In this chapter, we'll explore how to create effective to-do lists that help you stay organized and avoid the overwhelm that often accompanies the holiday season. You'll learn strategies for prioritizing tasks, breaking down large projects, and designing a system that works for your personal style, allowing you to tackle your holiday responsibilities with ease.

Why To-Do Lists Are Essential During the Holidays

To-do lists are more than just a tool for keeping track of tasks—they are a powerful way to reduce mental clutter, maintain focus, and ensure that nothing important slips through the cracks. During the busy holiday season, a well-organized to-do list can be a lifesaver for several reasons:

- **Reduce Stress:** Writing down your tasks allows you to offload them from your mind, reducing the mental load that can lead to stress and anxiety. When everything is clearly listed, you don't have to worry about forgetting something important.
- **Improve Productivity:** A well-structured to-do list helps you stay focused on what needs to be done. By breaking tasks into smaller, manageable steps, you can work more efficiently and feel a sense of accomplishment as you check off completed items.
- **Stay Organized:** The holidays involve juggling many different responsibilities, from shopping and cooking to social commitments and travel plans. A to-do list provides a clear roadmap for managing your time and ensures that you stay organized amidst the holiday chaos.
- **Enhance Time Management:** To-do lists allow you to prioritize your tasks and allocate your time more effectively. You can see at a glance what needs to be done immediately and what can wait, helping you avoid last-minute scrambles.

The Key Components of an Effective To-Do List

Not all to-do lists are created equal. To create a to-do list that truly works, it's important to include specific components that help you stay organized, prioritize your tasks, and break down large projects into manageable steps. Here are the key components of an effective to-do list:

1. Clear, Specific Tasks

The most effective to-do lists contain clear, specific tasks rather than vague goals. Instead of writing down broad objectives like "decorate the house" or "plan holiday dinner," break these tasks into smaller, actionable steps that are easier to tackle.

- **Example of Clear Tasks:** Instead of writing "decorate the house," break it down into tasks like "set up the tree," "hang outdoor lights," and "decorate the mantel." Similarly, rather than writing "plan holiday dinner," list specific steps like "choose menu," "make grocery list," and "order turkey."

Breaking down tasks into clear, actionable steps gives you a more concrete sense of what needs to be done and makes it easier to get started.

2. Prioritization

Not all tasks on your to-do list will carry the same level of urgency or importance. Prioritizing your tasks helps you focus on what needs to be done first and ensures that you're working on the most critical items rather than getting bogged down by less important ones.

- **Identify High-Priority Tasks:** Start by identifying the tasks that have the most pressing deadlines or that are most essential to your holiday plans. These might include things like buying gifts before shipping deadlines, finalizing travel arrangements, or preparing for an upcoming family gathering.
- **Use Categories or Codes:** You can use categories or codes to prioritize your tasks. For example, mark high-priority tasks with an "A," medium-priority tasks with a "B," and low-priority tasks with a "C." Alternatively, use symbols like stars or colors to highlight the most urgent items on your list.

3. Realistic Time Frames

To-do lists are most effective when they include realistic time frames for completing each task. Assigning deadlines to your tasks helps you stay on track and ensures that you're allocating your time wisely.

- **Estimate Time for Each Task:** For each item on your to-do list, estimate how much time it will take to complete. This will help you plan your day more effectively and prevent you from underestimating the time needed for certain tasks. For example, "wrap gifts for the family" might take two hours, while "mail holiday cards" could take 30 minutes.

- **Set Deadlines:** Assign specific deadlines to tasks that need to be completed by a certain date, such as ordering gifts online before the shipping cut-off or completing grocery shopping a few days before a holiday dinner. This ensures that you complete time-sensitive tasks on schedule.

4. Task Categories

Grouping similar tasks together can make your to-do list more organized and easier to navigate. By categorizing tasks by type or by context, you can streamline your workflow and reduce the mental effort of constantly switching between unrelated activities.

- **Create Categories for Different Types of Tasks:** For example, you might have categories such as "Shopping," "Decorating," "Cooking," "Travel," and "Gifts." This allows you to focus on related tasks at once. If you're out running errands, you can tackle multiple shopping-related tasks in one trip, rather than going out multiple times for different items.
- **Use Contextual Categories:** You can also group tasks by where or how they will be completed. For instance, "At Home," "Online," or "Errands" can help you focus on tasks that require similar tools or settings.

5. Manageable Chunks

Breaking down large tasks into smaller, manageable chunks is one of the most important elements of an effective to-do list. Large, vague tasks can feel overwhelming and lead to procrastination. By dividing them into smaller steps, you make progress more tangible and approachable.

- **Break Big Tasks into Subtasks:** For example, "Plan holiday dinner" can be broken down into smaller tasks such as "choose a menu," "make a grocery list," "shop for non-perishable items," and "prepare side dishes." These smaller tasks are easier to tackle and give you a clearer sense of progress.
- **Create Microtasks for Quick Wins:** Include microtasks that can be completed in just a few minutes, such as "make a phone call" or "write a holiday card." These quick wins help you build momentum and give you a sense of accomplishment early in the day.

Strategies for Creating Effective To-Do Lists

Now that we've covered the key components of an effective to-do list, let's dive into practical strategies that will help you create lists that work for your unique needs. Whether you're a digital list maker or prefer pen and paper, these strategies will help you stay organized and avoid feeling overwhelmed.

1. Use a Daily and Weekly List System

One of the best ways to stay organized and manage your time effectively is by using both daily and weekly to-do lists. This approach allows you to keep track of immediate tasks while also planning ahead for the longer-term.

- **Create a Weekly Master List:** At the beginning of each week, create a master to-do list that includes all the tasks you want to accomplish over the next seven days. This could include shopping, meal prep, attending events, wrapping gifts, and other holiday-related responsibilities. Having a weekly overview helps you allocate tasks more effectively and avoid overloading any single day.
- **Break the Weekly List into Daily Tasks:** Each day, create a more specific to-do list by pulling items from your weekly master list. Assign 3-5 tasks that you aim to complete each day. This ensures that your daily to-do list is manageable and that you're consistently making progress toward your weekly goals.

2. Prioritize the Most Important Tasks (MITs)

To avoid feeling overwhelmed by a long to-do list, focus on your Most Important Tasks (MITs) each day. These are the 1-3 tasks that are most critical to complete and that will have the biggest impact on your holiday preparations.

- **Choose 1-3 MITs for Each Day:** At the beginning of each day, identify your MITs. These could be high-priority tasks with upcoming deadlines, tasks that will free up time later in the week, or tasks that align most closely with your holiday goals. For example, if you need to finalize travel arrangements or complete a major shopping trip, those would be your MITs for the day.
- **Focus on MITs First:** Aim to complete your MITs early in the day, before tackling lower-priority tasks. This ensures that even if the rest of your day gets busy or interrupted, you've made significant progress on the most important items.

3. Use Time Blocking to Stay on Track

Time blocking is a powerful productivity technique that involves scheduling specific blocks of time for different tasks or categories of work. This approach can help you stay focused and prevent tasks from spilling over into other parts of your day.

- **Assign Time Blocks to Each Task:** Once you've created your daily to-do list, assign specific time blocks to each task. For example, you might block out an hour in the morning for holiday shopping, 30 minutes in the afternoon for wrapping gifts, and an hour in the evening for meal prep. Having dedicated time blocks for each task reduces the likelihood of distractions and helps you stay on schedule.
- **Group Similar Tasks into Time Blocks:** Time blocking is especially effective when you group similar tasks together. For example, you could block out two hours on Saturday afternoon for all your holiday shopping, rather than making multiple trips throughout the week. Similarly, you might dedicate a morning to writing and sending out holiday cards.

4. Tackle Small Tasks Immediately

Some tasks on your to-do list will be quick and easy to complete—things like sending an email, making a phone call, or running a quick errand. To keep your to-do list from becoming overwhelming, tackle these small tasks immediately rather than letting them pile up.

- **Apply the Two-Minute Rule:** If a task can be completed in two minutes or less, do it immediately rather than putting it off. This prevents small tasks from accumulating and frees up mental space for more important tasks. For example, if you need to confirm a holiday dinner reservation, send the email or make the phone call right away rather than adding it to your list for later.
- **Use Small Tasks as Breaks:** If you're working on a larger project and need a mental break, use small tasks as quick, productive breaks. For example, after spending an hour shopping online for gifts, take a break by writing a holiday card or sending a quick text to confirm holiday plans.

5. Review and Adjust Your List Daily

A to-do list is not a static document—it's a tool that should be reviewed and adjusted regularly to reflect changing priorities, completed tasks, and new responsibilities. Reviewing your list each day helps you stay organized and ensures that you're focusing on the right tasks.

- **Review Your List at the End of Each Day:** At the end of each day, review your to-do list and check off completed tasks. Celebrate your progress and take note of any tasks that didn't get finished. Move unfinished tasks to the next day's list, and adjust your priorities if needed.
- **Create Tomorrow's List the Night Before:** One of the best ways to start your day feeling organized and focused is to create your to-do list the night before. This allows you to wake up

with a clear plan for the day, reducing decision fatigue and helping you hit the ground running.

Avoiding To-Do List Overwhelm

Even with the best intentions, to-do lists can sometimes become overwhelming if they grow too long or unrealistic. To prevent overwhelm, it's important to keep your lists manageable and focus on progress rather than perfection.

1. Limit the Number of Tasks on Your Daily List

It's tempting to create an ambitious to-do list with dozens of tasks, but this can lead to frustration and burnout if you're unable to complete everything. Instead, focus on a smaller number of high-impact tasks each day.

- **Stick to 3-5 Tasks Per Day:** A good rule of thumb is to limit your daily to-do list to 3-5 tasks. This keeps your list manageable and ensures that you're focusing on the most important items. If you complete all your tasks early, you can always add more, but starting with a shorter list helps you stay focused and avoid overwhelm.

2. Be Realistic About Your Time and Energy

It's easy to underestimate how long tasks will take or overestimate how much energy you'll have to complete them. Being realistic about your time and energy levels will help you create more effective to-do lists.

- **Consider Your Energy Peaks:** Pay attention to when you have the most energy during the day and schedule your most challenging tasks for those times. For example, if you're a morning person, tackle your MITs first thing in the morning when you're most alert and focused. Leave lower-priority tasks for times when your energy dips.
- **Build in Buffer Time:** Avoid scheduling tasks back-to-back with no breaks in between. Build in buffer time between tasks to account for any delays, unexpected interruptions, or moments when tasks take longer than expected. This prevents your schedule from becoming too rigid and helps you stay flexible.

3. Give Yourself Grace

Finally, remember that no to-do list is perfect, and it's okay if not everything gets done. Give yourself grace and recognize that the holiday season is meant to be enjoyed, not just checked off a list.

- **Celebrate Progress, Not Perfection:** Focus on the progress you've made each day rather than stressing about unfinished tasks. Even if you don't complete everything on your list, the fact that you're moving forward is something to celebrate.

- **Prioritize Self-Care:** Make sure that your to-do list includes time for relaxation, rest, and self-care. Taking breaks and giving yourself time to recharge will help you stay productive and prevent burnout.

Conclusion

Creating to-do lists that work is an essential skill for managing the many tasks and responsibilities of the holiday season. By breaking down tasks into manageable chunks, prioritizing what's most important, and using strategies like time blocking and daily reviews, you can stay organized and avoid the overwhelm that often accompanies this busy time of year. Remember to keep your lists realistic, celebrate your progress, and give yourself permission to let go of perfection. With an effective to-do list system in place, you'll be able to navigate the holiday season with greater ease, focus, and enjoyment.

Chapter 15: Delegating Holiday Tasks Effectively

The holiday season is full of activities and responsibilities, from planning meals and decorating to buying gifts and attending family gatherings. For many people, the sheer number of tasks can feel overwhelming. However, trying to do everything yourself is a recipe for stress and burnout. One of the most effective ways to manage holiday responsibilities and maintain your sanity is by delegating tasks to family members. When done thoughtfully, delegating not only lightens your load but also creates opportunities for connection and shared experiences with loved ones.

That said, delegating tasks can sometimes lead to conflict, especially if family members feel like they're being given too much to do or don't understand the importance of their role. The key to delegating holiday tasks effectively is clear communication, mutual respect, and a willingness to work as a team. In this chapter, we'll explore how to get family members involved in holiday preparations without conflict, ensuring that everyone contributes to the festive season in a way that feels fair and enjoyable.

Why Delegating Holiday Tasks is Important

For many people, the holidays are synonymous with taking on too much. Whether it's planning elaborate meals, decorating the house from top to bottom, or buying gifts for every relative, the pressure to create a "perfect" holiday can lead to stress, exhaustion, and even resentment. Delegating tasks can help alleviate these feelings by:

- **Reducing Stress:** Sharing the workload helps prevent burnout and allows you to focus on the aspects of the holidays that are most important to you.
- **Building a Sense of Teamwork:** Delegating tasks encourages family members to work together and fosters a sense of shared responsibility for making the holidays special.
- **Encouraging Participation:** When everyone is involved in holiday preparations, family members feel more connected to the celebrations and more invested in the outcome.
- **Teaching Valuable Life Skills:** Delegating tasks to children and teens teaches them responsibility, teamwork, and the importance of contributing to family traditions.

However, for delegation to be successful, it must be done in a way that feels equitable and respectful to everyone involved. Let's explore how to delegate holiday tasks effectively without creating tension or conflict.

Step-by-Step Guide to Delegating Holiday Tasks

Delegating holiday tasks requires clear communication, thoughtful planning, and a willingness to be flexible. Here's a step-by-step guide to help you delegate effectively and avoid common pitfalls.

1. Assess the Tasks That Need to Be Delegated

Before you can delegate tasks, it's important to take a step back and assess what needs to be done. Start by making a list of all the tasks involved in your holiday preparations, from big responsibilities like planning a holiday meal to smaller tasks like setting the table or wrapping gifts.

- **Categorize Tasks by Type:** Break down your holiday responsibilities into categories, such as cooking, decorating, shopping, wrapping gifts, cleaning, and event planning. This will give you a clear picture of what needs to be done and help you identify which tasks can be delegated.
- **Identify Tasks That Can Be Delegated:** Once you've categorized your tasks, identify which ones can realistically be delegated to other family members. Consider factors like the difficulty of the task, the skills required, and the time commitment involved. For example, younger children might be able to help with decorating or setting the table, while teens or adults can take on more complex tasks like cooking or organizing holiday events.
- **Keep Personal Preferences in Mind:** While it's important to delegate, there may be certain tasks that you enjoy doing or that hold special meaning for you. Make a note of these tasks and consider keeping them for yourself, while delegating the ones that feel more like chores.

2. Assign Tasks Based on Strengths and Interests

One of the most effective ways to delegate tasks without conflict is to assign them based on each family member's strengths, interests, and preferences. When people feel that they are being asked to do something they enjoy or are good at, they are more likely to take ownership of the task and complete it with enthusiasm.

- **Consider Individual Strengths:** Think about each family member's skills and strengths when assigning tasks. For example, if one person is great at cooking, they might be responsible for preparing a side dish or dessert. If someone else enjoys decorating, they could take charge of setting up the holiday décor.
- **Ask for Input:** Instead of assigning tasks unilaterally, ask family members for their input on what they'd like to do. For example, you could say, "We have a few tasks that need to be done for the holiday dinner. Would you prefer to help with cooking, setting the table, or wrapping gifts?" Giving people a choice makes them feel more in control and increases their willingness to participate.
- **Match Tasks to Interests:** Whenever possible, try to match tasks to each person's interests. For example, if someone enjoys music, they could create a holiday playlist or be responsible

for entertainment during the gathering. If someone loves shopping, they might take on the responsibility of buying gifts or holiday groceries.

3. Communicate Expectations Clearly

Clear communication is the cornerstone of effective delegation. Family members need to know what is expected of them, when tasks need to be completed, and how their contributions fit into the larger picture of the holiday celebration.

- **Be Specific About Tasks:** When delegating a task, be as specific as possible about what needs to be done and when. For example, instead of saying, "Can you help with dinner?" say, "Can you prepare the mashed potatoes and bring them to the table by 6:00 p.m.?"
- **Set Clear Deadlines:** Make sure that everyone knows when their tasks need to be completed. This is especially important for time-sensitive tasks like cooking or setting up decorations before guests arrive. For example, "I need the table set by 5:00 p.m. so we can start dinner on time."
- **Explain the Importance of the Task:** Help family members understand why their task is important and how it contributes to the overall success of the holiday celebration. For example, you might say, "Your help with decorating the house will create a festive atmosphere for our guests," or "By handling the gift-wrapping, you're helping make sure everyone has a special moment when they open their presents."

4. Encourage Collaboration and Teamwork

Delegating tasks doesn't mean working in isolation. Encouraging collaboration and teamwork can make holiday preparations more enjoyable and help strengthen family bonds.

- **Pair Family Members for Tasks:** Pairing people together for certain tasks can make the work more fun and reduce the feeling of being overwhelmed. For example, you could pair a parent and child to bake cookies together, or ask two siblings to handle decorating the living room. Working in pairs or small groups fosters teamwork and allows family members to share the workload.
- **Make Tasks Social:** Turn holiday preparations into social events by playing music, chatting, or turning certain tasks into games. For example, you could have a gift-wrapping contest to see who can wrap the most presents in the shortest time or who can create the most creative wrapping designs. By making tasks more enjoyable, you'll reduce the sense of obligation and increase motivation.

5. Be Flexible and Willing to Compromise

Not every family member will have the same level of enthusiasm for certain tasks, and it's important to be flexible and willing to compromise. Some tasks may need to be divided differently, or you may need to adjust your expectations based on people's availability or preferences.

- **Negotiate When Needed:** If a family member feels overwhelmed or resistant to a certain task, be open to negotiating. For example, if someone doesn't want to cook, offer them an alternative task like cleaning up after the meal or handling the decorations. The key is to find a solution that works for everyone while still ensuring that the tasks get done.
- **Be Open to Different Approaches:** Delegating tasks means relinquishing some control over how things are done. Be open to the fact that family members might complete tasks differently than you would, and resist the urge to micromanage. For example, if someone decorates the tree in a different style than you would, embrace the creative input rather than focusing on perfection.
- **Respect Boundaries:** Some family members may have personal boundaries around how much they can contribute, whether due to time constraints, health reasons, or personal preferences. Be respectful of these boundaries and avoid pressuring anyone to take on more than they can handle. It's important to recognize that everyone has different capacities and that delegation should be about sharing the workload, not overburdening anyone.

6. Express Gratitude and Acknowledge Contributions

One of the best ways to ensure successful delegation is to express gratitude and acknowledge the contributions of each family member. When people feel appreciated for their efforts, they are more likely to participate willingly and take pride in their work.

- **Offer Genuine Thanks:** Take the time to thank family members for their help, both during the holiday preparations and after the celebration. For example, "I really appreciate you taking care of the gift-wrapping—it made everything look so special," or "Thanks for helping with dinner—everything came out perfectly."
- **Acknowledge Individual Contributions:** When expressing gratitude, be specific about what each person contributed. Acknowledging individual efforts helps family members feel valued and recognized. For example, "You did an amazing job with the decorations—the house looks so festive because of your hard work."
- **Celebrate Team Success:** At the end of the holiday celebration, take a moment to celebrate the success of everyone's efforts. Whether it's a toast at dinner or a simple "job well done" as you relax after the event, recognizing the collective effort creates a sense of accomplishment and strengthens family bonds.

Overcoming Common Challenges in Delegating Holiday Tasks

Even with the best intentions, delegating holiday tasks can sometimes lead to challenges, especially if family members are resistant or if conflicts arise. Here are some common challenges and strategies for overcoming them.

1. Resistance to Delegation

Some family members may be resistant to taking on tasks, either because they're used to someone else handling everything or because they feel they're too busy. To overcome resistance, it's important to communicate the importance of shared responsibility and make delegation feel less like a burden.

- **Explain the Importance of Sharing the Load:** Help family members understand that sharing the workload ensures that no one person is overwhelmed. For example, "I can't handle all the holiday preparations by myself, and it would mean a lot to have everyone pitch in so we can enjoy the day together."
- **Appeal to Fairness:** Frame delegation as a way to make the holiday experience fair for everyone. For example, "It's only fair that we all contribute to the preparations, so no one person is stuck doing everything."
- **Start with Small Tasks:** If someone is particularly resistant, start by assigning them small, manageable tasks that don't feel overwhelming. Over time, they may become more comfortable taking on larger responsibilities.

2. Conflict Over Task Distribution

Conflicts can arise when family members feel that tasks are not distributed fairly or when one person feels they are doing more than their share. To prevent this, it's important to ensure that tasks are distributed equitably and to address any concerns early on.

- **Ensure Fairness in Task Distribution:** Make sure that tasks are distributed fairly among family members, taking into account each person's abilities, availability, and preferences. If one person feels they are doing too much, reassess the distribution and make adjustments if needed.
- **Address Concerns Openly:** If conflicts arise over task distribution, address the issue openly and respectfully. For example, "I've noticed that you're feeling frustrated with the tasks you've been given. Let's talk about how we can redistribute things to make it fairer."
- **Use a Task Rotation System:** To prevent feelings of inequality, consider using a task rotation system where different family members take turns handling different responsibilities each year. For example, one year someone might be responsible for cooking, while the next year they take charge of decorations.

3. Managing Differing Standards

Different family members may have different standards for how tasks should be completed. For example, one person might be very detail-oriented about decorating, while another might prefer a more relaxed approach. To avoid conflict, it's important to let go of perfectionism and embrace flexibility.

- **Set Clear Expectations, but Be Flexible:** While it's important to communicate your expectations for certain tasks, be flexible and open to different approaches. For example, if someone wraps gifts in a way that's different from your usual style, embrace their creativity rather than focusing on the differences.
- **Prioritize What Matters Most:** If there are certain tasks where high standards are particularly important to you—such as setting the table for a formal dinner—communicate that clearly. For other tasks, be willing to let go of perfection and allow family members to put their own spin on things.

Conclusion

Delegating holiday tasks effectively is key to reducing stress, sharing the workload, and fostering a sense of teamwork among family members. By assessing tasks, assigning them based on strengths and interests, communicating clearly, and encouraging collaboration, you can involve your family in holiday preparations without conflict. Remember to stay flexible, express gratitude, and celebrate the collective effort. With the right approach, delegating tasks can not only lighten your load but also create opportunities for connection and shared experiences that make the holidays even more meaningful.

Chapter 16: Simplifying Holiday Travel Plans

For many people, the holiday season includes traveling to visit family and friends, attend special events, or take a much-needed vacation. While holiday travel can be exciting, it can also be a major source of stress, with crowded airports, busy roads, fluctuating prices, and the pressure to stay on budget. Managing travel logistics—planning, packing, budgeting, and coordinating schedules—can quickly become overwhelming if not handled strategically.

In this chapter, we will explore time-saving tips and strategies to help you organize your holiday travel, pack efficiently, and stay within your budget. With a well-thought-out plan, you can reduce the stress of holiday travel and ensure that your journey is as smooth and enjoyable as possible.

Common Holiday Travel Challenges

Holiday travel often comes with its own unique set of challenges that can lead to stress if not properly managed. Some of the most common difficulties include:

- **High Travel Costs:** Airfares, hotel rates, and rental car prices often skyrocket during the holiday season due to increased demand, making it difficult to stay within budget.
- **Crowded Airports and Roads:** The holiday season is one of the busiest travel times of the year, which means long lines, traffic jams, and potential delays at airports and on the road.
- **Last-Minute Travel Plans:** Whether due to unpredictable schedules or unexpected events, last-minute travel plans can add to the chaos, especially when flights and accommodations are limited.
- **Packing for Multiple Events or Weather Conditions:** Traveling during the holidays often means packing for a variety of events, such as family gatherings and holiday parties, or for different weather conditions, from winter cold to warmer climates.
- **Managing Family Schedules:** Coordinating travel plans with family members, especially when traveling with children or large groups, can be challenging and time-consuming.

By addressing these challenges head-on with thoughtful planning and organization, you can minimize stress and ensure that your holiday travel is more manageable and enjoyable.

Step-by-Step Guide to Simplifying Holiday Travel Plans

To simplify your holiday travel, it's important to break down the process into manageable steps, from booking transportation and accommodations to packing and staying on budget. Here's a step-by-step guide to help you navigate the complexities of holiday travel with ease.

1. Plan and Book Early

The earlier you start planning your holiday travel, the more options you'll have for flights, accommodations, and transportation. Early planning can save you both time and money, while also reducing the stress of last-minute decisions.

- **Start Researching Early:** Begin researching flights, hotels, and rental cars at least 2-3 months in advance of the holiday season. Use fare comparison tools like Google Flights, Kayak, or Skyscanner to track prices and find the best deals. These tools allow you to set up price alerts so that you'll be notified if prices drop.
- **Book Flights and Accommodations Early:** Flights and accommodations fill up quickly during the holiday season, so aim to book your travel as early as possible. Booking early not only gives you more flexibility in terms of flight times and hotel availability but also helps you lock in lower prices before they rise as the holidays approach.
- **Be Flexible with Travel Dates:** If possible, avoid traveling on peak travel days such as the day before Thanksgiving, Christmas Eve, or New Year's Eve. Flying or driving on less popular days—such as the days after a major holiday or mid-week—can help you save money and avoid the worst of the crowds.
- **Look for Alternate Airports or Routes:** If you live near a major city with multiple airports, consider flying out of a smaller, less congested airport to save time and reduce the stress of navigating a crowded hub. Similarly, look for alternate routes when driving to avoid heavy traffic.

2. Stay on Budget

Holiday travel can quickly become expensive if you're not careful with your spending. Between airfare, hotels, rental cars, and meals on the road, costs can add up quickly. Creating a travel budget and sticking to it can help you avoid financial stress.

- **Set a Realistic Budget:** Before you start booking flights or hotels, set a realistic budget for your holiday travel. Include all potential expenses, such as transportation, accommodation, meals, entertainment, and incidentals like parking fees or tips. Knowing your budget ahead of time will help you make informed decisions and avoid overspending.
- **Look for Travel Deals and Discounts:** Take advantage of travel deals, loyalty programs, and credit card rewards to save money on flights, hotels, and rental cars. Many airlines and hotel chains offer special holiday promotions or discounts for early bookings. If you have accumulated frequent flyer miles or credit card points, consider using them to offset the cost of your trip.

- **Consider Alternative Accommodations:** If hotel prices are too high during the holidays, consider staying in alternative accommodations like vacation rentals (Airbnb, Vrbo), hostels, or even with friends or family. Vacation rentals are especially cost-effective if you're traveling with a group, as you can split the cost and enjoy the benefits of a full kitchen, allowing you to save money by cooking some meals at home.
- **Limit Dining Out:** Meals can be one of the biggest travel expenses, especially if you're eating out for every meal. To stay on budget, plan to limit dining out by packing snacks or preparing simple meals in your hotel or vacation rental. If you're driving, pack a cooler with sandwiches, fruit, and drinks for the road.

3. Organize Your Travel Documents

Traveling during the holidays often means dealing with crowded airports and long lines at security checkpoints. To make your journey as smooth as possible, it's important to have all your travel documents organized and easily accessible.

- **Keep Documents in One Place:** Whether you're traveling by plane, train, or car, keep all your travel documents—tickets, boarding passes, identification, passports (if needed), hotel reservations, and rental car information—in one easy-to-access location. A travel document organizer or digital folder on your phone can help you keep everything in order.
- **Check Passport and ID Requirements:** If you're traveling internationally, make sure your passport is up to date and won't expire within six months of your travel date. For domestic travel, check your state's ID requirements, especially if your state requires a REAL ID for airport travel. Ensure that all family members have the appropriate identification before departure.
- **Check-in Online:** Many airlines allow you to check in online 24-48 hours before your flight, which can save you time at the airport. Take advantage of online check-in to choose your seats, print your boarding pass, or have it sent to your phone.
- **Download Travel Apps:** Travel apps like TripIt, Google Maps, or airline-specific apps can help you keep track of your itinerary, get real-time flight updates, and navigate your destination with ease.

4. Pack Efficiently

Packing can be one of the most stressful aspects of holiday travel, especially if you're trying to fit gifts, winter clothes, and holiday attire into your luggage. To simplify packing and avoid overpacking, focus on essentials and use smart packing strategies.

- **Make a Packing List:** Before you start packing, create a detailed packing list that includes everything you need for your trip. This helps you avoid forgetting important items and reduces the likelihood of overpacking. Divide your list into categories such as clothing, toiletries, electronics, and travel documents.
- **Pack Versatile Clothing:** Choose versatile, mix-and-match clothing items that can be worn in different combinations. This allows you to pack fewer clothes while still having plenty of outfit options. For example, pack neutral-colored tops and bottoms that can be dressed up or down depending on the occasion.
- **Layer for Different Weather Conditions:** If you're traveling to a destination with unpredictable weather, pack clothing that can be layered. Layering allows you to adjust to changing temperatures without needing to pack bulky clothing. For example, pack lightweight shirts that can be layered under sweaters or jackets.
- **Use Packing Cubes or Compression Bags:** Packing cubes or compression bags help you organize your luggage and save space. Use them to separate clothing by category (e.g., tops, bottoms, accessories) or by day, making it easier to find what you need without unpacking your entire suitcase.
- **Ship Gifts Ahead of Time:** If you're bringing gifts with you, consider shipping them ahead of time to avoid the hassle of packing bulky or fragile items in your luggage. Many retailers offer gift-wrapping and direct shipping options during the holidays, allowing you to have gifts delivered straight to your destination.

5. Prepare for Busy Airports and Roads

Traveling during the holiday season often means dealing with crowded airports, long security lines, and busy roads. Preparing for these challenges in advance can help you avoid frustration and delays.

- **Arrive Early:** Whether you're flying or driving, allow extra time for holiday travel. If you're flying, aim to arrive at the airport at least 2-3 hours before your flight, especially if you're flying during peak travel days. This gives you plenty of time to check in, pass through security, and deal with any unexpected delays.
- **Use TSA PreCheck or Global Entry:** If you're a frequent traveler, consider applying for TSA PreCheck or Global Entry to expedite your passage through security. These programs allow you to use dedicated security lanes, avoid removing shoes and belts, and save time at the airport.

- **Check Traffic Reports:** If you're driving, check traffic reports or use navigation apps like Waze or Google Maps to find the best routes and avoid traffic jams. Leave early in the day or travel during off-peak hours to avoid heavy traffic.
- **Pack Snacks and Entertainment:** Whether you're flying or driving, long delays are common during the holidays. Pack snacks, water, and entertainment (books, magazines, podcasts, or downloaded movies) to keep yourself and your family occupied while waiting at the airport or on long drives.

6. Coordinate Travel Plans with Family

If you're traveling with family or meeting up with relatives at your destination, clear communication and coordination are essential to avoid confusion or missed connections.

- **Share Travel Itineraries:** Make sure everyone in your group knows each other's travel plans, including flight numbers, arrival times, and hotel reservations. Share itineraries using travel apps or a shared document to keep everyone informed and on the same page.
- **Plan for Pickups and Drop-offs:** If you're being picked up from the airport or train station, coordinate with family members to ensure that everyone knows the meeting point and time. Use apps like WhatsApp or Messenger to communicate real-time updates, such as flight delays or traffic conditions.
- **Assign Responsibilities:** If you're traveling with a large group or family, assign responsibilities to different members of the group to keep things organized. For example, one person can be in charge of coordinating transportation, while another handles hotel check-ins or meal reservations.

7. Prepare for the Unexpected

Even with the best-laid plans, holiday travel can be unpredictable, and it's important to prepare for potential delays, cancellations, or other disruptions.

- **Purchase Travel Insurance:** Travel insurance can provide peace of mind if your trip is disrupted by cancellations, delays, or unexpected emergencies. Many travel insurance policies cover trip cancellations due to weather, illness, or other unforeseen circumstances, as well as lost luggage or medical emergencies.
- **Have a Backup Plan:** If your flight is delayed or canceled, it's helpful to have a backup plan in place. Keep a list of alternate flights, nearby hotels, and emergency contact numbers on hand. If you're driving, plan alternative routes in case of road closures or heavy traffic.
- **Stay Flexible and Patient:** Holiday travel can be stressful, especially when faced with unexpected challenges. Staying flexible, patient, and adaptable will help you navigate delays and changes with a positive attitude. Bring a sense of humor and remind yourself that the holiday season is about spending time with loved ones, even if the journey doesn't go exactly as planned.

Conclusion

Simplifying your holiday travel plans involves careful planning, smart packing, and staying on top of your budget. By booking early, setting a clear budget, organizing your travel documents, packing efficiently, and preparing for the unexpected, you can significantly reduce the stress of holiday travel and enjoy the journey as much as the destination. Remember that travel during the holidays is often unpredictable, so flexibility and patience are key to keeping the holiday spirit alive throughout your trip. With these strategies in place, you'll be well-equipped to navigate the challenges of holiday travel and focus on what matters most—spending time with the people you love.

Part 4: Mental and Emotional Well-Being

Chapter 17: Recognizing Holiday-Induced Anxiety

The holiday season, often portrayed as a time of joy and togetherness, can paradoxically be one of the most anxiety-inducing times of the year for many people. Amid the cheerful music, festive decorations, and gatherings, there are hidden stressors that can trigger feelings of overwhelm, worry, and even dread. Recognizing holiday-induced anxiety is the first step toward addressing it and ensuring that the holiday season remains a time of peace and enjoyment.

This chapter will explore the root causes of holiday-induced anxiety, help you identify the specific stressors that may be affecting you, and provide actionable strategies for managing and alleviating anxiety during the festive season. By understanding why the holidays can trigger anxiety and learning how to address it, you can create a more balanced, fulfilling holiday experience for yourself and those around you.

What is Holiday-Induced Anxiety?

Holiday-induced anxiety refers to the heightened levels of stress, worry, or unease that many people experience during the holiday season. Unlike clinical anxiety disorders, which are persistent and may occur year-round, holiday-induced anxiety is often temporary and linked to the unique pressures of the holiday season.

For some people, the holidays bring a range of emotions, from excitement and anticipation to anxiety and guilt. This emotional rollercoaster can make it difficult to manage day-to-day activities, leading to feelings of overwhelm. Symptoms of holiday-induced anxiety may include:

- **Physical Symptoms:** Tension headaches, stomach upset, fatigue, sleep disturbances, increased heart rate, or muscle tension.
- **Emotional Symptoms:** Irritability, frustration, sadness, or feelings of dread about upcoming events.
- **Cognitive Symptoms:** Difficulty concentrating, racing thoughts, worry about meeting expectations, or fear of judgment.
- **Behavioral Symptoms:** Avoidance of social gatherings, procrastination, overcommitting, or perfectionism.

Root Causes of Holiday-Induced Anxiety

To effectively address holiday-induced anxiety, it's important to identify the root causes that trigger these feelings. While each person's experience of holiday anxiety is unique, there are several common causes that many people share.

1. Unrealistic Expectations

One of the biggest sources of holiday-induced anxiety is the pressure to meet unrealistic expectations—whether it's the desire to create the "perfect" holiday, buy the ideal gifts, or host flawless family gatherings. These expectations are often influenced by societal norms, media portrayals of the holidays, or internalized beliefs about what the holiday season "should" look like.

- **Self-Imposed Pressure:** Many people place undue pressure on themselves to create an ideal holiday experience for their loved ones. This might involve spending hours planning elaborate meals, decorating the house to perfection, or buying expensive gifts in an attempt to live up to an unrealistic standard of holiday success.
- **External Expectations:** Family members, friends, or social circles may also have high expectations for holiday gatherings, gifts, or traditions. The pressure to meet these expectations can lead to feelings of inadequacy or anxiety, especially if there are financial constraints or time limitations.

2. Financial Strain

The holidays can be financially burdensome, particularly when there are high expectations around gift-giving, travel, and hosting events. Financial anxiety is one of the most common stressors during the holiday season, and it can lead to worry about spending more than you can afford or going into debt.

- **Gift-Giving Pressure:** The expectation to give expensive or numerous gifts can cause significant financial strain. Many people feel obligated to buy gifts for extended family, friends, coworkers, and others, which can quickly add up.
- **Travel and Entertainment Costs:** Holiday travel, hosting family gatherings, and attending parties can also be costly. Plane tickets, accommodations, festive meals, and social events can all take a toll on your budget, leading to anxiety about how to manage these expenses.

3. Overcommitment and Time Pressure

The holiday season is typically filled with social events, family gatherings, work parties, and holiday traditions. While these activities can be enjoyable, they can also lead to overcommitment and a sense of time pressure. Juggling multiple responsibilities—especially when combined with work or family duties—can leave little time for relaxation or self-care.

- **Too Many Events:** Trying to attend every holiday party, family dinner, or social gathering can be exhausting. Overcommitting to events leaves little time for rest, leading to burnout and increased anxiety.
- **Balancing Work and Personal Life:** Many people struggle to balance work commitments with holiday preparations. End-of-year deadlines, office parties, and personal obligations can create a packed schedule, making it difficult to manage everything without feeling overwhelmed.

4. Family Dynamics

Family gatherings during the holidays can be a major source of anxiety, especially if there are underlying conflicts, unresolved issues, or difficult relationships. The pressure to maintain harmony or avoid confrontation can cause emotional strain, particularly when family members have differing values, opinions, or personalities.

- **Tension with Family Members:** Whether it's sibling rivalry, parental expectations, or long-standing disagreements, holiday gatherings can bring unresolved family dynamics to the surface. The pressure to keep the peace or navigate difficult conversations can lead to anticipatory anxiety before family events.
- **Feelings of Obligation:** Many people feel obligated to attend family gatherings, even if these events are emotionally taxing. This sense of duty can lead to resentment or anxiety, especially if attending means spending time with individuals who trigger negative emotions.

5. Grief and Loneliness

The holidays can be a difficult time for those who have experienced loss, whether it's the death of a loved one, a recent breakup, or a feeling of isolation from friends and family. The emphasis on togetherness and celebration during the holidays can magnify feelings of grief or loneliness, making it harder to cope.

- **Missing Loved Ones:** If you've lost a family member or close friend, the holidays can be a painful reminder of their absence. Traditions that once brought joy may now feel bittersweet, and you may struggle with feelings of sadness or grief during what is supposed to be a festive time.

- **Loneliness or Isolation:** For some, the holidays highlight feelings of loneliness, particularly if they are far from family or don't have close social connections. Seeing others celebrate with loved ones can exacerbate feelings of isolation or sadness.

6. Perfectionism

Perfectionism is another common driver of holiday-induced anxiety. The desire to make everything "just right"—whether it's cooking the perfect meal, decorating the house flawlessly, or finding the perfect gifts—can lead to high levels of stress.

- **Fear of Judgment:** Perfectionism is often rooted in a fear of judgment or criticism from others. You may worry that your holiday preparations won't measure up to expectations, leading to anxiety about how you'll be perceived by family, friends, or colleagues.
- **Unrealistic Standards:** Perfectionists often set unrealistic standards for themselves, leading to a constant feeling of not being "good enough." This mindset can make holiday tasks feel overwhelming, as you strive to meet unattainable goals.

Recognizing the Signs of Holiday-Induced Anxiety

It's important to recognize the signs of holiday-induced anxiety early so that you can address them before they escalate. Here are some common signs that you may be experiencing holiday-related anxiety:

- **Persistent Worry:** You find yourself constantly worrying about upcoming events, whether you'll meet expectations, or how you'll handle holiday-related responsibilities.
- **Overwhelm and Procrastination:** You feel overwhelmed by the number of tasks on your to-do list, leading to procrastination or avoidance of holiday preparations.
- **Physical Symptoms:** You experience physical symptoms of anxiety, such as headaches, stomachaches, muscle tension, or difficulty sleeping, particularly when thinking about holiday-related tasks or events.
- **Irritability or Mood Swings:** You feel more irritable or emotionally volatile than usual, snapping at loved ones or feeling easily frustrated by minor issues.
- **Avoidance of Social Events:** You feel a desire to avoid social gatherings or family events due to feelings of anxiety or dread, even if you usually enjoy these activities.

Strategies for Addressing Holiday-Induced Anxiety

If you recognize that holiday-induced anxiety is affecting your well-being, there are several strategies you can use to address it. By taking proactive steps to manage stress and set realistic expectations, you can alleviate anxiety and enjoy the holiday season with greater peace of mind.

1. Set Realistic Expectations

One of the most effective ways to reduce holiday anxiety is to set realistic expectations for yourself and others. Let go of the pressure to create a perfect holiday and focus on what's truly important to you.

- **Embrace Imperfection:** Remind yourself that the holidays don't need to be perfect to be meaningful. It's okay if things don't go exactly as planned—whether it's a burned dish, a less-than-perfect gift, or a last-minute change of plans. Focus on the moments of connection and joy, rather than striving for perfection.
- **Communicate Expectations with Others:** Have open conversations with family members about what's realistic for the holiday season. If certain traditions or expectations are causing stress, discuss ways to simplify or adjust them. For example, if hosting a large dinner feels overwhelming, consider a potluck-style meal where everyone contributes.

2. Practice Mindfulness and Stress Management

Mindfulness and stress management techniques can help you stay grounded and calm during the holiday season. By practicing these techniques regularly, you can reduce feelings of overwhelm and prevent anxiety from taking over.

- **Deep Breathing Exercises:** When you start to feel anxious, practice deep breathing exercises to calm your nervous system. Try the 4-7-8 breathing technique: inhale for 4 seconds, hold your breath for 7 seconds, and exhale for 8 seconds. Repeat this cycle several times until you feel more relaxed.
- **Mindful Meditation:** Incorporate mindfulness meditation into your daily routine to help you stay present and reduce stress. Even just 10-15 minutes of meditation each day can help you manage anxiety and cultivate a sense of calm during the holiday season.
- **Progressive Muscle Relaxation:** Progressive muscle relaxation involves tensing and relaxing different muscle groups in your body, helping to release physical tension. This technique is especially helpful if you experience physical symptoms of anxiety, such as muscle tightness or headaches.

3. Simplify Your Holiday Plans

Simplifying your holiday plans can help you avoid overcommitment and reduce the pressure to do everything. By focusing on what matters most and letting go of unnecessary tasks, you can create a more manageable and enjoyable holiday experience.

- **Limit Social Commitments:** Be selective about which events and gatherings you attend. It's okay to decline invitations if your schedule is already full or if certain events cause more stress than joy. Prioritize the gatherings that are most meaningful to you and leave space in your schedule for rest and relaxation.
- **Scale Back Holiday Preparations:** If holiday preparations feel overwhelming, look for ways to simplify. For example, instead of cooking an elaborate meal, opt for a simpler menu. If decorating feels like a chore, focus on a few key areas rather than decorating the entire house.

4. Set Boundaries

Setting healthy boundaries during the holiday season is essential for managing anxiety. Boundaries help you protect your time, energy, and emotional well-being by ensuring that you don't overextend yourself.

- **Set Limits on Time and Energy:** Be honest with yourself and others about how much time and energy you have to dedicate to holiday activities. If you need to leave a gathering early or take a break during the day, give yourself permission to do so without guilt.
- **Say No When Necessary:** It's okay to say no to requests or invitations that feel overwhelming. Politely decline invitations or delegate tasks if you're feeling overburdened. For example, "I appreciate the invitation, but I'm going to take some time for myself this year."

5. Address Financial Anxiety

If financial anxiety is a major source of stress during the holidays, taking steps to manage your budget can help alleviate that burden.

- **Create a Holiday Budget:** Set a realistic holiday budget that accounts for all expenses, including gifts, travel, and entertainment. Stick to your budget to avoid overspending, and consider alternative ways to celebrate that don't involve excessive costs.
- **Simplify Gift-Giving:** Consider simplifying gift-giving by setting spending limits or opting for homemade gifts. For large families or groups of friends, suggest a Secret Santa gift exchange to reduce the number of gifts you need to buy.

6. Seek Support from Loved Ones

If you're struggling with holiday-induced anxiety, don't hesitate to seek support from loved ones. Talking about your feelings with a trusted friend, family member, or therapist can help you process your emotions and gain perspective.

- **Share Your Feelings:** Open up to a friend or family member about how you're feeling. Sometimes, simply expressing your anxiety can be a relief, and loved ones may offer emotional support or practical advice.
- **Seek Professional Help:** If holiday anxiety becomes overwhelming or persistent, consider seeking support from a therapist or counselor. Professional guidance can help you develop coping strategies and work through deeper emotional challenges.

Conclusion

Holiday-induced anxiety is a common experience, but it doesn't have to overshadow the joy and meaning of the season. By recognizing the root causes of your anxiety and implementing strategies to address them—such as setting realistic expectations, simplifying your plans, and practicing mindfulness—you can reduce stress and create a more balanced, peaceful holiday experience. Remember that it's okay to let go of perfection, set boundaries, and prioritize your well-being during the holidays. With the right tools in place, you can navigate holiday anxiety and focus on what truly matters: connection, gratitude, and joy.

Chapter 18: Practicing Self-Care During the Holidays

The holiday season, while often filled with joy, celebration, and connection, can also be a time of heightened stress and exhaustion. With the whirlwind of shopping, social gatherings, family obligations, and the pressure to meet expectations, it's easy to overlook your own needs. Practicing self-care during the holidays is essential for maintaining balance, staying grounded, and preserving your emotional and physical well-being. Prioritizing self-care not only benefits your overall health but also enables you to fully enjoy the season and give to others from a place of strength rather than depletion.

In this chapter, we will explore a variety of self-care routines and relaxation techniques designed to help you stay centered and calm amidst the holiday hustle. By incorporating these practices into your holiday schedule, you can reduce stress, manage overwhelm, and cultivate a greater sense of peace and joy.

Why Self-Care is Essential During the Holidays

Self-care is often misunderstood as a luxury, but in reality, it is a critical practice for maintaining health and well-being—especially during busy and stressful times like the holidays. When you're pulled in many directions and feel overwhelmed by obligations, self-care serves as a foundation that allows you to cope with stress, prevent burnout, and recharge your energy.

Here are some reasons why self-care is particularly important during the holiday season:

- **Prevents Burnout:** The holiday season can lead to physical and emotional burnout due to increased demands on your time, energy, and resources. Regular self-care practices help you manage stress and avoid reaching a point of exhaustion.
- **Supports Emotional Well-Being:** The holidays can bring up a range of emotions, from joy and excitement to sadness, anxiety, or grief. Practicing self-care helps you process these emotions and maintain emotional balance.
- **Boosts Physical Health:** Physical self-care, such as getting enough sleep, staying active, and eating nourishing foods, is crucial for staying healthy during the holidays, especially when the season is filled with rich meals, late nights, and frequent social events.
- **Promotes Mindfulness and Presence:** Self-care helps you stay present and mindful, allowing you to enjoy the special moments of the holiday season rather than getting lost in stress or distractions.

Self-Care Routines for the Holiday Season

To make self-care a priority during the holidays, it's helpful to develop a routine that includes practices for both physical and emotional well-being. By creating a daily or weekly self-care schedule, you can ensure that you're taking time for yourself even amidst the busyness of the season.

1. Start Your Day with Intention

Beginning your day with intention can set a positive tone for the rest of the day and help you feel more grounded and focused. Incorporating a morning self-care routine, even if it's just a few minutes long, can make a significant difference in how you manage stress throughout the day.

- **Morning Meditation or Mindfulness Practice:** Spend 5-10 minutes each morning practicing mindfulness or meditation. Simply sit in a quiet place, focus on your breath, and observe your thoughts without judgment. This practice helps calm your mind and prepares you to handle the day's challenges with clarity and composure.
- **Set Daily Intentions:** After your mindfulness practice, take a moment to set an intention for the day. This could be a word, phrase, or goal that aligns with how you want to feel or what you want to focus on. For example, your intention might be "calm," "gratitude," or "stay present." Setting an intention helps you approach the day with purpose and mindfulness.
- **Move Your Body:** Incorporating movement into your morning routine, even if it's just a short stretch or a quick walk, can boost your energy and improve your mood. Gentle exercises like yoga or stretching are excellent ways to release tension and prepare your body for the day ahead.

2. Practice Mindful Eating

Holiday gatherings often revolve around food, which can make it difficult to maintain healthy eating habits. While it's important to enjoy the festive treats, practicing mindful eating can help you find balance and nourish your body without overindulging.

- **Eat with Awareness:** Mindful eating involves paying attention to the experience of eating—savoring each bite, noticing the flavors, textures, and aromas, and being present in the moment. This practice helps you slow down, enjoy your food more fully, and avoid overeating.
- **Listen to Your Body's Signals:** During holiday meals, tune in to your body's hunger and fullness cues. Stop eating when you feel satisfied, rather than when you're uncomfortably full. This helps prevent the sluggishness and discomfort that often come with holiday indulgence.
- **Balance Treats with Nourishing Foods:** Enjoy holiday treats in moderation, but also make sure to incorporate nourishing, nutrient-rich foods into your meals. Focus on vegetables, lean proteins, whole grains, and healthy fats to keep your energy levels steady and support your overall health.

3. Incorporate Relaxation Breaks into Your Day

Amidst the hustle and bustle of the holiday season, it's important to carve out moments of relaxation to prevent stress from building up. Scheduling regular breaks throughout the day gives you a chance to recharge and reconnect with yourself.

- **Take Short Mindfulness Breaks:** Throughout the day, take 5-minute mindfulness breaks to pause, breathe, and check in with yourself. During these breaks, practice deep breathing, close your eyes, and focus on the present moment. This simple practice can help you reset your mind and reduce stress.
- **Create a Soothing Evening Routine:** In the evenings, set aside time to unwind and relax before bed. This could include reading a book, taking a warm bath, listening to calming music, or practicing gentle yoga. An evening self-care routine helps signal to your body that it's time to wind down and prepares you for restful sleep.
- **Practice Gratitude:** One of the most effective ways to shift your mindset from stress to joy is through gratitude. At the end of each day, take a few moments to reflect on what you're grateful for. This simple practice can improve your mood and help you focus on the positive aspects of the holiday season.

4. Protect Your Sleep

Quality sleep is one of the most important elements of self-care, but it's often neglected during the busy holiday season. Late-night gatherings, parties, or stress can disrupt your sleep schedule, leading to fatigue and irritability.

- **Prioritize a Consistent Sleep Schedule:** Aim to go to bed and wake up at the same time each day, even during the holidays. A consistent sleep schedule helps regulate your body's internal clock and promotes better quality sleep.
- **Create a Relaxing Sleep Environment:** Make your bedroom a calm, comfortable space that supports restful sleep. Keep the room cool, dark, and quiet, and avoid using electronics (such as your phone or computer) in the hour leading up to bedtime. Instead, focus on relaxing activities like reading or deep breathing exercises.
- **Limit Caffeine and Alcohol:** While holiday parties often involve caffeinated drinks or alcohol, these substances can interfere with your ability to fall asleep and stay asleep. Try to limit your consumption of caffeine and alcohol, especially in the evening, to protect your sleep quality.

5. Engage in Physical Activity

Staying active is a key component of self-care, as regular physical activity helps reduce stress, boost your mood, and improve your overall health. During the holiday season, it's especially important to make time for exercise, even if it's in short bursts.

- **Fit in Short Workouts:** If your schedule is packed with holiday activities, look for opportunities to fit in short workouts. This could be a 20-minute walk, a quick yoga session, or a home workout routine that you can do in the morning or between events.
- **Go for a Walk Outdoors:** Spending time in nature is an excellent way to reduce stress and recharge. If you can, go for a walk in a park, on a nature trail, or even around your neighborhood. Walking in fresh air helps clear your mind and provides a break from holiday chaos.
- **Incorporate Movement into Holiday Activities:** You can also integrate movement into holiday traditions—whether it's taking a family walk after a big meal, dancing to festive music, or engaging in winter activities like ice skating or hiking.

6. Set Boundaries Around Your Time

One of the most important forms of self-care during the holidays is learning to set healthy boundaries. Overcommitting to events, social gatherings, or obligations can lead to stress and exhaustion, so it's essential to protect your time and energy by saying no when necessary.

- **Limit Social Commitments:** Be mindful of how many social events or holiday gatherings you commit to. It's okay to say no to invitations if your schedule is already full or if you feel overwhelmed. Prioritize the events that are most meaningful to you and leave space in your calendar for rest and downtime.
- **Protect Personal Time:** Block off time in your calendar for personal self-care activities, such as relaxing at home, practicing yoga, or spending quiet time reading. Treat this time as non-negotiable and don't let other obligations encroach on it.
- **Communicate Your Boundaries Clearly:** When setting boundaries with others, be clear and respectful. For example, you might say, "I'm going to take some time for myself this afternoon to recharge, but I'm looking forward to seeing everyone at dinner tonight." Setting boundaries ensures that you're not overextending yourself and helps others respect your needs.

7. Practice Emotional Self-Care

Emotional self-care involves taking steps to protect and nurture your mental health, particularly when emotions run high during the holiday season. This is especially important if you're dealing with family conflicts, grief, or stress.

- **Acknowledge Your Emotions:** During the holidays, it's normal to experience a wide range of emotions, from joy and excitement to sadness or anxiety. Give yourself permission to feel whatever emotions arise without judgment. Acknowledging your feelings allows you to process them in a healthy way.
- **Practice Self-Compassion:** Be kind to yourself, especially when things don't go as planned. If you're feeling stressed, anxious, or overwhelmed, practice self-compassion by offering yourself the same understanding and care that you would offer a close friend. Remind yourself that it's okay not to be perfect and that you're doing your best.
- **Talk to Someone You Trust:** If you're struggling emotionally, don't hesitate to reach out to a friend, family member, or therapist. Sometimes, simply talking about your feelings with someone who listens and understands can help alleviate emotional burdens and provide perspective.

8. Incorporate Creativity into Your Self-Care Routine

Engaging in creative activities can be a powerful form of self-care, as it allows you to express yourself, relax, and tap into your imagination. Whether you enjoy crafting, painting, writing, or cooking, finding time for creative expression can bring joy and reduce stress.

- **Create Holiday Crafts:** Use the holiday season as an opportunity to engage in creative activities, such as making homemade decorations, creating DIY gifts, or designing your own holiday cards. Crafting can be a fun, relaxing way to take a break from more stressful holiday tasks.
- **Journal Your Thoughts and Feelings:** Journaling is a great way to process emotions, clarify thoughts, and reflect on your experiences. Set aside time each day or week to write in a journal, focusing on your feelings, what you're grateful for, or any stressors you're facing.
- **Cook or Bake for Fun:** If you enjoy cooking or baking, use it as a creative outlet during the holidays. Try new recipes, experiment with flavors, or bake festive treats as a way to relax and express your culinary creativity.

Relaxation Techniques to Stay Grounded

In addition to self-care routines, relaxation techniques can help you stay grounded and calm during the holiday season. These techniques are simple, effective ways to reduce stress and bring your mind and body back into balance.

1. Deep Breathing Exercises

Deep breathing exercises are one of the quickest and most effective ways to calm your nervous system and reduce stress. When you feel overwhelmed or anxious, practicing deep breathing can help you regain control and return to a state of calm.

- **Box Breathing:** One of the simplest deep breathing exercises is box breathing, also known as four-square breathing. Inhale through your nose for 4 counts, hold your breath for 4 counts, exhale through your mouth for 4 counts, and hold your breath again for 4 counts. Repeat this cycle several times until you feel more relaxed.
- **Diaphragmatic Breathing:** Focus on breathing deeply into your diaphragm, rather than shallow breaths into your chest. Place one hand on your chest and one hand on your abdomen. As you breathe in, your abdomen should rise while your chest remains still. Exhale fully, letting your abdomen fall. This type of breathing stimulates the body's relaxation response.

2. Progressive Muscle Relaxation (PMR)

Progressive muscle relaxation (PMR) is a technique that involves tensing and then relaxing different muscle groups in your body. This practice helps release physical tension and promotes a sense of relaxation.

- **How to Practice PMR:** Start by sitting or lying in a comfortable position. Beginning with your feet, tense the muscles for 5-10 seconds, then release the tension while focusing on how your muscles feel as they relax. Move up through your body, tensing and relaxing your legs, abdomen, arms, and finally your face and neck. By the end, your whole body should feel more relaxed.

3. Guided Imagery

Guided imagery is a relaxation technique that involves visualizing a peaceful, calming scene in your mind. This practice helps shift your focus away from stress and anxiety and allows you to immerse yourself in a relaxing mental environment.

- **How to Practice Guided Imagery:** Close your eyes and imagine yourself in a peaceful, soothing place—this could be a beach, forest, mountain retreat, or anywhere that feels calm and relaxing to you. As you visualize the scene, engage all your senses: feel the warmth of the sun, hear the sound of waves or birds, and smell the fresh air. Allow yourself to stay in this peaceful place for a few minutes, letting your body and mind relax.

4. Yoga and Stretching

Yoga and gentle stretching are excellent ways to relieve tension, reduce stress, and stay grounded during the holiday season. Even a short yoga session or simple stretches can help release physical stress and promote a sense of calm.

- **Gentle Yoga for Relaxation:** Incorporate gentle yoga poses into your self-care routine, focusing on poses that promote relaxation and stress relief. Poses like Child's Pose, Legs-Up-the-Wall, and Seated Forward Bend are particularly effective for calming the mind and body.
- **Stretching Routine:** If you don't have time for a full yoga session, a simple stretching routine can also help reduce tension. Focus on stretching areas that commonly hold stress, such as your neck, shoulders, back, and legs.

Conclusion

Practicing self-care during the holidays is not a luxury—it's a necessity for maintaining your physical, emotional, and mental well-being amidst the busyness of the season. By incorporating self-care routines, relaxation techniques, and healthy boundaries into your holiday schedule, you can reduce stress, prevent burnout, and stay grounded. Remember that the holidays are meant to be a time of joy, connection, and celebration, and prioritizing your well-being allows you to fully embrace those moments with a sense of calm and balance. With these self-care practices in place, you can navigate the holiday season with greater ease and enjoy the special moments that make this time of year truly meaningful.

Chapter 19: Holiday Mindfulness Practices

The holiday season can be a time of joy, connection, and celebration, but it can also be a period filled with stress, anxiety, and overwhelming expectations. Amidst the hustle and bustle of gift-giving, social gatherings, and endless to-do lists, it's easy to lose sight of the present moment and become consumed by the demands of the season. This is where mindfulness and meditation can be powerful tools to help you stay grounded, reduce stress, and fully enjoy the spirit of the holidays.

In this chapter, we will explore mindfulness practices and meditation techniques that can help you cultivate a sense of calm, presence, and awareness throughout the holiday season. These practices are designed to help you navigate holiday stress, manage overwhelming emotions, and savor the small moments that make this time of year special.

What is Mindfulness?

Mindfulness is the practice of bringing your attention to the present moment, without judgment. It involves paying attention to your thoughts, feelings, and bodily sensations as they arise, while staying anchored in the here and now. When you practice mindfulness, you allow yourself to observe your experiences—both positive and negative—with acceptance and curiosity, rather than being swept away by them.

During the holidays, mindfulness can help you:

- **Reduce Stress:** By staying present and aware, you can prevent stress from spiraling out of control and cultivate a sense of calm amidst the chaos.
- **Improve Emotional Regulation:** Mindfulness allows you to recognize and manage your emotions more effectively, preventing frustration or anxiety from taking over.
- **Enhance Joy and Gratitude:** When you're fully present, you're more able to appreciate the small, meaningful moments of the holiday season, from a shared meal to the laughter of loved ones.
- **Prevent Overwhelm:** Mindfulness can help you slow down, take a deep breath, and approach holiday tasks with a sense of clarity and intention.

Mindfulness Techniques for the Holiday Season

Incorporating mindfulness into your daily routine during the holidays doesn't require hours of meditation or complicated rituals. Even a few minutes of mindfulness each day can have a profound impact on your mental and emotional well-being. Here are some simple yet effective mindfulness practices to help you stay present and reduce stress during the holiday season.

1. Mindful Breathing

Mindful breathing is one of the most accessible and effective mindfulness practices for reducing stress. It involves focusing your attention on your breath, allowing you to reconnect with the present moment and calm your mind.

- **How to Practice Mindful Breathing:** Find a quiet place where you can sit comfortably. Close your eyes and bring your attention to your breath. Notice the sensation of the air entering your nostrils, filling your lungs, and then leaving your body as you exhale. If your mind begins to wander, gently bring your focus back to your breath. You can practice mindful breathing for as little as 2-5 minutes whenever you feel stressed or overwhelmed.
- **Box Breathing Technique:** Box breathing is a simple, structured form of mindful breathing that helps calm the nervous system. Inhale for 4 counts, hold your breath for 4 counts, exhale for 4 counts, and hold your breath again for 4 counts. Repeat this cycle for several minutes to reduce stress and anxiety.

2. Body Scan Meditation

Body scan meditation is a mindfulness technique that involves bringing awareness to different parts of your body, one at a time. This practice helps you release physical tension and become more aware of how stress manifests in your body.

- **How to Practice Body Scan Meditation:** Begin by lying down or sitting in a comfortable position. Close your eyes and take a few deep breaths to relax. Start by focusing on your toes and slowly work your way up your body, paying attention to each area as you go. Notice any sensations, tension, or discomfort without trying to change anything. As you move through your body, simply observe how each part feels and invite relaxation into those areas. A body scan meditation can last anywhere from 5 to 20 minutes, depending on how much time you have.
- **Use During Stressful Moments:** The body scan meditation is especially helpful during stressful moments when you may feel tense or physically uncomfortable. It allows you to check in with your body and release any tension that has accumulated, helping you feel more relaxed and centered.

3. Mindful Eating

With holiday meals, parties, and indulgent treats all around, the season can often lead to mindless eating—eating too quickly, overeating, or not fully enjoying your food. Mindful eating is a practice that encourages you to slow down, savor each bite, and bring awareness to the experience of eating.

- **How to Practice Mindful Eating:** During your next meal, take a moment to pause before you begin eating. Notice the colors, smells, and textures of your food. As you eat, chew slowly and pay attention to the taste and texture of each bite. Put your fork down between bites and take time to fully experience the flavors. By eating mindfully, you can enhance your enjoyment of holiday meals and prevent overeating.
- **Tune into Your Hunger and Fullness Cues:** Mindful eating also involves paying attention to your body's hunger and fullness signals. Before you begin eating, ask yourself if you're truly hungry or if you're eating out of habit or stress. Similarly, stop eating when you feel satisfied, rather than waiting until you're overly full.

4. Mindful Walking

Walking can be a meditative and mindful activity, especially when you're feeling overwhelmed by holiday preparations or social obligations. Mindful walking allows you to reconnect with your body, breathe deeply, and clear your mind while engaging in gentle movement.

- **How to Practice Mindful Walking:** Find a quiet space where you can walk slowly and undisturbed, whether it's outside in nature or inside your home. Begin by focusing on the sensation of your feet touching the ground with each step. Pay attention to the rhythm of your breathing as you walk, and notice the sights, sounds, and smells around you. If your mind starts to wander, gently bring your attention back to the act of walking.
- **Incorporate Mindful Walking into Your Routine:** Mindful walking can be practiced at any time of day—whether it's a short walk during your lunch break, a stroll in the evening, or simply walking from one room to another. It's a great way to incorporate mindfulness into your daily life without needing to set aside a separate block of time.

5. Gratitude Meditation

The holiday season is a time for gratitude, and practicing gratitude meditation can help you cultivate a sense of appreciation for the people, experiences, and things that bring joy into your life. This practice shifts your focus away from stress and anxiety, allowing you to experience more positive emotions.

- **How to Practice Gratitude Meditation:** Find a quiet place to sit comfortably. Close your eyes and take a few deep breaths to center yourself. Begin by bringing to mind something or someone you are grateful for. This could be a loved one, a meaningful experience, or even a small moment of joy from your day. Focus on the feeling of gratitude and allow it to fill your heart. Continue reflecting on different aspects of your life that you're grateful for, allowing the positive feelings to grow with each one.

- **Create a Daily Gratitude Practice:** Incorporate gratitude meditation into your daily routine by setting aside a few minutes each morning or evening to reflect on what you're grateful for. You can also keep a gratitude journal, writing down three things you're grateful for each day. This practice helps shift your mindset from stress and scarcity to appreciation and abundance.

6. Loving-Kindness Meditation

Loving-kindness meditation (also known as "metta" meditation) is a mindfulness practice that involves sending positive thoughts and well-wishes to yourself and others. This practice is especially helpful during the holidays when emotions may run high, or you may be dealing with difficult family dynamics.

- **How to Practice Loving-Kindness Meditation:** Sit comfortably and close your eyes. Begin by focusing on yourself and silently repeat phrases like, "May I be happy, may I be healthy, may I be safe, may I be at peace." After a few minutes, extend these wishes to others, starting with someone you love, then to friends, acquaintances, and finally to all living beings. You can customize the phrases to suit your preferences, but the key is to focus on sending feelings of kindness and compassion.
- **Use Loving-Kindness to Navigate Difficult Emotions:** If you're dealing with challenging relationships during the holidays, practicing loving-kindness meditation can help you cultivate empathy and patience. It allows you to approach others from a place of compassion rather than frustration, easing tension and promoting harmony.

7. Mindful Listening

The holiday season often involves spending time with family and friends, which can be both joyful and stressful. Practicing mindful listening during conversations can help you stay present, deepen your connections, and reduce the tendency to become distracted or overwhelmed.

- **How to Practice Mindful Listening:** When you're in a conversation with someone, focus your full attention on what they're saying without interrupting or thinking about your response. Notice their tone of voice, body language, and emotions. Try to listen with empathy and an open heart, without judgment. If your mind starts to wander, gently bring your focus back to the speaker.
- **Mindful Listening in Social Settings:** Mindful listening is particularly valuable during social gatherings when conversations can become rushed or superficial. By practicing mindful listening, you can foster more meaningful interactions and show genuine interest in others, enhancing the quality of your relationships.

Mindfulness in Holiday Activities

The holiday season offers countless opportunities to practice mindfulness, even in the midst of your usual holiday activities. By incorporating mindfulness into tasks like decorating, cooking, or wrapping gifts, you can transform everyday moments into opportunities for presence and joy.

1. Mindful Gift Wrapping

Instead of rushing through the task of wrapping gifts, turn it into a mindful activity by focusing on the textures, colors, and sounds of the materials. As you wrap each gift, take a moment to reflect on the person you're giving it to and the joy you hope it brings them. This simple shift in focus can make the task more meaningful and enjoyable.

2. Mindful Decorating

As you decorate your home for the holidays, practice mindfulness by paying attention to the colors, lights, and textures of your decorations. Instead of hurrying to finish, savor the process and allow yourself to enjoy each step. Notice how the act of decorating makes you feel and the way it transforms your living space.

3. Mindful Cooking and Baking

Cooking and baking are often central to holiday traditions, and these activities can be opportunities for mindfulness. As you prepare food, focus on the smells, textures, and sounds of the ingredients. Pay attention to each step of the process, from chopping vegetables to stirring dough. Cooking mindfully helps you stay present and can make the experience more enjoyable and less stressful.

4. Mindful Holiday Gatherings

Holiday gatherings can be busy and chaotic, but by approaching them with mindfulness, you can create moments of connection and presence. As you engage with loved ones, practice being fully present. Listen mindfully, savor the food, and take in the sights and sounds around you. Allow yourself to experience the joy of being with others without worrying about what's next on your to-do list.

Managing Holiday Stress with Mindfulness

Mindfulness practices are particularly helpful for managing stress and overwhelm during the holiday season. When stress levels rise, mindfulness can help you pause, breathe, and regain a sense of calm and perspective. Here are some mindfulness strategies for managing stress during the holidays:

1. Pause and Breathe

When you feel stressed or overwhelmed, take a mindful pause. Close your eyes, take a deep breath, and focus on the sensation of the air entering and leaving your body. This simple practice helps interrupt the cycle of stress and gives you a moment to reset before moving forward.

2. Focus on One Task at a Time

Multitasking can increase stress and reduce your ability to be present. Instead of trying to juggle multiple tasks at once, practice focusing on one task at a time. Whether you're wrapping gifts, cooking, or cleaning, give your full attention to the task at hand and complete it mindfully before moving on to the next.

3. Practice Non-Judgmental Awareness

During the holidays, it's easy to become critical of yourself or others—whether it's worrying about how things should be or feeling frustrated by family dynamics. Mindfulness invites you to practice non-judgmental awareness by accepting things as they are, without trying to control or change them. This mindset helps reduce frustration and fosters greater peace of mind.

4. Use Mindful Transitions

Holiday schedules can be packed with back-to-back events, errands, and tasks. To manage the pace, use mindful transitions between activities. Before starting a new task, take a moment to pause, breathe, and check in with yourself. This practice helps you stay grounded and prevents the feeling of being rushed or overwhelmed.

Conclusion

Mindfulness and meditation practices offer powerful tools for navigating the holiday season with a greater sense of calm, presence, and joy. By incorporating mindful breathing, meditation, and everyday mindfulness into your holiday routine, you can reduce stress, manage emotions, and fully enjoy the special moments that make the holidays meaningful. Remember that mindfulness is not about perfection—it's about being present with whatever arises, whether it's joy, stress, or something in between. With these mindfulness practices in place, you can embrace the holiday season with greater peace and awareness, savoring each moment as it comes.

Chapter 20: Balancing Your Mental Health with Holiday Expectations

The holiday season, while filled with joy, tradition, and celebration, can also be a time of immense pressure. Many people feel the need to create the "perfect" holiday experience—whether it's hosting flawless family gatherings, buying the best gifts, or meeting the expectations of friends and family. The desire to meet these high standards can lead to stress, anxiety, and even a sense of inadequacy, ultimately impacting your mental health.

In this chapter, we will explore how to balance your mental health with the expectations that come with the holiday season. We'll examine strategies for managing the pressure to create the "perfect" holiday, discuss how to set healthy boundaries, and provide tips for letting go of unrealistic ideals. The goal is to help you enjoy the holidays without sacrificing your well-being, allowing you to focus on what truly matters.

Understanding the Pressure to Create "Perfect" Holidays

Holiday perfectionism often stems from internal and external pressures. Many of us have an idealized image of what the holidays should look like—whether it's inspired by childhood memories, social media, or cultural norms. The pressure to live up to these expectations can make the holidays feel more like a test of worthiness than a time of joy.

1. Internal Pressures

Internal pressures are the expectations you place on yourself to create a flawless holiday experience. This might involve trying to recreate past traditions perfectly, ensuring that everyone around you is happy, or attempting to meet an idealized version of the holidays.

- **Perfectionism:** Perfectionism can drive you to set unrealistic goals for yourself, whether it's preparing an elaborate meal, decorating your home to magazine standards, or finding the perfect gifts. The desire for everything to go smoothly can lead to excessive planning, stress, and disappointment if things don't go as expected.
- **Guilt and Obligation:** You may feel obligated to meet certain holiday standards because of your own expectations or a sense of duty. This can manifest as guilt about not spending enough money on gifts, not attending every event, or not keeping up with family traditions. Guilt-driven holiday behavior often leads to overextending yourself and neglecting your own well-being.

2. External Pressures

External pressures come from societal norms, family expectations, and cultural portrayals of the holidays. These pressures often push us to conform to a certain vision of what the holidays should be like, even if it doesn't align with our current circumstances.

- **Family Expectations:** Family members may have their own expectations about how the holidays should be celebrated, from adhering to traditions to attending certain gatherings. The pressure to meet these expectations can be overwhelming, especially if they conflict with your own desires or needs.
- **Social Media and Cultural Influences:** Social media can intensify holiday-related stress by showcasing idealized, curated versions of the holidays. Seeing perfectly decorated homes, extravagant parties, and happy families can lead to feelings of inadequacy or pressure to keep up with others.
- **Cultural Norms:** Holiday movies, advertisements, and cultural narratives often emphasize the idea of a "perfect" holiday filled with joy, love, and togetherness. While these portrayals can be heartwarming, they can also create unrealistic expectations that don't account for the complexities of real life, such as financial struggles, family conflicts, or personal challenges.

The Impact of Holiday Perfectionism on Mental Health

The pressure to create perfect holidays can take a toll on your mental health, leading to increased stress, anxiety, and burnout. It's important to recognize how perfectionism can affect your emotional well-being so that you can take steps to protect your mental health during the holiday season.

1. Stress and Anxiety

Trying to live up to unrealistic holiday expectations can lead to chronic stress and anxiety. The constant need to plan, prepare, and perform at a high level can leave you feeling overwhelmed and emotionally drained. You may worry about disappointing others or fear that your efforts won't be "good enough," leading to heightened anxiety.

- **Signs of Stress and Anxiety:** Symptoms of holiday-related stress and anxiety can include irritability, difficulty sleeping, fatigue, tension headaches, and racing thoughts. You may also find yourself feeling emotionally detached or on edge.

2. Burnout

When you overcommit to holiday responsibilities without giving yourself time to rest, you risk experiencing burnout. Burnout occurs when prolonged stress leads to physical and emotional exhaustion, making it difficult to enjoy the holidays or engage with loved ones.

- **Signs of Burnout:** Signs of burnout include feeling constantly tired, emotionally distant or numb, having difficulty concentrating, and feeling resentful of holiday obligations. You may also feel a sense of disillusionment or apathy toward the holidays.

3. Feelings of Inadequacy

Holiday perfectionism often leads to feelings of inadequacy, as it's nearly impossible to meet every expectation or create a flawless holiday experience. You may compare yourself to others, worry about being judged, or feel like you're failing if things don't go as planned.

- **Self-Criticism:** Perfectionism is often accompanied by harsh self-criticism. If you make a mistake, such as burning the holiday roast or forgetting a gift, you may beat yourself up and focus on your perceived failures rather than the joy of the occasion.

Strategies for Managing Holiday Expectations

To protect your mental health during the holiday season, it's essential to manage both internal and external pressures. By setting realistic expectations, practicing self-compassion, and letting go of perfectionism, you can reduce stress and enjoy the holidays in a more balanced, fulfilling way.

1. Set Realistic Expectations

One of the most effective ways to manage holiday stress is to set realistic expectations for yourself and others. Let go of the need for everything to be perfect and focus on what's truly important to you.

- **Reevaluate Holiday Traditions:** Take a moment to reflect on which holiday traditions bring you joy and which ones feel like burdens. It's okay to let go of traditions that no longer serve you or your family. For example, if hosting a large dinner every year is too stressful, consider simplifying the meal or hosting a potluck instead.
- **Focus on Meaning Over Perfection:** Shift your focus away from achieving perfection and toward creating meaningful experiences. What matters most is spending quality time with loved ones, sharing moments of connection, and appreciating the spirit of the season. Remember that the small imperfections are often what make the holidays memorable.
- **Communicate Expectations with Family:** If family expectations are causing stress, have an open conversation with your loved ones about what's realistic for you this year. For example, if you're feeling overwhelmed by multiple family gatherings, suggest splitting time between households or hosting a smaller, more intimate celebration.

2. Practice Self-Compassion

Self-compassion is essential for managing the emotional toll of holiday perfectionism. It involves treating yourself with the same kindness and understanding that you would offer to a friend, especially when things don't go as planned.

- **Let Go of Self-Criticism:** If you make a mistake or things don't turn out perfectly, practice self-compassion by reminding yourself that it's okay to be imperfect. Instead of focusing on what went wrong, focus on the effort you put in and the positive moments that came out of the experience.
- **Talk to Yourself Kindly:** When you notice negative self-talk, challenge it with more compassionate, realistic thoughts. For example, if you're thinking, "I ruined the holiday dinner," reframe it as, "It didn't turn out the way I planned, but we still had a great time together."
- **Acknowledge Your Efforts:** Take time to acknowledge and appreciate the effort you're putting into the holidays, even if everything isn't perfect. Recognizing your hard work can help you feel more positive about the holiday season, rather than focusing solely on the outcome.

3. Set Healthy Boundaries

Setting healthy boundaries is crucial for managing holiday expectations and protecting your mental health. Boundaries help you avoid overcommitting to events, activities, and responsibilities that may lead to stress or burnout.

- **Say No When Necessary:** It's okay to say no to holiday invitations or requests if they don't align with your capacity or well-being. Politely decline with a simple explanation, such as, "I'm prioritizing time with my immediate family this year," or, "I won't be able to attend, but I hope you have a wonderful celebration."
- **Prioritize Your Well-Being:** Set boundaries around your time and energy, making sure you leave space for rest and self-care. This may mean limiting the number of events you attend, scaling back on holiday preparations, or carving out time for yourself amidst the busyness.
- **Limit Social Media Exposure:** Social media can amplify the pressure to create a picture-perfect holiday, so consider limiting your exposure to it during the holiday season. If scrolling through holiday photos and posts leads to feelings of inadequacy or comparison, take a break or curate your feed to focus on content that uplifts you.

4. Simplify Holiday Preparations

Simplifying your holiday preparations can help reduce stress and free up time to focus on what matters most. Rather than striving to do it all, look for ways to streamline tasks and make the holiday season more manageable.

- **Simplify Gift-Giving:** Consider scaling back on gift-giving by setting spending limits, organizing a Secret Santa exchange, or giving homemade gifts. Simplifying your approach to gifts can alleviate financial stress and reduce the pressure to find "perfect" presents for everyone on your list.
- **Delegate Responsibilities:** If you're hosting a holiday gathering, don't be afraid to delegate tasks to others. Ask family members to bring a dish, help with decorating, or assist with cleanup. Sharing the workload ensures that you're not shouldering all the responsibility on your own.
- **Embrace Imperfections:** When it comes to holiday meals, decorations, and events, embrace imperfection. Rather than aiming for an elaborate spread or perfectly coordinated decorations, focus on creating a warm, welcoming atmosphere. For example, choose simple, easy-to-make recipes or decorate with items you already have on hand, rather than trying to replicate Pinterest-worthy setups.

5. Prioritize Self-Care

Taking care of your mental and physical well-being is essential during the holidays. Make self-care a priority by incorporating activities that help you relax, recharge, and stay grounded.

- **Schedule Time for Relaxation:** Block off time in your calendar for relaxation and self-care, whether it's reading a book, taking a bath, going for a walk, or practicing mindfulness. Scheduling downtime helps ensure that you're not constantly in "go" mode and gives you the opportunity to recharge.
- **Incorporate Mindfulness Practices:** Mindfulness practices, such as deep breathing, meditation, or yoga, can help you manage stress and stay present. Even a few minutes of mindfulness each day can make a significant difference in how you approach the holiday season.
- **Stay Active:** Physical activity is a great way to manage stress and improve your mood during the holidays. Whether it's a morning workout, a walk with family, or a yoga session, make time for movement as part of your self-care routine.

6. Manage Financial Stress

Financial stress is a common source of anxiety during the holidays, particularly when it comes to gift-giving, travel, and hosting gatherings. Managing your holiday budget can help alleviate some of this stress and prevent overspending.

- **Set a Holiday Budget:** Create a holiday budget that outlines how much you're willing to spend on gifts, travel, entertainment, and other holiday-related expenses. Stick to this budget to avoid financial strain or guilt about overspending.
- **Communicate with Family About Finances:** If financial concerns are causing stress, have an open conversation with family members about adjusting holiday plans. For example, suggest doing a Secret Santa gift exchange, setting spending limits, or focusing on non-material ways to celebrate, such as sharing experiences or time together.
- **Focus on Meaningful Gifts:** Rather than focusing on expensive or material gifts, consider giving meaningful, thoughtful presents that align with your budget. For example, you could give homemade gifts, create a photo album, or write a heartfelt letter expressing your appreciation.

7. Accept That It's Okay to Disappoint Others

It's natural to want to make everyone happy during the holidays, but it's important to recognize that it's okay if you don't meet everyone's expectations. Sometimes, despite your best efforts, you may need to disappoint others to protect your own well-being.

- **Let Go of the Need to Please Everyone:** Remind yourself that it's impossible to please everyone, and that's okay. Focus on creating a holiday experience that works for you and your immediate family, rather than trying to accommodate every expectation or demand from others.
- **Release Guilt:** If you feel guilty about not meeting someone's expectations, practice self-compassion and remind yourself that it's not your responsibility to make everyone happy. Your well-being is just as important as anyone else's, and setting boundaries is a healthy, necessary step in maintaining balance.

Conclusion

Balancing your mental health with holiday expectations requires a shift in mindset and a willingness to let go of perfectionism. By setting realistic expectations, practicing self-compassion, setting healthy boundaries, and simplifying your holiday plans, you can protect your mental health and reduce the pressure to create a "perfect" holiday. Remember that the holidays are meant to be a time of joy, connection, and reflection—focusing on what truly matters will help you experience the season with greater peace and fulfillment.

Chapter 21: Overcoming Holiday Burnout

The holiday season is often associated with joy, celebration, and time spent with loved ones. However, for many, it can also bring stress, exhaustion, and burnout. With the endless to-do lists, family obligations, financial pressures, and social commitments, it's easy to feel overwhelmed and stretched too thin. Holiday burnout occurs when the demands of the season surpass your emotional, physical, and mental capacity, leaving you feeling drained and unable to enjoy the festivities.

In this chapter, we will explore how to recognize the signs of holiday burnout and provide practical strategies for recovering before the season is over. By learning to manage stress, set boundaries, and prioritize your well-being, you can prevent burnout and make the most of the holiday season with renewed energy and enjoyment.

What is Holiday Burnout?

Holiday burnout occurs when the accumulated stress, overcommitment, and high expectations of the season leave you feeling physically, mentally, and emotionally exhausted. Unlike regular stress, which might come and go, burnout is a state of prolonged and chronic exhaustion that can affect your ability to function effectively and enjoy the holidays.

Burnout during the holiday season is often caused by a combination of factors:

- **Overcommitment:** Trying to attend every party, host multiple gatherings, shop for everyone on your list, and meet all holiday obligations can leave you feeling overextended.
- **High Expectations:** The pressure to create a "perfect" holiday—whether in terms of gifts, decorations, or family gatherings—can lead to excessive stress and disappointment.
- **Emotional Strain:** Managing family dynamics, dealing with grief or loss, and navigating personal or financial challenges can take an emotional toll, contributing to burnout.
- **Neglecting Self-Care:** Focusing solely on holiday preparations without taking time for self-care can quickly lead to burnout, as you deplete your physical and emotional reserves.

Recognizing the Signs of Holiday Burnout

It's essential to recognize the early signs of burnout so that you can address it before it escalates. Burnout doesn't happen overnight—it builds up over time, often starting with small symptoms that gradually intensify if left unchecked.

1. Physical Exhaustion

One of the most common signs of burnout is feeling physically exhausted, even after a full night's sleep. You may find it difficult to get out of bed in the morning, experience chronic fatigue, or feel physically drained after completing routine tasks.

- **Signs of Physical Exhaustion:** Constant tiredness, lack of energy, headaches, muscle tension, difficulty sleeping, or a weakened immune system (resulting in frequent colds or illnesses).

2. Emotional and Mental Fatigue

Burnout can leave you feeling emotionally numb or mentally checked out. You may notice that you're more irritable, frustrated, or short-tempered than usual, or you may feel emotionally detached from the holiday activities you normally enjoy.

- **Signs of Emotional and Mental Fatigue:** Feeling emotionally drained, struggling to concentrate, experiencing mood swings, feeling indifferent or apathetic about holiday events, or having difficulty making decisions.

3. Increased Irritability and Frustration

When you're burned out, even small annoyances can feel overwhelming, and you may find yourself becoming easily frustrated or irritable with family, friends, or coworkers.

- **Signs of Irritability:** Snapping at loved ones, feeling easily annoyed or overwhelmed, and having little patience for everyday challenges.

4. Feeling Overwhelmed or Hopeless

Burnout can create a sense of overwhelm, where every task feels insurmountable, and it's hard to see a way forward. You may feel like there's too much to do and not enough time or energy to accomplish it all.

- **Signs of Overwhelm:** Feeling like you're constantly behind, avoiding tasks because they feel too daunting, or feeling hopeless about getting everything done.

5. Withdrawal from Social Interactions

Another sign of burnout is withdrawing from social interactions, even with people you usually enjoy spending time with. You may feel like you don't have the energy to attend holiday events or engage with loved ones, leading to social isolation.

- **Signs of Withdrawal:** Avoiding social gatherings, canceling plans, or feeling detached or disengaged during family or social events.

6. Loss of Joy or Interest in Holiday Activities

When burnout sets in, the activities that once brought you joy—whether it's decorating, cooking, or celebrating with family—may start to feel like burdens. You may find yourself going through the motions without feeling the usual excitement or enjoyment.

- **Signs of Loss of Joy:** Feeling indifferent about holiday traditions, dreading activities that you used to enjoy, or finding little pleasure in holiday events or celebrations.

Causes of Holiday Burnout

To effectively address holiday burnout, it's important to understand its root causes. While each person's experience of burnout is unique, there are several common factors that contribute to burnout during the holiday season.

1. Overcommitment and Lack of Boundaries

One of the primary causes of holiday burnout is overcommitment. The desire to please everyone, meet expectations, and attend every event can lead to an overloaded schedule, leaving little time for rest or self-care. Without setting healthy boundaries, you may find yourself saying yes to every invitation or task, even when it's beyond your capacity.

- **The Cost of Overcommitment:** When you overcommit, you risk spreading yourself too thin, leading to exhaustion, stress, and a feeling of being constantly "on." Over time, this can result in burnout as you struggle to keep up with the demands of the season.

2. Perfectionism and High Expectations

Many people feel pressured to create the "perfect" holiday, whether it's through meticulously planned meals, perfectly wrapped gifts, or an immaculately decorated home. The pursuit of perfection can lead to heightened stress and disappointment when things don't go as planned.

- **The Burden of Perfectionism:** Perfectionism can create unrealistic expectations, leading you to spend excessive time and energy on tasks that may not be essential. This constant striving for perfection can prevent you from enjoying the holiday season and contribute to burnout.

3. Neglecting Self-Care

During the holiday season, it's easy to prioritize everything and everyone else over yourself. Neglecting self-care—such as getting enough sleep, eating well, staying active, and taking time to relax—can quickly deplete your energy reserves and lead to burnout.

- **The Importance of Self-Care:** Self-care is essential for maintaining your physical and emotional well-being, especially during times of stress. Without it, you may find yourself feeling exhausted, overwhelmed, and unable to cope with the demands of the holiday season.

4. Financial Stress

The financial pressures of the holidays—buying gifts, hosting gatherings, and traveling—can also contribute to burnout. Worrying about money or overspending can add an extra layer of stress, leading to anxiety and a sense of overwhelm.

- **The Impact of Financial Stress:** When financial concerns are at the forefront of your mind, it can be difficult to fully enjoy the holidays. The constant worry about expenses can drain your mental and emotional energy, making burnout more likely.

5. Family Dynamics and Emotional Strain

Navigating complex family dynamics during the holidays can be emotionally draining, especially if there are unresolved conflicts, difficult relationships, or differing expectations. The pressure to maintain harmony or meet family obligations can contribute to emotional burnout.

- **The Toll of Family Strain:** Managing family conflicts, dealing with challenging personalities, or trying to live up to family expectations can be emotionally taxing, leading to burnout if not addressed.

Recovering from Holiday Burnout

If you're already experiencing the symptoms of holiday burnout, it's important to take immediate steps to recover and restore your well-being. Recovery from burnout involves slowing down, setting boundaries, and prioritizing self-care to regain your energy and emotional balance.

1. Acknowledge the Burnout

The first step in recovering from holiday burnout is acknowledging that you're experiencing it. Many people push through burnout, hoping they can make it to the end of the season without addressing the underlying stress. However, this often leads to further exhaustion.

- **Be Honest with Yourself:** Take a moment to reflect on how you're feeling. Are you constantly tired, overwhelmed, or irritable? Do you feel disconnected from the holiday activities you used to enjoy? Recognizing the signs of burnout allows you to take action before it worsens.

2. Prioritize Rest and Relaxation

One of the most important steps in recovering from burnout is giving yourself permission to rest. Burnout often occurs when you've been running on empty for too long, so taking time to relax and recharge is essential.

- **Schedule Downtime:** Block off time in your schedule for rest and relaxation, whether it's a quiet evening at home, a weekend without plans, or simply taking a break during the day. Use this time to do activities that help you relax, such as reading, meditating, or taking a bath.
- **Get Enough Sleep:** Sleep is critical for recovering from burnout. Make sure you're getting enough rest by establishing a consistent bedtime routine and prioritizing sleep, even if it means skipping late-night events or parties.

3. Set Boundaries and Say No

If you're feeling burned out, it's essential to set boundaries around your time and energy. This may mean saying no to additional invitations, delegating tasks to others, or scaling back on holiday commitments.

- **Practice Saying No:** It's okay to decline invitations or requests that feel overwhelming. For example, if you're invited to a party but you're feeling too exhausted, politely decline by saying, "I appreciate the invitation, but I need some time to rest." Setting boundaries helps protect your well-being and prevents further burnout.
- **Delegate Tasks:** If you're hosting a holiday event or have a long to-do list, don't be afraid to delegate tasks to others. Ask family members to help with cooking, cleaning, or shopping, and trust that they can handle the responsibility.

4. Let Go of Perfectionism

To recover from burnout, it's important to let go of the need for everything to be perfect. Perfectionism can drive you to overwork and overextend yourself, leaving little room for relaxation or enjoyment.

- **Embrace Imperfection:** Remind yourself that the holidays don't have to be perfect to be meaningful. If something doesn't go as planned—whether it's a meal that doesn't turn out right or a gift that isn't perfect—let it go and focus on the moments of connection and joy.
- **Simplify Your Holiday Plans:** If you're feeling burned out, consider simplifying your holiday plans. For example, scale back on the number of events you attend, reduce the complexity of your holiday meals, or limit your gift-giving. Simplifying your plans allows you to focus on what truly matters without feeling overwhelmed.

5. Practice Self-Care Daily

Recovering from burnout requires consistent self-care. Make self-care a non-negotiable part of your daily routine, even if it's just for a few minutes each day.

- **Engage in Activities That Recharge You:** Identify the activities that help you feel relaxed and recharged, whether it's going for a walk, practicing yoga, journaling, or spending time with loved ones. Incorporate these activities into your routine to help you recover from burnout.
- **Eat Nourishing Foods:** During times of stress, it's easy to turn to comfort foods or skip meals, but proper nutrition is essential for recovering from burnout. Focus on eating balanced, nourishing meals that provide you with energy and support your overall health.
- **Stay Active:** Physical activity is a great way to relieve stress and boost your mood. Even light exercise, such as stretching or walking, can help reduce feelings of burnout and improve your energy levels.

6. Reconnect with What Brings You Joy

Burnout can make it difficult to enjoy the holiday season, but reconnecting with activities that bring you joy can help you recover emotionally and mentally.

- **Identify What Makes the Holidays Special for You:** Take a moment to reflect on what aspects of the holidays bring you the most joy. Is it spending time with loved ones, engaging in traditions, or simply taking time to relax? Focus on these activities and let go of the ones that feel like obligations.
- **Engage in Joyful Activities:** Once you've identified what brings you joy, make time for these activities in your schedule. Whether it's watching your favorite holiday movie, baking cookies with your family, or taking a peaceful walk, prioritizing joy helps counteract the stress of burnout.

7. Seek Support

Recovering from burnout is often easier when you have the support of loved ones. Don't hesitate to reach out to friends, family members, or a therapist if you need help managing stress or recovering from burnout.

- **Talk to a Loved One:** Share your feelings of burnout with a trusted friend or family member. Sometimes, simply talking about your experience can provide relief and perspective. Your loved ones may also offer support by helping you with tasks or providing emotional encouragement.
- **Consider Professional Support:** If burnout is severely impacting your mental health, consider seeking support from a therapist or counselor. Professional guidance can help you develop coping strategies, manage stress, and recover from burnout.

Preventing Future Holiday Burnout

Once you've recovered from burnout, it's important to take steps to prevent it from happening again in future holiday seasons. By learning to manage your time, set boundaries, and prioritize self-care, you can enjoy the holidays without feeling overwhelmed.

1. Plan Ahead and Pace Yourself

One of the best ways to prevent burnout is to plan ahead and pace yourself throughout the holiday season. Rather than trying to do everything at once, spread out tasks over several weeks to avoid last-minute stress.

- **Create a Holiday Timeline:** Make a list of all the tasks you need to complete during the holidays, from shopping and decorating to hosting events. Break these tasks down into smaller, manageable steps and schedule them throughout the season. This will help you avoid the stress of cramming everything into the last few days before the holidays.
- **Leave Room for Flexibility:** While planning ahead is important, it's also essential to leave room for flexibility. Allow yourself to adjust your plans as needed, especially if unexpected events or stressors arise.

2. Set Boundaries Early

Setting boundaries early in the holiday season can help you avoid overcommitting and protect your energy.

- **Communicate Boundaries with Family and Friends:** If you know that certain activities or events will be too much for you, communicate your boundaries with family and friends early. For example, let them know how many events you're willing to attend, or set expectations around gift-giving.
- **Respect Your Own Limits:** Be mindful of your own limits and respect them. If you feel yourself approaching burnout, take a step back and reassess your commitments.

3. Prioritize Self-Care Throughout the Season

Self-care isn't just for when you're feeling burned out—it's something you should prioritize throughout the holiday season to maintain your well-being.

- **Make Self-Care a Daily Practice:** Incorporate small self-care practices into your daily routine, such as deep breathing exercises, mindfulness meditation, or spending time doing something you love. Consistent self-care helps prevent stress from building up and keeps you balanced.
- **Take Breaks When Needed:** Don't wait until you're completely burned out to take a break. If you're feeling tired or overwhelmed, give yourself permission to rest, even if it means rescheduling or canceling non-essential commitments.

Conclusion

Overcoming holiday burnout requires recognizing the signs early, taking steps to recover, and prioritizing your mental and physical well-being. By acknowledging burnout, setting healthy boundaries, letting go of perfectionism, and practicing self-care, you can recover before the season is over and fully enjoy the holidays. Remember that the holidays don't have to be perfect to be meaningful—what matters most is taking care of yourself and spending time with the people and activities that bring you joy. With these strategies in place, you can prevent burnout in the future and create a more balanced, fulfilling holiday experience.

Part 5: Simplifying the Festive Experience

Chapter 22: Minimalist Holiday Décor Ideas

The holiday season is often associated with lavish decorations, glittering lights, and homes transformed into winter wonderlands. While festive décor can certainly bring joy and enhance the holiday spirit, it can also lead to stress, clutter, and an overwhelming sense of obligation to create a picture-perfect holiday setting. For many, the pressure to decorate extensively—both inside and outside the home—can detract from the simple pleasures of the season.

In recent years, minimalist holiday décor has gained popularity as a way to reduce stress, simplify holiday preparations, and focus on what truly matters. By embracing minimalist décor, you can create a peaceful, beautiful holiday atmosphere without the overwhelm of excess. In this chapter, we will explore how to simplify your holiday decorations, reduce clutter, and create a festive environment that aligns with minimalist principles.

Why Choose Minimalist Holiday Décor?

Minimalist holiday décor is about paring down your decorations to focus on simplicity, beauty, and intentionality. It's not about sacrificing holiday spirit or foregoing festive traditions—it's about making thoughtful choices that enhance your space without overwhelming it. Here are some reasons to consider a minimalist approach to holiday decorating:

1. Reduces Stress

One of the biggest advantages of minimalist holiday décor is that it reduces the stress associated with decorating, maintaining, and eventually taking down holiday decorations. With fewer items to organize and manage, you'll spend less time decorating and more time enjoying the season.

2. Less Clutter

Minimalist décor helps eliminate visual clutter, creating a more peaceful and serene environment in your home. Clutter can contribute to feelings of overwhelm and anxiety, especially during the busy holiday season. A minimalist approach ensures that your holiday décor enhances your space rather than overcrowds it.

3. Focuses on Meaningful Items

By simplifying your decorations, you can focus on the pieces that truly matter—whether they're sentimental heirlooms, handmade ornaments, or natural elements that reflect the season. Minimalist décor encourages you to be intentional about what you display, emphasizing quality over quantity.

4. Eco-Friendly and Sustainable

Minimalist holiday décor often incorporates natural, reusable, and sustainable elements, reducing waste and environmental impact. By focusing on fewer, high-quality pieces and natural materials, you can create an eco-friendly holiday atmosphere that aligns with sustainable living.

5. Saves Time and Money

Fewer decorations mean less time spent shopping, setting up, and cleaning up after the holidays. Minimalist décor also saves money, as you'll be purchasing fewer items and may even be able to re-purpose or use what you already have.

Key Principles of Minimalist Holiday Décor

To create a minimalist holiday aesthetic, it's important to focus on simplicity, intentionality, and balance. Here are some key principles to keep in mind as you approach holiday decorating with a minimalist mindset:

1. Focus on Quality, Not Quantity

Minimalism emphasizes quality over quantity. Instead of covering every surface with decorations, choose a few high-quality, meaningful pieces that will have a greater impact. Opt for timeless, versatile items that can be used year after year, rather than following fleeting trends that require constant updating.

2. Incorporate Natural Elements

Nature plays a central role in minimalist décor. Incorporating natural elements such as greenery, pinecones, branches, and seasonal flowers adds warmth and texture to your space while maintaining a simple, organic feel. These items can often be sourced from your own backyard or local environment, reducing the need for store-bought decorations.

3. Limit Your Color Palette

A minimalist holiday décor scheme typically features a limited, cohesive color palette. Neutral tones such as white, beige, and soft grays create a serene and sophisticated backdrop, while accents of green, metallics (such as gold or silver), or muted reds can add a festive touch. Limiting your color palette prevents visual clutter and creates a more harmonious look.

4. Embrace Negative Space

Negative space—empty areas in your home that aren't filled with decorations—is an important component of minimalist décor. Rather than filling every corner with holiday items, allow space for your home to breathe. Negative space helps balance the visual elements and creates a more open, calming atmosphere.

5. Prioritize Functionality

Minimalist décor isn't just about aesthetics—it's also about functionality. Choose decorations that are easy to store, reusable, and practical. This might mean investing in long-lasting, high-quality pieces or creating multi-functional décor that can be repurposed for other occasions.

Minimalist Holiday Décor Ideas

Now that we've covered the key principles of minimalist holiday décor, let's explore some specific ideas for creating a simple, elegant holiday atmosphere in your home. These ideas focus on natural elements, thoughtful design, and minimal clutter.

1. Simplified Christmas Tree

The Christmas tree is often the centerpiece of holiday décor, but it doesn't need to be extravagant to make an impact. A minimalist Christmas tree embraces simplicity and elegance.

- **Natural or Bare Tree:** A simple tree with minimal decorations can be incredibly striking. Choose a natural evergreen tree or even a small, bare branch from a tree outside. This brings the beauty of nature indoors without the need for excessive ornaments.
- **Monochromatic Decorations:** Instead of using a variety of colors, opt for a monochromatic theme with ornaments in a single color, such as white, gold, or silver. This creates a cohesive, elegant look. You can also consider limiting your decorations to just a few carefully chosen ornaments that have personal meaning.
- **Natural Ornaments:** Decorate your tree with natural ornaments, such as dried orange slices, cinnamon sticks, wooden beads, or pinecones. These items add a rustic, organic touch to your tree and can be composted or reused after the holidays.

2. Minimalist Wreaths

Wreaths are a traditional holiday decoration, but they don't have to be ornate or over-the-top. A minimalist wreath can be just as beautiful and festive.

- **Simple Greenery Wreath:** Create or purchase a wreath made from simple greenery, such as eucalyptus, pine, or fir branches. Leave the wreath undecorated or add just one or two accents, such as a simple ribbon or a few berries, for a subtle festive touch.
- **Asymmetrical Design:** An asymmetrical wreath, where only part of the wreath is decorated with greenery or ornaments, is a modern, minimalist take on a classic holiday decoration. This style keeps the design balanced yet understated.
- **DIY Natural Wreath:** If you enjoy crafting, consider making your own minimalist wreath using natural materials like twigs, leaves, and flowers. This is an eco-friendly option that allows you to create a unique, personalized piece of décor.

3. Simple Table Settings

Holiday gatherings often center around the dining table, so creating a minimalist tablescape can set a calm, inviting tone for your meal.

- **Neutral Linens:** Start with a neutral tablecloth or runner in soft, natural tones like beige, white, or gray. This creates a clean canvas for your table setting and complements a minimalist aesthetic.
- **Greenery Centerpiece:** Instead of an elaborate centerpiece, use simple greenery, such as sprigs of pine or eucalyptus, arranged along the center of the table. You can also add a few candles or natural elements like pinecones or berries for a subtle pop of color.
- **Minimalist Place Settings:** Keep place settings simple and uncluttered. Use white or neutral-colored plates, minimal glassware, and plain silverware. You can add a festive touch by tying a piece of twine or ribbon around each napkin, or placing a small sprig of greenery on each plate.

4. Natural Garlands

Garlands are a versatile and festive addition to any holiday décor, but a minimalist approach favors natural, simple garlands that enhance your space without overwhelming it.

- **Greenery Garland:** A plain garland made from pine, cedar, or eucalyptus branches can be draped over a mantel, staircase, or doorway. Keep the garland natural and undecorated for a simple, elegant look, or add a few accents like berries, dried flowers, or a strand of fairy lights for a soft, warm glow.
- **Dried Citrus Garland:** For a minimalist yet colorful touch, create a garland from dried orange slices. String them together with twine and hang the garland on your tree, mantel, or wall. This natural garland is eco-friendly, easy to make, and adds a subtle pop of color.

5. Candles and Soft Lighting

Lighting plays a crucial role in creating a warm, cozy atmosphere, especially during the darker winter months. Minimalist holiday décor focuses on soft, ambient lighting rather than bright, flashy displays.

- **Candles Everywhere:** Candles are a simple yet effective way to create a calming, festive atmosphere. Place white or neutral-colored candles in various sizes throughout your home—on your dining table, windowsills, or mantel. The soft glow of candlelight adds warmth and intimacy to any space.
- **Fairy Lights:** Instead of bold, multicolored lights, opt for soft white fairy lights. Drape them across your tree, along your mantel, or around windows to create a gentle, twinkling effect. Fairy lights are subtle yet magical, enhancing the holiday spirit without being overwhelming.

6. Minimalist Stockings

Hanging stockings is a cherished holiday tradition, but you can take a minimalist approach to this classic décor item by focusing on simplicity and quality.

- **Neutral Stockings:** Choose stockings in neutral tones like white, beige, or gray, made from natural materials such as wool, linen, or cotton. These simple stockings add a cozy, rustic touch to your décor and blend seamlessly into a minimalist design scheme.
- **Personalized Touches:** Personalize each stocking with a simple name tag or a small, natural ornament like a pinecone or sprig of greenery. This adds a personal, festive touch without cluttering the space.

7. Thoughtful Outdoor Décor

Minimalist holiday décor can extend to the outside of your home as well. Instead of elaborate light displays and extensive decorations, focus on a few simple, thoughtful elements that enhance the natural beauty of your home's exterior.

- **Simple Greenery:** Adorn your front door with a minimalist wreath made from greenery, and consider placing small potted evergreen trees or plants by your entrance. These natural elements add a festive touch without overwhelming your outdoor space.
- **Subtle Lighting:** Instead of covering your house with strings of bright lights, consider using simple, white lights to highlight key features, such as a tree in your yard or your front porch. This creates a warm, inviting glow without the clutter of extensive lighting displays.

Minimalist Holiday Decluttering Tips

Adopting a minimalist approach to holiday décor often involves decluttering and letting go of decorations that no longer serve you. Here are some tips for decluttering your holiday décor and creating a more streamlined, intentional collection:

1. Assess Your Current Collection

Before you start decorating, take a moment to assess your current holiday décor collection. Pull out everything you have and go through each item, asking yourself whether it still fits your aesthetic, brings you joy, or has sentimental value.

- **Keep Only What You Love:** Only keep the decorations that you truly love or that hold special meaning for you. Let go of items that are outdated, broken, or that no longer align with your minimalist vision.
- **Donate or Recycle Unwanted Items:** If you have decorations that are in good condition but no longer suit your style, consider donating them to a charity or local thrift store. This helps reduce waste and allows someone else to enjoy the items.

2. Simplify Storage

Once you've decluttered your holiday décor, simplify your storage by organizing the remaining items in a way that's easy to access and manage.

- **Use Clear Storage Bins:** Store your holiday decorations in clear, labeled bins so you can easily see what's inside. This helps prevent overbuying and ensures that you only use what you need each year.
- **Store Items by Category:** Organize your decorations by category (e.g., tree ornaments, garlands, lights) to make decorating and taking down decorations more efficient.

3. Practice Intentional Purchasing

As you embrace minimalist holiday décor, be mindful of what you bring into your home. Avoid impulse purchases and focus on buying only high-quality, meaningful items that will enhance your space.

- **Buy Less, Buy Better:** Rather than purchasing multiple inexpensive decorations, invest in a few high-quality pieces that will last for years. Look for timeless, versatile items that can be used year after year.
- **Opt for Sustainable Décor:** When purchasing new decorations, consider eco-friendly and sustainable options. Natural materials, reusable items, and ethically sourced products are

great choices for creating a holiday décor scheme that aligns with minimalist and sustainable values.

Conclusion

Minimalist holiday décor is about creating a beautiful, intentional space that enhances the holiday season without overwhelming you with clutter or stress. By focusing on simplicity, quality, and natural elements, you can design a festive environment that feels calm, peaceful, and meaningful. Whether it's a simple wreath, a pared-down Christmas tree, or a few well-placed candles, minimalist holiday décor allows you to celebrate the season in a way that aligns with your values and brings you joy. Embrace the less-is-more philosophy this holiday season, and enjoy a more serene, stress-free approach to decorating.

Chapter 23: Hosting the Holidays Without the Hassle

Hosting a holiday party can be one of the most enjoyable aspects of the season, bringing friends and family together to celebrate, share a meal, and create lasting memories. However, the pressures of planning, preparing, and managing the event can often lead to stress and overwhelm. Many hosts feel the need to create a perfect experience for their guests, from the décor to the food to the entertainment, which can quickly turn a joyful occasion into a daunting task.

The good news is that hosting a holiday gathering doesn't have to be stressful. With a little planning, organization, and a focus on simplicity, you can throw a memorable holiday party without feeling overwhelmed. In this chapter, we will explore practical tips and strategies for hosting a hassle-free holiday event, from planning the menu and setting the atmosphere to managing your time and staying relaxed. The goal is to create a festive, welcoming environment where both you and your guests can enjoy the occasion.

Why Hosting Can Feel Overwhelming

Before diving into solutions, it's helpful to understand why hosting holiday gatherings can feel overwhelming. Recognizing these common sources of stress allows you to address them proactively and minimize their impact on your experience as a host.

1. High Expectations

Many hosts put pressure on themselves to create a flawless, picture-perfect event. Whether inspired by social media, holiday movies, or past experiences, these high expectations can lead to feelings of inadequacy or stress when things don't go exactly as planned.

2. Overcommitting

Trying to do too much—whether it's preparing an elaborate meal, decorating every inch of your home, or planning multiple activities—can quickly lead to burnout. Overcommitting often results in exhaustion, making it difficult to enjoy your own party.

3. Last-Minute Planning

Procrastination or a lack of planning can create unnecessary stress as the event approaches. Scrambling to prepare everything at the last minute can leave you feeling frazzled and overwhelmed, especially when unexpected challenges arise.

4. Fear of Judgment

Worrying about how your event will be perceived by guests can add to the pressure of hosting. Concerns about whether the food, décor, or overall experience will meet others' expectations can detract from your enjoyment and increase anxiety.

5. Lack of Help

Trying to handle every aspect of the event on your own can quickly become overwhelming. Without help or delegation, even a small gathering can feel like a major undertaking, leading to feelings of being overwhelmed.

How to Host a Holiday Party Without the Hassle

To host a holiday party without feeling overwhelmed, it's important to simplify the process and focus on what truly matters: spending time with your loved ones and creating a warm, inviting atmosphere. Here are practical strategies for hosting a hassle-free holiday event, from planning to execution.

1. Start with a Plan

One of the best ways to reduce stress as a host is to start with a clear, simple plan. By organizing your event in advance, you can avoid last-minute scrambling and ensure that you have everything under control.

- **Set a Realistic Date and Time:** Choose a date and time for your party that works for both you and your guests, allowing plenty of time for preparation. Avoid hosting an event too close to other major commitments or holidays, which can add unnecessary pressure.
- **Create a Guest List:** Decide who you want to invite and create a guest list that fits your space and your comfort level. Be realistic about how many people you can accommodate without feeling overwhelmed. If you prefer a smaller, more intimate gathering, don't feel pressured to invite everyone.
- **Send Invitations Early:** Whether you're sending formal invitations or casual digital invites, do so early to give your guests plenty of notice. This will also help you get an accurate headcount, making it easier to plan your food, drinks, and seating.

2. Keep the Menu Simple

One of the biggest sources of stress for hosts is planning and preparing food for the event. While it's tempting to create an elaborate spread, a simple, well-thought-out menu can be just as satisfying—and much easier to manage.

- **Stick to a Few Key Dishes:** Rather than trying to cook an extensive menu with multiple courses, focus on a few crowd-pleasing dishes that you can prepare easily. Choose recipes you're comfortable with and that don't require complicated techniques or last-minute prep.
- **Incorporate Make-Ahead Dishes:** Whenever possible, prepare dishes that can be made ahead of time, such as casseroles, salads, or desserts. This reduces the amount of cooking you need to do on the day of the event and allows you to spend more time with your guests.
- **Consider Potluck-Style Hosting:** If you're hosting a larger gathering or simply want to reduce your workload, consider making your event potluck-style. Ask guests to bring a dish to share, specifying what type of dish they should bring (e.g., appetizer, side dish, dessert) to en-

sure variety. This not only lightens your cooking responsibilities but also makes the event feel more communal.

- **Serve Finger Foods or a Buffet:** For a casual, stress-free party, consider serving finger foods, appetizers, or a buffet-style meal. These options allow guests to serve themselves, reducing the pressure on you to plate and serve each dish.

3. Create a Relaxed Atmosphere with Minimalist Décor

Holiday décor can quickly become overwhelming if you try to do too much. Instead of going overboard with decorations, focus on creating a simple, cozy atmosphere that reflects the holiday spirit without adding stress.

- **Choose a Theme or Color Palette:** Sticking to a specific theme or color palette can simplify your décor decisions. For example, choose a minimalist winter theme with natural elements like greenery, pinecones, and candles, or a classic red-and-white holiday color scheme. This helps create a cohesive look without the need for excessive decorations.
- **Focus on a Few Key Areas:** Instead of decorating every corner of your home, focus on a few key areas where guests will spend the most time, such as the dining table, living room, or entryway. A simple centerpiece, a few candles, and some greenery can go a long way in setting a festive tone.
- **Use What You Already Have:** There's no need to buy new decorations every year. Use what you already have, such as string lights, candles, and holiday ornaments, and arrange them in new ways to create a fresh look. Incorporating natural elements like branches, pine boughs, or fresh flowers can also add beauty without the need for store-bought décor.

4. Delegate and Accept Help

You don't have to handle everything on your own. Delegating tasks and accepting help from others can make hosting much more manageable and reduce the pressure on you to do it all.

- **Assign Tasks to Family or Friends:** If you have close family or friends attending the event, don't hesitate to ask for help. For example, someone could be in charge of setting up the buffet, another could manage drinks, and someone else could help with cleanup. Delegating tasks allows you to focus on being present with your guests rather than running around.
- **Ask Guests to Bring Something:** In addition to food, you can ask guests to contribute in other ways, such as bringing drinks, napkins, or a dessert. Many guests are happy to help, and this takes some of the burden off your shoulders.

5. Create a Manageable Timeline

A well-organized timeline can help you stay on track and prevent last-minute panic. By breaking down your tasks into manageable steps, you can spread out your preparations and avoid feeling rushed.

- **Make a To-Do List:** Create a detailed to-do list for everything that needs to be done before the party, including shopping, cooking, cleaning, and setting up. Break tasks into smaller, manageable steps, and assign deadlines for each one.
- **Do as Much as Possible in Advance:** Prepare as much as you can in advance, such as cooking make-ahead dishes, setting the table, and arranging decorations. This will leave you with only a few last-minute tasks on the day of the event, allowing you to stay calm and relaxed.
- **Give Yourself Plenty of Time to Get Ready:** On the day of the party, leave enough time for yourself to get dressed, relax, and mentally prepare before guests arrive. Rushing to finish tasks right before the event can leave you feeling frazzled and exhausted.

6. Focus on Connection Over Perfection

One of the most important aspects of hosting a holiday party is creating a welcoming environment where guests feel comfortable and connected. Instead of striving for perfection, focus on making your guests feel at home and enjoying the moment.

- **Be Present with Your Guests:** Once the party starts, shift your focus away from managing every detail and toward connecting with your guests. Greet each person warmly, engage in conversations, and enjoy the company of those around you.
- **Let Go of Perfection:** Remember that your guests are there to spend time with you, not to judge your cooking or décor. If something doesn't go as planned—a dish doesn't turn out perfectly, or you forget to put out a decoration—don't stress. Embrace the imperfections and focus on the positive aspects of the event.
- **Encourage a Relaxed Atmosphere:** Set the tone for your party by keeping the atmosphere relaxed and informal. Play soft music, light some candles, and let your guests mingle at their own pace. By creating a low-pressure environment, you can help everyone—including yourself—feel more at ease.

7. Enjoy the Event

As the host, it's easy to get caught up in managing the event and forget to enjoy it yourself. Make it a priority to relax and savor the experience alongside your guests.

- **Take Breaks During the Party:** Don't be afraid to step away from hosting duties to enjoy the party. Sit down, chat with your guests, and take a moment to appreciate the festive atmosphere you've created.
- **Celebrate the Small Moments:** Hosting a holiday gathering isn't about grand gestures or perfect execution—it's about celebrating the small, meaningful moments. Whether it's laughter around the table, a heartfelt conversation with a friend, or simply enjoying a quiet moment by the fire, take time to savor the joy of the season.
- **Keep Things in Perspective:** If something doesn't go exactly as planned, remind yourself that it's not the end of the world. Hosting a successful holiday party isn't about perfection—it's about bringing people together and creating a warm, welcoming space for connection.

Handling Unexpected Challenges

Even with careful planning, unexpected challenges can arise during your holiday party. The key to managing these situations without feeling overwhelmed is to stay calm, be flexible, and focus on solutions rather than stressing over the problem.

1. Dealing with Food Issues

If a dish doesn't turn out as expected, or you run out of food, don't panic. There are always workarounds.

- **Have Backup Snacks or Easy-to-Prepare Items:** Keep some backup snacks, appetizers, or frozen foods on hand in case you need to quickly supplement the meal. A simple cheese and cracker plate, some chips and dip, or a frozen pizza can save the day if you run out of food.
- **Ask Guests to Bring Extra Dishes:** If you're worried about not having enough food, ask guests ahead of time to bring additional appetizers or sides. This way, you won't feel as much pressure to provide everything yourself.

2. Managing Guest Dynamics

At any gathering, there may be moments of awkwardness or tension, especially if you're hosting guests with differing personalities or opinions.

- **Encourage Positive Interactions:** As the host, you can help create a positive atmosphere by engaging guests in conversations, introducing people who may not know each other, and steering the conversation away from sensitive topics.
- **Provide Discreet Help:** If you notice a guest who seems uncomfortable or out of place, check in with them privately to see how you can make them feel more at ease. Sometimes a simple gesture, such as offering a drink or introducing them to someone, can help break the ice.

3. Staying Calm Under Pressure

If you find yourself feeling stressed during the party, take a deep breath and remind yourself that you've done your best to prepare. It's okay to step away for a moment to collect your thoughts, re-focus, and return with a calm mindset.

- **Practice Deep Breathing or Mindfulness:** If you're feeling overwhelmed, take a few deep breaths or practice a quick mindfulness exercise to calm your nerves. Focus on the present moment, and remind yourself that the event doesn't need to be perfect for it to be successful.

Conclusion

Hosting a holiday party doesn't have to be stressful or overwhelming. By planning ahead, simplifying your menu and décor, delegating tasks, and focusing on connection over perfection, you can create a memorable event that both you and your guests will enjoy. Remember, the true spirit of the holidays is about bringing people together, sharing meaningful moments, and creating a warm, welcoming atmosphere. With these strategies in place, you can host a holiday gathering that's festive, fun, and stress-free.

Chapter 24: Quick and Easy Holiday Meal Planning

The holiday season is a time for gathering with loved ones and sharing delicious meals, but for many, the prospect of planning and preparing a holiday meal can be a source of stress. Between co-ordinating menus, shopping for ingredients, and cooking for a crowd, it's easy to feel overwhelmed. However, with a bit of organization and a focus on simplicity, you can create a festive and delicious meal without the hassle.

In this chapter, we'll explore strategies for simplifying holiday meal planning, from choosing easy-to-make dishes to organizing your time in the kitchen. Whether you're hosting a small family dinner or a larger gathering, these tips will help you streamline the process and take the stress out of holiday cooking.

The Benefits of Simple Holiday Meal Planning

Taking a simplified approach to holiday meal planning offers several benefits, allowing you to enjoy the season without feeling burdened by the demands of the kitchen:

- **Reduces Stress:** A well-organized meal plan helps you avoid last-minute scrambling and reduces the pressure of preparing complex dishes. Simpler meals require less time and effort, leaving you with more time to relax and enjoy the holiday with your guests.
- **Saves Time:** By focusing on dishes that are quick to prepare or can be made in advance, you can cut down on the time you spend in the kitchen on the day of the event. This frees up time for other holiday activities and allows you to be present with your family and friends.
- **Prevents Overwhelm:** Simplifying your meal plan means fewer ingredients to shop for, fewer pots and pans to clean, and fewer opportunities for things to go wrong. A simple, straightforward menu keeps you from feeling overwhelmed by the complexity of holiday cooking.
- **Allows for Flexibility:** A simple meal plan is often more flexible, making it easier to accommodate dietary restrictions, unexpected guests, or changes in plans.

Step-by-Step Guide to Easy Holiday Meal Planning

Creating a stress-free holiday meal starts with good planning. By breaking down the process into manageable steps, you can streamline your meal preparation and avoid feeling rushed or overwhelmed.

1. Plan Your Menu Around Simple, Crowd-Pleasing Dishes

When planning your holiday meal, focus on simple, crowd-pleasing dishes that are easy to prepare and sure to satisfy your guests. You don't need to create a five-course gourmet feast—often, it's the familiar, comforting dishes that are the biggest hits.

- **Stick to Classics with a Twist:** Rather than experimenting with unfamiliar, complex recipes, stick to classic holiday dishes that you know how to make well. You can add a modern twist or seasonal variation to keep things interesting, but there's no need to reinvent the wheel.
- **Limit the Number of Dishes:** Don't feel pressured to serve a large variety of dishes. Focus on a few high-quality, well-executed dishes that complement each other. A typical holiday meal might include a main course, two or three side dishes, and a dessert—more than enough to create a festive spread without overwhelming yourself.
- **Choose Recipes You're Comfortable With:** Pick recipes you're familiar with and confident in preparing. Holiday meals are not the time to test new, complicated techniques or unfamiliar ingredients. If you want to try something new, opt for a simple, foolproof recipe that won't add unnecessary stress.

2. Incorporate Make-Ahead and No-Cook Dishes

One of the best ways to simplify your holiday meal is by incorporating make-ahead dishes that can be prepared in advance. This not only saves time on the day of the event but also reduces the pressure of having to juggle multiple dishes at once.

- **Make-Ahead Casseroles and Sides:** Many side dishes, such as casseroles, stuffing, mashed potatoes, or roasted vegetables, can be made the day before and reheated just before serving. Make-ahead dishes free up your oven and stovetop on the day of the meal, allowing you to focus on the main course.
- **No-Cook Appetizers:** For a stress-free start to your meal, opt for no-cook appetizers like cheese platters, charcuterie boards, or vegetable crudités with dip. These can be assembled quickly and require minimal preparation, allowing you to focus on the main meal.

3. Simplify the Main Course

The main course is often the centerpiece of the holiday meal, but it doesn't need to be overly complicated to impress your guests. Focus on easy-to-prepare main dishes that are flavorful and satisfying.

- **One-Pan or One-Pot Meals:** Dishes that can be cooked in a single pan or pot, such as roasted meats, stews, or casseroles, simplify both the cooking and the cleanup process. A roast chicken or turkey, for example, can be cooked alongside vegetables in the same pan, minimizing dishes and maximizing flavor.
- **Slow Cooker or Instant Pot Recipes:** If you have a slow cooker or Instant Pot, consider using it for your main course. These appliances allow you to prepare dishes like pot roast, ham, or braised meats with minimal effort. Simply set it and forget it, freeing you up to focus on other tasks.
- **Consider Vegetarian Options:** For a simpler, lighter meal, consider a vegetarian main course like a vegetable tart, stuffed squash, or a savory bread pudding. Vegetarian dishes are often quicker to prepare than meat-based mains and can be just as hearty and festive.

4. Use a Detailed Shopping List

A well-organized shopping list is essential for efficient meal planning. A clear list ensures that you don't forget any key ingredients, reduces the number of trips to the store, and helps you stick to your budget.

- **Organize Your List by Section:** Group your shopping list by sections of the grocery store (e.g., produce, dairy, pantry staples) to make your trip more efficient. This prevents backtracking and saves time during a busy holiday shopping season.
- **Double-Check Ingredients:** Before heading to the store, double-check your pantry, fridge, and freezer to see what ingredients you already have. This not only saves money but also ensures you're not buying duplicates of items you don't need.
- **Shop Early:** Avoid the stress of last-minute grocery shopping by purchasing your non-perishable ingredients well in advance. For perishable items, try to shop a few days before your event to avoid the crowds and ensure you have everything you need.

5. Create a Cooking Timeline

To avoid feeling rushed in the kitchen, create a cooking timeline that breaks down when each dish needs to be prepared. This allows you to stay organized and ensures that everything is ready to serve at the same time.

- **Work Backward from Serving Time:** Start by determining what time you want to serve the meal, then work backward to plan when each dish needs to be started and finished. For example, if your roast turkey takes three hours to cook and you want to serve dinner at 6 p.m., plan to put the turkey in the oven by 2:30 p.m.

- **Factor In Prep Time:** Don't forget to factor in the time needed to chop vegetables, assemble dishes, or allow meats to rest before carving. If you're making multiple dishes, stagger the prep and cooking times so that you're not trying to do everything at once.
- **Delegate Tasks:** If you have family members or friends who are willing to help, delegate specific tasks to them, such as chopping vegetables, setting the table, or managing the drinks. This not only lightens your load but also creates a more communal, enjoyable experience.

6. Simple Holiday Meal Ideas

Here are some quick and easy holiday meal ideas that are perfect for a low-stress, delicious celebration:

Main Courses:

- **Roast Chicken or Turkey Breast:** Instead of cooking a whole bird, opt for a roast chicken or turkey breast, which cooks faster and is easier to manage. You can roast it with vegetables like carrots, potatoes, and onions for a simple, one-pan meal.
- **Baked Salmon:** Salmon is quick to prepare and adds an elegant touch to your holiday meal. Bake it with lemon, garlic, and herbs for a flavorful yet simple dish.
- **Vegetarian Lasagna:** A vegetarian lasagna made with layers of ricotta, spinach, and marinara sauce is a comforting, make-ahead main dish that can be prepared the day before and baked just before serving.

Side Dishes:

- **Garlic Mashed Potatoes:** A classic side dish that can be made ahead and reheated, mashed potatoes are always a crowd-pleaser. Add garlic and butter for extra flavor.
- **Roasted Vegetables:** Roasted vegetables like carrots, Brussels sprouts, and sweet potatoes are simple to prepare and can be roasted alongside your main dish.
- **Stuffing:** A traditional holiday side, stuffing can be made with just a few ingredients—bread, onions, celery, and herbs—and baked in the oven while your main dish is cooking.

Appetizers:

- **Cheese and Charcuterie Board:** A beautifully arranged cheese and charcuterie board requires no cooking and is a great way to start the meal. Include a variety of cheeses, cured meats, crackers, and fruit.
- **Vegetable Crudités with Dip:** Arrange fresh vegetables like carrots, cucumbers, and cherry tomatoes with a simple dip, such as hummus or ranch dressing, for a light, no-cook appetizer.
- **Caprese Skewers:** Skewer cherry tomatoes, fresh mozzarella, and basil leaves, and drizzle with balsamic glaze for a fresh and easy appetizer.

Desserts:

- **Simple Fruit Tart:** A store-bought pie crust filled with fresh fruit and a light custard or cream makes for a quick and elegant dessert.
- **Holiday Cookies:** Bake a batch of holiday cookies in advance, such as sugar cookies or gingerbread, and serve them with coffee or tea.
- **No-Bake Cheesecake:** A no-bake cheesecake is easy to prepare ahead of time and can be stored in the fridge until it's time to serve.

7. Relax and Enjoy the Process

One of the most important aspects of holiday meal planning is to remember that the holidays are meant to be enjoyable, not stressful. Embrace the process, focus on the joy of bringing people together, and let go of the need for perfection.

- **Accept Imperfections:** If something doesn't go exactly as planned—a dish doesn't turn out quite right, or the timing is off—don't stress. Most guests won't notice, and they're there to enjoy your company, not to critique your cooking.
- **Take Time to Enjoy the Meal:** Once everything is ready, take a moment to sit down, relax, and enjoy the meal with your guests. You've worked hard to prepare the food, so give yourself permission to savor the experience.

Conclusion

Holiday meal planning doesn't have to be overwhelming or complicated. By focusing on simple, crowd-pleasing dishes, planning ahead, and using time-saving strategies, you can create a festive, delicious meal without the hassle. Remember, the true spirit of the holidays lies in spending time with loved ones and sharing meaningful moments around the table. By simplifying your approach to meal planning, you'll reduce stress, enjoy the process, and create a memorable holiday experience for yourself and your guests.

Chapter 25: Healthy Holiday Eating Without Deprivation

The holiday season is filled with indulgent treats, large meals, and festive gatherings centered around food. While it's a time to celebrate and enjoy delicious dishes, it's also easy to go overboard, leading to feelings of guilt or discomfort after the holidays. Striking a balance between indulging in festive meals and maintaining your overall well-being can feel like a challenge. However, with mindful eating strategies and a balanced approach, it's possible to enjoy the holiday season without feeling deprived or compromising your health.

In this chapter, we'll explore how to maintain a healthy approach to eating during the holidays, focusing on balance, mindful choices, and strategies that allow you to enjoy your favorite holiday foods while supporting your well-being. This isn't about strict dieting or avoiding holiday treats but about finding harmony between indulgence and health.

The Challenge of Holiday Eating

Holiday meals often involve larger portions, richer foods, and more frequent eating than your typical routine. Combined with the emotional and social aspects of the season, it's easy to lose track of mindful eating habits. Here are some common challenges associated with holiday eating:

1. Social Pressure to Overeat

Holiday gatherings are often centered around food, and there can be social pressure to indulge in large portions or multiple courses. Whether it's a family member encouraging you to try every dish or a festive buffet tempting you to fill your plate, it can be difficult to say no.

2. Abundance of Rich, High-Calorie Foods

From buttery mashed potatoes to sugary desserts, holiday meals tend to feature rich, calorie-dense foods. While these foods can be delicious and festive, overindulging regularly can lead to discomfort, weight gain, and fatigue.

3. Emotional Eating

The holidays can bring up a range of emotions, from joy and excitement to stress, anxiety, or loneliness. Many people turn to food for comfort, using it to manage their emotions. This can lead to overeating, especially when faced with abundant holiday treats.

4. Frequent Celebrations and Leftovers

With multiple gatherings, holiday parties, and leftover meals, it's easy to find yourself in a continuous cycle of indulgence. The frequency of celebrations makes it more challenging to balance indulgent eating with healthier habits.

How to Maintain Balance Without Deprivation

The key to healthy holiday eating is finding a balance between enjoying indulgent foods and making mindful, nourishing choices. You don't need to deprive yourself of your favorite holiday dishes—instead, focus on moderation, listening to your body, and making choices that support both your well-being and your enjoyment of the season.

1. Practice Mindful Eating

Mindful eating is one of the most effective ways to enjoy holiday meals without overindulging. By paying attention to your body's hunger and fullness cues and savoring each bite, you can enjoy your favorite foods in a more balanced way.

- **Slow Down and Savor Each Bite:** Take the time to truly enjoy your food by eating slowly and savoring each bite. Notice the flavors, textures, and aromas of the dishes you're eating. This not only enhances your enjoyment but also gives your body time to register when it's full.
- **Eat Without Distractions:** During holiday meals, try to focus on the food and the company around you, rather than eating while distracted by conversations, TV, or other activities. When you eat mindfully, you're more likely to notice when you're satisfied, helping you avoid overeating.
- **Listen to Your Body's Signals:** Pay attention to your body's hunger and fullness cues. Before reaching for seconds, check in with yourself to see if you're truly hungry or if you're eating out of habit or social pressure. Stopping when you're comfortably full, rather than stuffed, will help you feel better throughout the day.

2. Enjoy Indulgent Foods in Moderation

Holiday meals are meant to be enjoyed, and it's perfectly okay to indulge in your favorite dishes. The key is to do so in moderation, allowing yourself to enjoy the flavors of the season without overdoing it.

- **Use the "80/20 Rule":** A helpful strategy is the "80/20 rule," where you aim to make 80% of your food choices healthy and balanced, while allowing 20% to be more indulgent. This gives you the flexibility to enjoy holiday treats without feeling deprived, while still maintaining a focus on nutritious eating.
- **Choose Your Indulgences:** Be selective about the indulgent foods you truly love, and skip those that don't bring you as much joy. For example, if you love holiday pie but aren't as excited about mashed potatoes, enjoy a slice of pie and skip the potatoes. This way, you can indulge in what matters most to you without overloading on calories.
- **Watch Portion Sizes:** One of the simplest ways to enjoy indulgent foods without overdoing it is to watch your portion sizes. Take small portions of richer dishes and balance them with

larger servings of vegetables or lighter options. This allows you to taste everything without feeling overly full.

3. Incorporate Healthier Versions of Holiday Classics

You don't have to completely avoid your favorite holiday dishes to maintain a healthier approach. By making a few simple swaps or adjustments, you can create lighter, healthier versions of classic holiday dishes that are just as delicious.

- **Swap Ingredients for Healthier Options:** Look for ways to swap high-calorie or high-fat ingredients for lighter alternatives. For example, use Greek yogurt in place of sour cream in dips, substitute mashed cauliflower for mashed potatoes, or use olive oil instead of butter in certain recipes.
- **Include More Vegetables:** Adding more vegetables to your holiday meal is an easy way to increase the nutritional value of your dishes. Consider roasting a variety of seasonal vegetables as a side dish, or add extra greens to your stuffing or salads.
- **Lighten Up Desserts:** If you're baking holiday treats, look for ways to reduce sugar or fat without sacrificing flavor. You can often reduce the amount of sugar in dessert recipes, use whole wheat flour instead of white flour, or substitute applesauce for some of the butter or oil.

4. Balance Your Plate

A balanced plate is the foundation of healthy eating, even during the holidays. By including a variety of foods in appropriate portions, you can enjoy a festive meal without overindulging in any one type of dish.

- **Fill Half Your Plate with Vegetables:** Start by filling half your plate with non-starchy vegetables, such as roasted Brussels sprouts, green beans, or salad. Vegetables are low in calories, high in fiber, and packed with nutrients, making them a great way to balance richer holiday dishes.
- **Include Protein and Healthy Fats:** Add a serving of lean protein, such as turkey, chicken, or fish, and healthy fats like avocado, nuts, or olive oil. Protein and healthy fats help keep you full and satisfied, reducing the likelihood of overeating.
- **Limit High-Carb or Rich Dishes:** For starches like mashed potatoes, stuffing, or dinner rolls, take smaller portions and balance them with plenty of vegetables. This allows you to enjoy these festive dishes without feeling overly full or sluggish afterward.

5. Stay Hydrated

It's easy to forget about hydration during holiday meals, especially with festive drinks like wine, cocktails, and hot cocoa readily available. However, staying hydrated is important for maintaining energy and avoiding overeating.

- **Drink Water Throughout the Day:** Make a habit of drinking water throughout the day, especially before and during holiday meals. Sometimes, thirst can be mistaken for hunger, leading to overeating. Drinking water helps keep you hydrated and can aid digestion.
- **Alternate Alcoholic Drinks with Water:** If you're enjoying alcoholic beverages at a holiday gathering, alternate each drink with a glass of water. This not only helps you stay hydrated but also reduces the chances of overindulging in alcohol, which can be high in calories.
- **Start with a Glass of Water Before Meals:** Before sitting down to a large holiday meal, drink a glass of water. This can help you feel more hydrated and may prevent you from eating too quickly or overloading your plate.

6. Don't Skip Meals

It might be tempting to skip breakfast or lunch in anticipation of a big holiday dinner, but this can backfire by leading to overeating later in the day. Skipping meals can leave you overly hungry, making it harder to make mindful food choices.

- **Eat Balanced Meals Throughout the Day:** Instead of skipping meals, focus on eating balanced, nutrient-dense meals earlier in the day. A breakfast that includes protein, fiber, and healthy fats—such as eggs with avocado and whole-grain toast—will keep you satisfied and help you avoid overeating later.
- **Have a Light Snack Before Big Meals:** If you're attending a holiday party in the evening, have a light snack beforehand, such as a piece of fruit with nuts or a small salad. This can prevent you from arriving too hungry and making impulsive food choices.

7. Practice Gratitude and Enjoyment

The holidays are about more than just the food on your plate—they're also about connecting with loved ones, reflecting on the past year, and celebrating together. Shifting your focus from food to gratitude and enjoyment can help you feel more satisfied and less reliant on overindulging.

- **Practice Gratitude for Your Meal:** Take a moment before eating to express gratitude for the food in front of you, the effort that went into preparing it, and the people you're sharing it with. This mindfulness practice can enhance your enjoyment of the meal and help you eat more intentionally.
- **Focus on Social Connection:** Engage in meaningful conversations with your family and friends, and savor the opportunity to connect with others. When you focus on the people

around you rather than solely on the food, you're more likely to eat at a slower pace and feel satisfied with smaller portions.

- **Relish the Experience:** Enjoy the experience of the holidays as a whole, from the festive atmosphere to the traditions and celebrations. This broader focus helps reduce the temptation to overeat as a way of enhancing the holiday experience.

8. Get Moving

Incorporating physical activity into your holiday routine is a great way to support both your mental and physical well-being. Exercise helps balance out the extra calories from holiday meals, boosts your energy, and reduces stress.

- **Take a Walk After Meals:** After a big holiday meal, consider taking a walk with family or friends. Walking aids digestion, helps prevent the post-meal slump, and gives you an opportunity to enjoy some fresh air and movement.
- **Stay Active During the Holidays:** Look for fun, festive ways to stay active during the holiday season, whether it's ice skating, playing a game of touch football, or dancing at a holiday party. Staying active helps keep your metabolism moving and provides a healthy outlet for holiday stress.

Sample Healthy Holiday Menu

To give you some inspiration for balancing indulgence with healthy eating, here's a sample holiday menu that includes both festive and nutritious options:

Appetizers:

- **Vegetable Crudités with Hummus:** A fresh and light appetizer that provides a healthy start to the meal.
- **Stuffed Mushrooms:** Mushrooms stuffed with a mixture of herbs, garlic, and whole-grain breadcrumbs are flavorful and lower in calories than many traditional appetizers.

Main Course:

- **Roast Turkey or Chicken with Herbs:** A classic holiday main course that's high in protein and can be made with minimal added fat.

Side Dishes:

- **Roasted Brussels Sprouts with Balsamic Glaze:** Brussels sprouts roasted to perfection and drizzled with a light balsamic glaze for a burst of flavor.
- **Garlic Mashed Cauliflower:** A healthier, lower-carb alternative to mashed potatoes that's creamy and satisfying.

- **Quinoa and Cranberry Salad:** A light and refreshing side dish made with quinoa, dried cranberries, spinach, and a lemon vinaigrette.

Dessert:

- **Dark Chocolate Dipped Fruit:** Fresh fruit dipped in dark chocolate provides a sweet and indulgent dessert with health benefits.
- **Greek Yogurt Parfaits with Berries:** Layers of Greek yogurt, fresh berries, and a drizzle of honey create a light, protein-rich dessert option.

Conclusion

Maintaining healthy eating habits during the holidays doesn't mean depriving yourself of festive foods or feeling guilty about indulging in your favorite treats. By practicing mindful eating, balancing indulgence with nutritious choices, and focusing on enjoying the overall experience, you can navigate holiday meals in a way that supports both your well-being and your enjoyment of the season. Remember, the goal is not perfection but balance—enjoy the delicious flavors of the holidays while also taking care of your body and mind. With these strategies, you can create a holiday experience that is both festive and health-conscious.

Chapter 26: Incorporating Gratitude Practices into the Holidays

The holiday season is often portrayed as a time of joy, togetherness, and celebration, but it can also bring about stress, overwhelm, and anxiety. Between family gatherings, holiday shopping, financial pressures, and endless to-do lists, it's easy to lose sight of what really matters during this time of year. One powerful tool to shift your mindset and reduce stress during the holidays is the practice of gratitude.

Gratitude involves recognizing and appreciating the positive aspects of your life—both big and small. It's about acknowledging the good things you often take for granted and expressing thankfulness for the people, experiences, and even challenges that shape your life. By incorporating gratitude practices into your holiday season, you can transform your outlook, enhance your well-being, and experience the true joy and meaning of the holidays.

In this chapter, we'll explore how gratitude can improve your mental and emotional health, reduce stress, and help you cultivate a sense of peace and presence during the holiday season. We'll also provide practical gratitude exercises and ideas that you can incorporate into your holiday traditions, helping you and your loved ones shift from a mindset of stress to one of appreciation and joy.

The Power of Gratitude

Gratitude is more than just saying "thank you"—it's a mindset and practice that has the potential to change how you experience the world. Numerous studies have shown that practicing gratitude can improve mental health, enhance relationships, and increase overall life satisfaction. Here's how gratitude can shift your mindset and reduce holiday stress:

1. Reduces Stress and Anxiety

Gratitude helps reduce stress by shifting your focus away from what's wrong or stressful and toward what's positive in your life. When you're caught up in the demands of the holiday season, it's easy to focus on what's overwhelming, from endless to-do lists to family tensions. Gratitude helps you take a step back and refocus on the aspects of your life that bring you peace, joy, and fulfillment.

- **Interrupts Negative Thought Patterns:** Practicing gratitude interrupts the cycle of negative thinking, helping you focus on the present moment rather than worrying about what's missing or what could go wrong. This shift in perspective can reduce feelings of anxiety and help you manage holiday stress with a clearer, more positive mindset.

2. Improves Mental Health

Regular gratitude practice has been linked to improved mental health, including increased happiness, reduced depression, and greater emotional resilience. By fostering a sense of appreciation for the good things in your life, gratitude helps combat feelings of dissatisfaction or unhappiness that can arise during the holidays.

- **Promotes Emotional Balance:** Gratitude encourages you to recognize the positive aspects of your life, even when things aren't perfect. This can help you maintain emotional balance during challenging or stressful times, such as navigating family conflicts or managing holiday expectations.
- **Boosts Happiness:** Gratitude has been shown to increase feelings of happiness and contentment. By focusing on what you're thankful for, you cultivate a sense of fulfillment that can improve your overall mood and well-being during the holidays.

3. Strengthens Relationships

The holiday season is often centered around spending time with family and friends. Gratitude can help strengthen these relationships by fostering deeper connections, improving communication, and increasing feelings of closeness.

- **Enhances Connection:** Expressing gratitude to loved ones deepens your bond by showing them that you appreciate their presence in your life. Whether it's through a heartfelt conversation, a note of thanks, or simply acknowledging their efforts, gratitude helps you build stronger, more meaningful relationships.
- **Reduces Conflict:** Gratitude helps reduce tension and conflict by shifting your focus away from frustration and toward appreciation. Instead of dwelling on what's not going right in your relationships, you can focus on what you value and appreciate about the people in your life, which fosters a more positive and harmonious atmosphere.

4. Increases Mindfulness and Presence

The holidays can feel chaotic, with endless tasks to complete, events to attend, and expectations to meet. Practicing gratitude helps ground you in the present moment and cultivate mindfulness, allowing you to savor the simple joys of the season.

- **Brings You Back to the Moment:** Gratitude encourages you to pause, reflect, and appreciate the present. This practice helps you slow down and be fully present in your holiday experiences, whether it's enjoying a meal with loved ones, admiring holiday decorations, or simply taking a walk in nature.
- **Fosters Appreciation for Small Moments:** When you practice gratitude, you begin to notice and appreciate the small, meaningful moments that often go overlooked in the rush of the season. This could be a quiet moment by the fire, the laughter of children, or a kind gesture from a friend.

5. Shifts Focus from Materialism to Meaning

The holiday season is often associated with consumerism and the pressure to buy, give, and receive material gifts. Gratitude helps shift your focus away from the material aspects of the season and toward the deeper, more meaningful experiences and connections that truly matter.

- **Reduces Pressure to Buy More:** When you focus on what you're grateful for, you're less likely to feel pressured to keep up with materialistic holiday trends or overspend on gifts. Gratitude helps you appreciate what you already have, reducing the need for more "stuff" to feel fulfilled.

- **Emphasizes Connection Over Possessions:** Gratitude encourages you to prioritize relationships and shared experiences over material possessions. This shift in focus helps you find greater joy in the time you spend with loved ones, rather than in the gifts exchanged.

Practical Gratitude Practices for the Holidays

Incorporating gratitude into your holiday season doesn't have to be complicated. There are many simple, practical ways to bring gratitude into your daily life and holiday traditions. Here are some gratitude practices that you can start using today to reduce stress and enhance your well-being during the holidays.

1. Start a Gratitude Journal

One of the most effective ways to cultivate gratitude is to keep a gratitude journal. This simple practice involves writing down the things you're grateful for each day, helping you focus on the positive aspects of your life.

- **How to Start:** Set aside a few minutes each morning or evening to write down three to five things you're grateful for. These can be big or small—anything from a meaningful conversation with a loved one to the beauty of a sunset. The key is to focus on what brought you joy, peace, or fulfillment that day.
- **Holiday Twist:** During the holiday season, use your gratitude journal to reflect on holiday-specific blessings, such as time spent with family, festive traditions, or acts of kindness. This practice helps you stay grounded in the positive aspects of the season, even amidst the busyness.

2. Express Gratitude to Loved Ones

The holidays provide a perfect opportunity to express gratitude to the people in your life. Whether it's through a handwritten note, a phone call, or a heartfelt conversation, taking the time to thank others for their support, love, and presence can strengthen your relationships and spread holiday cheer.

- **Write Gratitude Letters:** Write a letter or note to someone who has made a positive impact on your life. This could be a family member, friend, mentor, or colleague. Express your appreciation for their support, kindness, or the role they've played in your life. This simple act of gratitude can deepen your connection and bring joy to both you and the recipient.
- **Verbal Gratitude:** If writing isn't your style, express your gratitude verbally. During holiday gatherings, take a moment to tell your loved ones how much you appreciate them. You can do this privately in one-on-one conversations or share your gratitude with the whole group during a meal or toast.

3. Practice Gratitude as a Family

Incorporating gratitude into your family's holiday traditions can create meaningful connections and help everyone focus on the positive aspects of the season. Practicing gratitude together fosters a sense of togetherness and helps shift the focus from stress or materialism to appreciation and joy.

- **Gratitude at the Dinner Table:** During holiday meals, go around the table and ask each person to share something they're grateful for. This simple practice helps everyone reflect on the positive aspects of their lives and creates an atmosphere of gratitude and connection.
- **Create a Gratitude Tree or Jar:** As a family, create a "gratitude tree" by writing down things you're thankful for on paper leaves and attaching them to a tree-shaped decoration. Alternatively, you can use a jar to collect notes of gratitude throughout the holiday season. On New Year's Eve, read through the notes together and reflect on the year's blessings.

4. Use Gratitude as a Daily Reminder

Incorporating small moments of gratitude into your daily routine can help you stay grounded and reduce stress during the holidays. These reminders don't have to be elaborate—just brief moments of reflection that help you refocus on the positive.

- **Morning Gratitude:** Start your day by reflecting on something you're grateful for. This could be as simple as appreciating the warmth of your bed, the quiet of the morning, or the opportunity to spend time with loved ones during the holidays. Setting a positive tone in the morning helps you carry a grateful mindset throughout the day.
- **Gratitude Breaks:** Throughout the day, take short "gratitude breaks" to pause and reflect on something positive. This could be while you're waiting in line at the store, sitting in traffic, or taking a break from holiday preparations. These brief moments of gratitude help shift your focus away from stress and toward the good things in your life.

5. Shift Your Perspective on Challenges

The holidays aren't always easy, and challenges like family conflicts, financial stress, or loneliness can make the season difficult. Practicing gratitude doesn't mean ignoring these challenges—it means finding ways to appreciate the growth, lessons, or silver linings that come from difficult experiences.

- **Reframe Challenges with Gratitude:** When faced with a challenge, try to reframe it with gratitude. For example, if you're feeling stressed about holiday finances, reflect on what you do have—whether it's a stable income, supportive relationships, or good health. Reframing challenges helps you maintain a positive perspective, even when things are tough.
- **Find Gratitude in the Small Things:** Even on challenging days, there are always small things to be grateful for. Whether it's a cup of coffee, a friendly smile from a stranger, or a moment of peace, focusing on these small blessings can help you get through difficult times with greater resilience.

6. Create Gratitude-Focused Holiday Traditions

Incorporating gratitude into your holiday traditions can add deeper meaning to the season and help you focus on what truly matters. These traditions can become cherished parts of your holiday celebrations, reminding you and your family to stay grounded in appreciation.

- **Host a "Gratitude Thanksgiving":** Instead of focusing solely on the food, host a Thanksgiving celebration where gratitude is the main event. Encourage each guest to share something they're thankful for, and consider making gratitude a theme for the evening by decorating with quotes or reminders of thankfulness.
- **Start a New Year's Gratitude Tradition:** As the new year approaches, reflect on the past year's blessings with a gratitude tradition. You can write down what you're grateful for from the past year, make a gratitude collage, or create a family gratitude list to display in your home.

7. Incorporate Gratitude into Gift-Giving

Gift-giving is a central part of the holiday season, but it can sometimes feel transactional or stressful. By incorporating gratitude into your gift-giving, you can transform the experience into something more meaningful and intentional.

- **Give Gifts of Gratitude:** Instead of focusing on material gifts, consider giving gifts that express gratitude or appreciation. This could be a heartfelt letter, a homemade gift, or a meaningful experience, such as spending quality time with someone you love.
- **Gratitude Gift Tags:** When giving material gifts, add a personal touch by including a note or tag that expresses your gratitude for the recipient. A simple message like "I'm so grateful for your friendship" can make the gift more meaningful and thoughtful.

Conclusion

Gratitude is a powerful tool for shifting your mindset and reducing stress during the holiday season. By focusing on what you're thankful for, you can cultivate a sense of peace, joy, and fulfillment amidst the busyness of the holidays. Whether through journaling, expressing appreciation to loved ones, or incorporating gratitude into your holiday traditions, these practices help you stay grounded in what truly matters. As you move through the season, remember that gratitude isn't about perfection—it's about recognizing and appreciating the blessings, both big and small, that make the holidays special.

Part 6: Preparing for Post-Holiday Success

Chapter 27: Reflecting on the Holiday Experience

The holiday season is often a whirlwind of activities, from family gatherings and festive meals to gift exchanges and travel. After the celebrations wind down and life returns to its normal rhythm, taking time to reflect on the holiday experience can be an invaluable practice. Reflecting allows you to process your feelings, identify what went well, and recognize areas for improvement in the future. This intentional reflection helps you learn from the experience, enhance your holiday planning skills, and ensure that next year's holidays are even more meaningful and enjoyable.

In this chapter, we will explore the importance of reflecting on the holiday season, how to evaluate both the successes and challenges, and how to plan for improvements in the coming year. By adopting a reflective mindset, you can approach each holiday season with greater clarity, balance, and intentionality, ultimately creating a more fulfilling experience for yourself and your loved ones.

Why Reflection is Important After the Holidays

Reflection is a powerful tool for personal growth and continuous improvement. After the holidays, taking a step back to reflect on your experience offers several key benefits:

1. Celebrates Successes

Reflection allows you to acknowledge and celebrate what went well during the holiday season. Whether it was a meaningful family gathering, a stress-free event, or a small victory in sticking to your budget, recognizing these positive moments helps you appreciate the effort and thought you put into making the holidays special.

- **Gratitude for Positive Moments:** Reflecting on the high points of the holiday season fosters a sense of gratitude. You can savor the memories of the good times shared with loved ones, successful events, and personal achievements.
- **Building Confidence:** Acknowledging your successes, even small ones, boosts your confidence as a holiday planner and host. By recognizing what you did well, you can build on these strengths in the future.

2. Identifies Areas for Improvement

No holiday season is without its challenges, whether it's managing stress, dealing with family dynamics, or navigating a packed schedule. Reflecting on these areas helps you pinpoint what didn't work as well as you'd hoped and what changes could be made to improve your experience next year.

- **Learn from Challenges:** Reflection helps you learn from any difficulties or setbacks you encountered, allowing you to approach similar situations with more wisdom and preparedness next time.

- **Prevents Repeating Mistakes:** By analyzing what didn't go well, you can make adjustments to avoid the same issues in the future, leading to a smoother, more enjoyable holiday season.

3. Encourages Mindful Planning for the Future

Reflecting on the holiday season sets the foundation for more mindful, intentional planning in the future. You can use what you've learned from your reflection to design holidays that better align with your values, priorities, and personal well-being.

- **Clarify Priorities:** Reflection helps you identify what aspects of the holidays are most important to you and your family. You can then focus on these elements in the future, letting go of unnecessary obligations or traditions that no longer serve you.
- **Prepare for Next Year:** The insights gained from reflecting on this year's holidays can guide your planning for next year. You can start thinking about changes you'd like to make, from simplifying your celebrations to setting more realistic goals or boundaries.

How to Reflect on the Holiday Experience

Effective reflection involves looking at the holiday season with a balanced perspective—celebrating the successes while also identifying areas that could be improved. To get the most out of your reflection, follow these steps to break down your holiday experience.

1. Create a Quiet Space for Reflection

Reflection requires time and focus, so find a quiet, comfortable space where you can think clearly without distractions. This could be done in a favorite chair with a cup of tea, during a relaxing walk, or while journaling at your desk. The goal is to give yourself the mental space to process your thoughts and experiences.

- **Set Aside Dedicated Time:** Allocate specific time for reflection, whether it's an hour or just a few minutes a day for a week. Reflection is more effective when you approach it thoughtfully rather than rushing through it.
- **Be Honest and Open:** Reflection is most meaningful when you're honest with yourself about both the positive and negative aspects of the holiday season. Give yourself permission to acknowledge challenges without judgment, as well as to celebrate successes.

2. Review Your Goals and Expectations

Start by revisiting any goals or expectations you had for the holiday season. Did you have specific plans in mind, such as hosting a party, managing your budget, or maintaining a healthy work-life balance? Reflecting on these goals can help you evaluate how well they were met and whether your expectations were realistic.

- **What Were Your Priorities?** Reflect on the priorities you set at the beginning of the holiday season. For example, did you prioritize spending quality time with family, sticking to a budget, or avoiding holiday burnout? How well did you achieve these priorities?

- **Did Expectations Match Reality?** Consider whether your expectations for the holiday season aligned with reality. Did you expect a stress-free holiday, only to find yourself overwhelmed? Or did you have concerns that turned out to be less challenging than anticipated? Identifying mismatches between expectations and reality can help you set more realistic goals in the future.

3. Celebrate What Went Well

Before focusing on challenges, take the time to celebrate the aspects of the holiday season that went well. Reflecting on your successes allows you to recognize your efforts, appreciate the positive experiences, and build on these strengths next year.

- **What Worked Well?** Think about the moments or events that were particularly enjoyable or successful. Did a party or family gathering go smoothly? Were you able to stick to your budget or avoid holiday stress? Reflect on what made these successes possible—whether it was good planning, clear communication, or setting boundaries.
- **Personal Wins:** Consider your personal achievements during the holiday season. Did you manage to stay organized? Did you navigate family dynamics more smoothly than in past years? Reflecting on your personal growth can help you feel more empowered and prepared for future challenges.

4. Identify What Could Be Improved

Next, think about the aspects of the holiday season that didn't go as smoothly or caused stress. These are the areas where you can focus on making changes or improvements for next year.

- **What Were the Biggest Challenges?** Identify any challenges you faced during the holiday season, such as time management issues, financial stress, or family conflicts. What specific factors contributed to these challenges? For example, did you overcommit to too many events, or did you underestimate the amount of time needed to prepare for a gathering?
- **What Could Be Done Differently?** Reflect on what you might do differently next year to address these challenges. This could involve setting clearer boundaries, simplifying your plans, delegating more tasks, or adjusting your expectations. Consider practical solutions that would make the holiday season more manageable and enjoyable.

5. Assess Your Well-Being

One of the most important aspects of holiday reflection is assessing your overall well-being during the season. The holidays can be a time of heightened stress, and it's important to reflect on how you felt physically, emotionally, and mentally throughout the celebrations.

- **Did You Feel Overwhelmed or Burnt Out?** Reflect on whether you experienced feelings of overwhelm, exhaustion, or burnout during the holiday season. If so, what contributed to these feelings, and how can you better protect your well-being next year?

- **Did You Make Time for Self-Care?** Think about whether you made time for self-care during the holidays. Did you prioritize rest, relaxation, and activities that helped you recharge, or did you find yourself constantly busy and stressed? If self-care fell by the wayside, consider ways to make it a more integral part of your holiday routine in the future.
- **How Did You Manage Stress?** Reflect on the ways you managed holiday stress. Were there particular strategies that helped you stay calm and grounded, such as mindfulness, setting boundaries, or simplifying your schedule? Take note of these strategies so you can use them again next year.

6. Consider Family Dynamics and Relationships

The holidays often bring together family and friends, which can be both joyful and challenging. Reflecting on the dynamics of your relationships during the holiday season can help you understand what worked well and what may need attention in the future.

- **Were There Any Conflicts or Tensions?** If you experienced family conflicts or tensions during the holidays, reflect on the causes of these issues and how they were handled. What could be done differently next year to improve communication, reduce tension, or resolve conflicts before they escalate?
- **What Strengthened Relationships?** On the positive side, consider what helped strengthen your relationships during the holidays. Did you have meaningful conversations, share special moments, or reconnect with loved ones? Reflect on how you can nurture these connections throughout the year, not just during the holidays.

7. Evaluate Time and Budget Management

Two of the most common sources of holiday stress are time management and financial pressures. Reflecting on how you managed both your time and your budget during the holidays can help you plan more effectively for the future.

- **Time Management:** Did you feel rushed or pressed for time during the holiday season? Were you able to complete your holiday tasks (shopping, decorating, hosting) without feeling overwhelmed? If time management was a challenge, consider ways to improve your planning for next year, such as starting preparations earlier or simplifying your to-do list.
- **Budget Management:** Reflect on how well you managed your holiday spending. Did you stick to your budget, or did you find yourself overspending? If you faced financial stress, think about what caused it—whether it was unexpected expenses, pressure to buy more gifts, or a lack of planning. Consider setting a more realistic budget for next year or finding creative ways to reduce costs.

8. Plan for Next Year

Once you've reflected on this year's holiday experience, use what you've learned to start planning for next year. By identifying areas for improvement and setting new goals, you can create a more balanced, enjoyable holiday season in the future.

- **Set Realistic Goals:** Based on your reflections, set realistic goals for next year's holiday season. These could include simplifying your plans, setting clearer boundaries, sticking to a budget, or making more time for self-care.
- **Adjust Traditions as Needed:** If certain holiday traditions felt more like obligations than sources of joy, consider adjusting or letting go of them. Focus on traditions that bring meaning and happiness to your holiday experience, and don't be afraid to create new ones that better align with your values.
- **Create a Rough Timeline:** While it may seem early, consider creating a rough timeline for next year's holiday preparations. If you struggled with last-minute shopping or planning this year, setting deadlines for key tasks—such as gift buying, meal planning, or sending invitations—can help you stay organized and reduce stress.

Reflection Prompts for the Holiday Season

To guide your reflection process, here are some prompts you can use to evaluate your holiday experience and plan for next year:

- **What was the best moment of the holiday season for you, and why?**
- **Which holiday traditions brought you the most joy, and which felt like obligations?**
- **What challenges did you face, and how did you handle them?**
- **Did you feel overwhelmed or stressed at any point? What contributed to these feelings?**
- **How well did you manage your time and budget? What could be improved?**
- **What steps did you take to prioritize your well-being, and how did they affect your experience?**
- **What do you want to do differently next year to make the holidays more enjoyable and less stressful?**
- **How can you nurture your relationships and strengthen connections with loved ones in the future?**

Conclusion

Reflecting on the holiday experience is a valuable practice that allows you to celebrate successes, learn from challenges, and plan for a more fulfilling and balanced holiday season in the future. By taking the time to evaluate what worked well and what can be improved, you can approach each holiday season with greater clarity, intention, and mindfulness. Whether it's simplifying your plans, setting more realistic goals, or focusing on what truly matters, reflection helps you create a holiday experience that brings joy, meaning, and lasting memories for you and your loved ones.

Chapter 28: Creating a Financial Plan for Next Year's Holidays

The holiday season is one of the most expensive times of the year for many people, with gifts, travel, decorations, and special meals adding up quickly. While the joy of the holidays often makes these expenses feel worthwhile, financial stress can overshadow the festivities if you find yourself overspending or facing post-holiday debt. The good news is that by creating a financial plan for next year's holidays and starting to save early, you can enjoy the season without financial worries.

In this chapter, we will explore strategies for creating a holiday financial plan that helps you save throughout the year, manage your spending, and avoid the stress of last-minute financial decisions. With careful planning and discipline, you can take control of your holiday budget and ensure that the financial aspects of the holidays enhance your experience rather than diminish it.

Why Planning for Holiday Expenses is Important

Taking the time to plan for holiday expenses well in advance provides several key benefits:

1. Reduces Financial Stress

One of the main reasons people experience financial stress during the holidays is a lack of preparation. When expenses are unplanned and unexpected, it's easy to overspend, accumulate debt, or feel overwhelmed by last-minute costs. Starting early allows you to save gradually, which spreads the financial load over several months and reduces the pressure on your budget.

2. Prevents Post-Holiday Debt

Without a financial plan, many people resort to credit cards to cover holiday expenses, leading to debt that lingers long after the season is over. By saving ahead of time and setting a clear budget, you can avoid the need for credit cards or loans, allowing you to enter the new year debt-free.

3. Allows for Smarter Spending

Having a financial plan enables you to be more intentional with your spending. Rather than making impulsive purchases or succumbing to holiday pressure, you can allocate your resources more thoughtfully, ensuring that your money goes toward meaningful experiences and gifts that truly matter.

4. Provides Flexibility

When you plan ahead, you have more flexibility to take advantage of sales, discounts, or deals throughout the year. This not only helps you save money but also reduces the need for rushed, expensive purchases during the peak holiday season.

5. Aligns Spending with Values

A well-crafted financial plan helps you prioritize spending on the aspects of the holidays that align with your values, whether it's gift-giving, travel, charitable donations, or hosting family gatherings. By defining what matters most to you, you can allocate your financial resources in a way that brings the most joy and meaning to the season.

Step-by-Step Guide to Creating a Holiday Financial Plan

Creating a financial plan for next year's holidays requires intentionality, organization, and a commitment to saving throughout the year. Here is a step-by-step guide to help you develop a solid plan that reduces financial stress and ensures a more enjoyable holiday season.

1. Review Last Year's Holiday Spending

The first step in creating a financial plan for next year's holidays is to review your spending from the previous holiday season. This will give you a clear understanding of where your money went, how much you spent, and what areas could be adjusted.

- **Analyze Your Expenses:** Look at your holiday spending in categories such as gifts, travel, meals, decorations, events, and charitable donations. How much did you spend in each category? Were there any unexpected or last-minute expenses that you didn't account for?
- **Identify Overspending:** Did you go over your budget or spend more than you intended in certain areas? If so, reflect on why this happened. Were there unplanned expenses, impulse purchases, or social pressures to spend more? Identifying areas of overspending will help you make more informed decisions next year.
- **Assess What Worked:** Consider what went well with your financial planning last year. Were there areas where you stuck to your budget, found ways to save, or made financially sound decisions? Recognizing these successes will help you continue those practices in the future.

2. Set a Realistic Holiday Budget for Next Year

Based on your review of last year's spending, set a realistic budget for next year's holiday expenses. Having a clear, predetermined budget allows you to stay within your financial limits and avoid overspending.

- **Break Down Your Budget by Category:** Divide your holiday budget into key categories such as gifts, travel, food, decorations, and entertainment. Estimate how much you're willing to spend in each category based on last year's spending and any adjustments you want to make.
- **Be Honest About Your Priorities:** Focus your budget on the aspects of the holiday season that are most important to you. If you value spending time with family, allocate more of your budget to travel or hosting gatherings. If gift-giving is a priority, make sure you budget accordingly, but also look for ways to be thoughtful without overspending.
- **Factor in Hidden Costs:** Don't forget to account for hidden or smaller costs that can add up, such as postage for holiday cards, wrapping paper, stocking stuffers, or holiday party contributions. Including these smaller expenses in your budget helps you avoid unexpected financial surprises.

3. Set a Monthly Savings Goal

Once you have a clear holiday budget, the next step is to break it down into a manageable savings goal. By starting early and saving a small amount each month, you can accumulate the funds you need by the time the holidays arrive, without putting strain on your finances.

- **Divide Your Total Budget by the Number of Months Until the Holidays:** To calculate how much you need to save each month, divide your total holiday budget by the number of months remaining until the start of the holiday season. For example, if you plan to spend $1,200 and you have 12 months until the holidays, you would need to save $100 per month.
- **Automate Your Savings:** Set up an automatic transfer to a separate savings account specifically for holiday expenses. By automating your savings, you can ensure that money is consistently set aside without having to remember to do it manually. This also helps you avoid the temptation to dip into your holiday fund for other expenses.
- **Start Small If Needed:** If saving a significant amount each month feels overwhelming, start small and gradually increase your savings over time. Even putting aside a small amount each month can make a big difference when the holidays roll around.

4. Take Advantage of Sales and Discounts

One of the benefits of starting your holiday financial planning early is that you can take advantage of sales, discounts, and deals throughout the year. By spreading out your purchases, you reduce the pressure to buy everything at once during the peak holiday season, when prices are often higher.

- **Shop During Sales:** Keep an eye out for sales events throughout the year, such as Black Friday, Cyber Monday, or mid-year clearance sales. If you find items on your gift list or holiday décor at a discounted price, purchase them early and store them for the holidays.
- **Use Coupons and Loyalty Programs:** Sign up for store loyalty programs or email newsletters to receive exclusive discounts, coupons, and promotions. Many retailers offer significant savings to loyal customers, which can help you stretch your holiday budget further.
- **Buy in Bulk:** For certain holiday expenses, such as gift wrapping supplies, decorations, or party essentials, buying in bulk can save you money. Look for bulk discounts on non-perishable items that you can use across multiple holidays or years.

5. Create a Gift-Giving Strategy

Gift-giving is often one of the largest holiday expenses, and without a clear strategy, it's easy to overspend. By planning your gift-giving early and thoughtfully, you can stay within your budget while still giving meaningful, personalized gifts.

- **Set a Budget for Each Person:** Determine how much you're willing to spend on each person on your gift list. This helps you allocate your gift budget evenly and prevents overspending on one individual while neglecting others.
- **Consider Group Gifts or Secret Santa:** If you have a large family or friend group, consider organizing a Secret Santa exchange or giving group gifts. This way, each person only has to buy one gift instead of multiple, which significantly reduces costs.
- **DIY and Handmade Gifts:** Handmade or DIY gifts are a great way to give thoughtful, personalized presents without spending a lot of money. Consider making baked goods, crafting homemade candles, or creating custom photo albums or scrapbooks for loved ones.
- **Shop Throughout the Year:** If you come across the perfect gift for someone months before the holidays, don't hesitate to buy it early. Shopping throughout the year allows you to spread out your expenses and avoid the last-minute rush.

6. Manage Travel and Event Costs

Holiday travel and events, such as parties or family gatherings, can be expensive, especially if you don't plan ahead. Whether you're traveling to visit family or hosting a holiday dinner, incorporating these costs into your financial plan early on can help you avoid financial strain.

- **Book Travel Early:** If you're planning to travel during the holidays, book your transportation and accommodations as early as possible to lock in lower rates. Airlines and hotels often offer the best prices months in advance, and you can save money by booking early rather than waiting until peak travel times.
- **Budget for Holiday Events:** If you're hosting a holiday party or gathering, make sure to include the cost of food, decorations, and entertainment in your holiday budget. Plan the event according to your financial means, and consider potluck-style meals where guests contribute dishes to reduce your overall costs.
- **Use Travel Rewards and Points:** If you travel frequently, consider using travel rewards points or airline miles to offset the cost of holiday travel. Many credit cards offer rewards programs that allow you to accumulate points throughout the year, which you can then redeem for flights, hotel stays, or rental cars during the holidays.

7. Prepare for Unexpected Expenses

No matter how carefully you plan, unexpected expenses can arise during the holiday season. Setting aside a small portion of your holiday budget as a buffer for unanticipated costs will help you handle any surprises without derailing your financial plan.

- **Set Aside an Emergency Fund:** Allocate a portion of your savings to cover unexpected holiday expenses, such as last-minute gifts, additional travel costs, or unforeseen event fees. Having this buffer in place reduces the need to dip into other funds or rely on credit cards.
- **Be Flexible with Your Budget:** If an unexpected expense arises, adjust your budget in other areas to accommodate it. For example, if you end up spending more on travel than anticipated, you may need to reduce your budget for gifts or events.

8. Review and Adjust Your Plan as Needed

Your financial situation and holiday plans may evolve throughout the year, so it's important to review and adjust your holiday financial plan as needed. Regularly checking in on your savings progress and budget allows you to stay on track and make changes if necessary.

- **Monitor Your Savings Progress:** Periodically check your savings account to ensure that you're meeting your monthly savings goals. If you're falling behind, consider increasing your contributions or adjusting your budget to make up the difference.
- **Adjust for Life Changes:** If your circumstances change—such as a new job, relocation, or changes in your family situation—revisit your holiday financial plan to make sure it still aligns with your current needs and priorities. You may need to adjust your budget, savings goals, or gift-giving plans based on these changes.
- **Plan a Mid-Year Review:** Midway through the year, conduct a review of your holiday financial plan to assess whether you're on track. If you find that certain areas of your plan need adjustment—such as increasing your savings or modifying your gift list—make the necessary changes to ensure you're prepared when the holidays arrive.

Practical Tips for Reducing Holiday Expenses

In addition to creating a financial plan and saving early, there are several practical ways to reduce your holiday expenses without sacrificing the joy and meaning of the season.

1. Set Clear Boundaries for Gift-Giving

Communicate with family and friends about gift-giving expectations ahead of time. Agree on spending limits or opt for alternative approaches, such as Secret Santa exchanges, homemade gifts, or charitable donations in each other's names.

2. Reuse and Repurpose Decorations

Rather than buying new holiday decorations every year, reuse and repurpose the ones you already have. Get creative with DIY decorations made from natural elements like pinecones, greenery, and twine, or repurpose materials like old wrapping paper or ribbons.

3. Host a Potluck or Casual Gathering

If you're hosting a holiday event, consider making it a potluck-style gathering where guests bring a dish to share. This reduces the financial burden on you as the host and creates a more communal, festive atmosphere.

4. Focus on Experiences Over Material Gifts

Consider giving the gift of experiences rather than material items. This could include tickets to a show, a day trip, or a special activity you can enjoy together. Experience-based gifts often have lasting value and can be more meaningful than physical items.

5. Avoid Last-Minute Shopping

Last-minute shopping often leads to impulse buying and overspending. Start your holiday shopping early, and take the time to compare prices, find deals, and make thoughtful purchases.

Conclusion

Creating a financial plan for next year's holidays is one of the most effective ways to reduce stress and ensure a more joyful, financially secure season. By starting early, setting a budget, saving gradually, and planning for all aspects of the holiday experience—from gifts to travel—you can approach the season with confidence and peace of mind. With a clear financial plan in place, you'll be able to focus on what truly matters during the holidays: spending quality time with loved ones, creating meaningful memories, and enjoying the spirit of the season without the weight of financial worry.

Chapter 29: Recharging After the Holidays

The holiday season, while often filled with joy, celebration, and time with loved ones, can also be physically and mentally draining. From the hustle of planning events and traveling to the emotional energy spent navigating family dynamics and gift-giving pressures, it's not uncommon to feel exhausted once the festivities are over. As the new year begins, it's important to take time to restore your energy, reset your mind, and focus on your well-being. This period of post-holiday recovery allows you to step into the new year with renewed energy, clarity, and balance.

In this chapter, we will explore the importance of recharging after the holidays and provide practical strategies for restoring your mental, physical, and emotional health. Whether you're feeling burnt out from the holiday rush or simply need time to decompress, these strategies will help you regain your equilibrium and start the new year on a positive, energized note.

The Need for Post-Holiday Recovery

After weeks of holiday celebrations, many people find themselves feeling depleted, both physically and emotionally. While the holidays bring joy, they also come with their own set of stressors—overpacked schedules, disrupted routines, financial strain, and even feelings of loneliness or disappointment. The post-holiday period is a time to reflect, rest, and recharge.

1. Physical Fatigue

The physical demands of the holidays—cooking, traveling, attending parties, shopping, and late-night celebrations—can leave you feeling physically drained. Many people push themselves to keep up with the busy holiday pace, often sacrificing sleep, proper nutrition, and exercise in the process.

2. Emotional and Mental Exhaustion

The holidays can also take an emotional toll. The pressure to create a "perfect" holiday, manage family dynamics, or meet social obligations can lead to feelings of stress, anxiety, or emotional fatigue. For some, the holidays may also bring up feelings of loneliness or disappointment, especially if expectations weren't met or if they experienced grief or loss during the season.

3. Financial Stress

The financial pressures of the holidays—whether from gift-giving, travel, or hosting events—can also contribute to post-holiday stress. Many people find themselves facing financial strain or even debt after the holidays, which can add to feelings of anxiety and fatigue.

4. Disrupted Routines

During the holiday season, normal routines are often disrupted by travel, social events, and holiday preparations. This can throw off sleep schedules, eating habits, and exercise routines, leaving you feeling out of balance. Once the holidays are over, it's important to re-establish a sense of structure and routine to help restore your well-being.

How to Recharge After the Holidays

Recharging after the holiday season requires intentional self-care, mindfulness, and a commitment to restoring balance in your life. The following strategies will help you recover physically, mentally, and emotionally, allowing you to enter the new year feeling refreshed and energized.

1. Prioritize Rest and Sleep

One of the most important aspects of post-holiday recovery is getting enough rest. The holiday season is often packed with activities, late nights, and disrupted sleep patterns, which can leave you feeling exhausted. Prioritizing rest helps your body and mind recover from the holiday rush.

- **Get Enough Sleep:** Aim for 7-9 hours of sleep each night to allow your body to fully rest and restore its energy levels. If you've been staying up late or missing out on sleep during the holidays, take a few days to catch up by going to bed earlier and creating a restful bedtime routine.
- **Take Short Breaks or Naps:** If you're still feeling tired during the day, take short breaks or naps to recharge. Even a 15-20 minute power nap can help improve your energy levels and mental clarity.
- **Create a Relaxing Sleep Environment:** Ensure that your sleep environment is conducive to rest by keeping your bedroom cool, dark, and quiet. Avoid screens before bed and engage in relaxing activities like reading or listening to calming music to help you unwind.

2. Re-establish Healthy Eating Habits

Holiday celebrations are often filled with indulgent foods and large meals, which can leave you feeling sluggish and out of balance. Once the holidays are over, it's important to return to a more balanced, nutritious diet to support your physical and mental health.

- **Focus on Whole Foods:** Replenish your body with nutrient-dense, whole foods, such as fruits, vegetables, lean proteins, and whole grains. These foods provide essential vitamins and minerals that help boost your energy, improve digestion, and support overall well-being.
- **Hydrate:** After the holiday indulgences, staying hydrated is essential for restoring your body's balance. Drink plenty of water throughout the day to help flush out toxins, improve digestion, and combat fatigue. Herbal teas and infused water can also be refreshing options to keep you hydrated.
- **Avoid Overeating:** Returning to regular, balanced meal portions after the holiday feasts helps your digestive system reset. Focus on eating smaller, more frequent meals if you feel heavy or sluggish from holiday indulgence.
- **Limit Sugar and Alcohol:** While holiday treats and festive drinks are fun, they can leave you feeling drained afterward. Reduce your intake of sugar and alcohol to help stabilize your blood sugar levels and prevent energy crashes.

3. Return to Regular Exercise

Exercise is one of the most effective ways to boost your energy, improve your mood, and reduce stress. After the holidays, returning to a regular exercise routine can help you recharge both physically and mentally.

- **Start Slowly:** If you took a break from exercise during the holidays, ease back into it gradually. Start with low-impact activities like walking, stretching, or yoga to help your body recover without overexertion.
- **Incorporate Movement into Your Day:** If you're feeling too tired for a full workout, incorporate small movements into your day. Take short walks, stretch at your desk, or do a few minutes of light exercise to get your blood flowing and improve your mood.
- **Focus on Enjoyable Activities:** Exercise doesn't have to feel like a chore. Choose physical activities that you enjoy, whether it's dancing, swimming, or playing a sport. Doing something you love will make it easier to stick to your routine and help you feel more energized.

4. Practice Mindfulness and Relaxation

Recharging after the holidays also involves taking care of your mental and emotional well-being. Practicing mindfulness and relaxation techniques can help you manage stress, process any lingering emotions, and restore your sense of balance.

- **Meditation and Deep Breathing:** Incorporate mindfulness practices such as meditation, deep breathing, or progressive muscle relaxation into your daily routine. These techniques help calm the mind, reduce anxiety, and promote a sense of inner peace.
- **Journaling:** Reflect on your holiday experience through journaling. Writing down your thoughts and feelings can help you process any lingering emotions, whether it's joy, gratitude, stress, or disappointment. Journaling also helps you gain clarity on how you want to approach the new year.
- **Gratitude Practice:** Practicing gratitude can shift your mindset from stress or frustration to appreciation and positivity. Take a few moments each day to reflect on what you're grateful for, whether it's the meaningful moments you shared during the holidays or the opportunity to rest and recharge now.

5. Rebuild a Routine

During the holiday season, routines often fall by the wayside as schedules become more unpredictable. Re-establishing a regular routine after the holidays is an important part of regaining your sense of balance and control.

- **Set a Regular Sleep Schedule:** Consistency is key when it comes to re-establishing your sleep routine. Set a regular bedtime and wake-up time to help regulate your internal clock and improve your energy levels.

- **Create a Daily Structure:** Rebuild a daily routine that includes time for work, self-care, exercise, and relaxation. Having a structure to your day helps reduce feelings of overwhelm and gives you a sense of purpose as you transition back to everyday life.
- **Plan Ahead:** If you have upcoming responsibilities or work projects, start planning for them gradually rather than diving in all at once. Break tasks into smaller, manageable steps to ease back into your routine without feeling rushed or stressed.

6. Declutter and Organize Your Space

After the holidays, your home may feel cluttered with gifts, decorations, or remnants from holiday gatherings. Taking the time to declutter and organize your space can help you feel more mentally and emotionally clear, creating a sense of calm and order.

- **Put Away Holiday Decorations:** Start by putting away holiday decorations and returning your home to its usual state. This simple task can help you transition out of the holiday mindset and create a sense of closure for the season.
- **Declutter Gift Wrapping Supplies and Leftovers:** If you have leftover wrapping paper, ribbons, or holiday cards, organize them neatly for future use or donate any excess items. Similarly, if you have holiday leftovers or excess food, use or freeze what you can and clear out the rest.
- **Tidy Up Common Areas:** Focus on decluttering and organizing the areas of your home where you spend the most time, such as the living room, kitchen, or bedroom. A clean, organized space helps reduce stress and promotes a sense of calm as you recharge.

7. Address Financial Stress

If holiday spending has left you feeling financially stressed, taking steps to address and manage your finances will help reduce anxiety and create a more stable foundation for the new year.

- **Review Your Holiday Budget:** Reflect on your holiday spending and compare it to the budget you set for yourself. If you overspent or accumulated debt, identify the areas where you went off track and consider how you can adjust your spending habits next year.
- **Make a Post-Holiday Debt Repayment Plan:** If you have holiday-related debt, create a plan to pay it off as quickly as possible. Set a specific timeline for repayment and prioritize paying down high-interest credit cards or loans. Even small, regular payments can help you regain control of your finances.
- **Start Saving for Next Year:** Once you've addressed any holiday-related debt, consider setting up a savings plan for next year's holidays. By saving a small amount each month, you can reduce financial stress when the holidays come around again.

8. Set Intentions for the New Year

The post-holiday period is an ideal time to set intentions for the new year. Rather than setting rigid resolutions, focus on setting intentions that align with your values, well-being, and personal growth.

- **Reflect on Your Goals:** Take time to reflect on your personal and professional goals for the coming year. What areas of your life would you like to focus on—whether it's your health, relationships, career, or personal development?
- **Set Realistic, Actionable Intentions:** Set intentions that are realistic and actionable, rather than vague or overly ambitious resolutions. For example, instead of resolving to "get healthier," you might set an intention to "exercise three times a week" or "cook more nutritious meals at home."
- **Create a Self-Care Plan:** As part of your new year's intentions, create a self-care plan that prioritizes your physical, mental, and emotional well-being. This could include regular exercise, mindfulness practices, creative hobbies, or simply taking time to rest and recharge when needed.

Conclusion

Recharging after the holiday season is essential for restoring your energy, mental health, and overall sense of balance. By prioritizing rest, re-establishing healthy routines, practicing mindfulness, and addressing any lingering financial or emotional stress, you can recover from the holiday rush and start the new year feeling refreshed and revitalized. Remember, post-holiday recovery is a process that takes time, so be patient with yourself and make self-care a priority as you transition back to everyday life. With these strategies in place, you'll be well-equipped to enter the new year with a clear mind, a recharged body, and a renewed sense of purpose.

Chapter 30: Setting New Year Intentions for a Fresh Start

The start of a new year brings with it a sense of renewal, possibility, and the chance to make positive changes in our lives. Many people use this time to set resolutions and goals, hoping to improve various aspects of their personal and professional lives. However, traditional New Year's resolutions can often feel overwhelming or rigid, leading to frustration when we fall short of meeting them. Instead of setting strict resolutions that may add pressure, shifting your focus to setting meaningful intentions for the new year can foster a more positive, balanced, and sustainable approach.

In this chapter, we will explore how to set thoughtful and intentional goals that reflect your values, support your well-being, and create a clear, stress-free mindset for the year ahead. You'll learn how to approach the process of setting intentions, how to break them down into actionable steps, and how to maintain motivation throughout the year. By focusing on purpose-driven intentions rather than rigid resolutions, you can cultivate a fresh start that feels empowering, inspiring, and attainable.

The Difference Between Resolutions and Intentions

Traditional New Year's resolutions often focus on specific, external outcomes—such as losing weight, saving money, or achieving a career milestone. While these goals can be valuable, they can also feel limiting or daunting, particularly if they are set without considering the deeper reasons behind them. Resolutions often emphasize what you *should* do, which can lead to feelings of guilt or failure if they aren't achieved.

Intentions, on the other hand, are more focused on the internal process and mindset that guide your actions. Instead of being purely outcome-driven, intentions reflect the way you want to live, grow, and feel throughout the year. They align with your values and are adaptable to your evolving needs, helping you stay connected to your purpose even when challenges arise. Here's how intentions differ from traditional resolutions:

1. Focus on the Journey, Not Just the Destination

Resolutions are typically tied to a specific outcome, such as "lose 20 pounds" or "get a promotion." Intentions, however, focus on how you want to approach the journey—whether it's living a healthier lifestyle, being more present, or nurturing your personal growth. Intentions allow for flexibility, recognizing that growth is a process, not a one-time achievement.

2. Aligned with Personal Values

Intentions are rooted in your core values and reflect what matters most to you. While resolutions often focus on external achievements, intentions are about how you want to feel and who you want to become. They help guide your actions in a way that aligns with your deeper sense of purpose.

3. Less Pressure, More Empowerment

Traditional resolutions can feel like a set of rules or benchmarks that need to be met, which can create stress or disappointment if they're not achieved. Intentions, however, are more empowering because they focus on progress rather than perfection. They encourage you to approach each day with mindfulness and self-compassion, without the fear of failure.

4. Adaptable and Evolving

While resolutions are often rigid and have a defined end point, intentions are flexible and can evolve over time. They adapt to your changing circumstances, allowing you to adjust your focus as needed. This adaptability makes intentions more sustainable in the long term, helping you stay committed even when life's challenges arise.

How to Set Meaningful New Year Intentions

Setting intentions requires a reflective and thoughtful approach. Instead of simply listing goals, take time to connect with what truly matters to you and how you want to experience the year ahead. Here's a step-by-step guide to setting meaningful New Year intentions that will help you start the year with clarity and a stress-free mindset.

1. Reflect on the Past Year

Before setting intentions for the new year, take time to reflect on the past year—both the successes and the challenges. This reflection helps you understand what worked well, what didn't, and how you've grown. Consider the following questions as you reflect:

- **What were your biggest accomplishments?** Celebrate the successes, big or small, that you achieved in the past year. Reflect on the hard work and dedication that contributed to these accomplishments.
- **What challenges did you face?** Think about the obstacles or difficulties you encountered and how you navigated them. What lessons did you learn, and how did they shape your growth?
- **What brought you joy and fulfillment?** Reflect on the moments or experiences that brought you happiness and meaning. These are key indicators of what matters most to you and can help guide your intentions for the new year.
- **What habits or patterns didn't serve you?** Consider any behaviors, routines, or mindsets that held you back or caused stress. Reflecting on these areas can help you identify what needs to change or be let go.

2. Identify Your Core Values

Your intentions should be aligned with your core values—the principles that guide your decisions, relationships, and actions. Identifying your values helps you set intentions that feel authentic and meaningful, rather than goals driven by external pressure or societal expectations.

- **What do you value most in life?** Consider what is most important to you, whether it's family, health, creativity, growth, connection, or something else. Your values are the foundation of your intentions, so it's essential to identify them before setting goals.
- **How do you want to feel in the new year?** Instead of focusing solely on what you want to achieve, think about how you want to feel in the coming year. Do you want to feel more at peace, energized, or fulfilled? Setting intentions based on how you want to feel can help guide your actions toward greater well-being.

3. Set Intentions in Different Areas of Life

Once you've reflected on the past year and identified your values, it's time to set intentions for the year ahead. Consider setting intentions across different areas of your life to create a holistic approach to growth and well-being. Here are some common areas to consider:

- **Health and Wellness:** How do you want to care for your body and mind in the new year? This could involve setting intentions for physical activity, nutrition, mental health practices, or self-care routines.

Example intention: "I intend to prioritize my mental and physical well-being by practicing mindfulness daily and incorporating movement into my routine."

- **Relationships and Connection:** What kind of relationships do you want to nurture in the new year? Consider how you want to show up for your loved ones, build deeper connections, or improve communication.

Example intention: "I intend to cultivate deeper connections with my family and friends by being fully present and actively listening during our time together."

- **Personal Growth and Learning:** How do you want to grow or expand your knowledge in the coming year? This could involve learning new skills, exploring creative outlets, or committing to personal development.

Example intention: "I intend to embrace lifelong learning by dedicating time each week to reading, taking courses, or pursuing creative projects."

- **Career and Professional Development:** How do you want to grow in your career or professional life? Consider setting intentions that focus on skill development, work-life balance, or pursuing meaningful opportunities.

Example intention: "I intend to find more balance in my work by setting boundaries and prioritizing tasks that align with my long-term career goals."

- **Financial Well-Being:** How do you want to manage your finances in the new year? This could involve setting intentions for saving, budgeting, or reducing financial stress.

Example intention: "I intend to create financial stability by setting a monthly savings goal and sticking to a realistic budget that aligns with my values."

- **Spirituality and Inner Peace:** How do you want to connect with your inner self or cultivate a sense of peace? This could involve spiritual practices, meditation, or finding more moments of stillness.

Example intention: "I intend to cultivate inner peace by incorporating meditation and quiet reflection into my daily routine."

4. Break Down Intentions into Actionable Steps

Intentions are more effective when they are supported by concrete actions. Once you've set your overarching intentions, break them down into small, actionable steps that you can incorporate into your daily or weekly routine. These steps should be manageable and aligned with your capacity, ensuring that you can make steady progress throughout the year.

- **Start Small:** Begin with small, achievable steps that build momentum over time. For example, if your intention is to improve your physical health, start by incorporating a 15-minute walk into your routine each day, and gradually build from there.
- **Set Milestones:** Break your larger intentions into milestones or checkpoints throughout the year. This helps you track your progress and stay motivated. For example, if your intention is to save more money, set monthly or quarterly savings goals that allow you to measure your progress.
- **Incorporate Intentions into Your Routine:** Look for ways to integrate your intentions into your existing routines. For example, if your intention is to practice mindfulness, you could start by adding a 5-minute meditation session to your morning or evening routine.

5. Create a Support System

Achieving your intentions is often easier with the support of others. Whether it's through friends, family, or a professional mentor, having people in your life who encourage and hold you accountable can help you stay on track.

- **Share Your Intentions:** Consider sharing your intentions with someone you trust, whether it's a friend, family member, or partner. Sharing your goals can provide additional motivation and accountability, as well as a sense of connection and support.
- **Find an Accountability Partner:** Having someone to check in with regularly can help keep you accountable. Choose an accountability partner who shares similar goals, or someone who can encourage and support you along your journey.
- **Join a Community:** If your intention involves learning a new skill or engaging in personal growth, consider joining a community, class, or group that aligns with your interests. Being part of a community can provide a sense of belonging and motivation as you work toward your goals.

6. Be Kind to Yourself

One of the most important aspects of setting intentions is practicing self-compassion. While it's natural to encounter setbacks or challenges along the way, it's important to approach these moments with kindness and understanding, rather than self-criticism.

- **Allow Flexibility:** Life is unpredictable, and sometimes circumstances change. If you need to adjust your intentions or the timeline for achieving them, give yourself the grace to do so without feeling like you've failed.
- **Celebrate Progress:** Celebrate your progress, no matter how small. Acknowledge the steps you've taken and the effort you've put in, even if you haven't yet reached your ultimate goal. Every bit of progress is a step toward growth.
- **Practice Gratitude:** Cultivate a sense of gratitude for the journey itself. Be thankful for the opportunities you have to grow, learn, and evolve, and recognize the positive changes that come from setting intentional goals.

7. Reflect and Adjust Throughout the Year

Intentions are not static—they can evolve as you grow and as your circumstances change. Regularly reflecting on your progress allows you to stay connected to your intentions, make adjustments if needed, and recommit to your goals.

- **Schedule Regular Check-Ins:** Set aside time each month or quarter to reflect on your progress and assess how your intentions are unfolding. Are you making progress? Do your intentions still feel aligned with your values? Use these check-ins to recalibrate if necessary.
- **Adjust Intentions as Needed:** If you find that certain intentions no longer resonate or if new priorities emerge, feel free to adjust your intentions accordingly. Life is dynamic, and your intentions should reflect the natural ebb and flow of your experiences and growth.

Conclusion

Setting New Year intentions provides a powerful, flexible framework for personal growth and self-improvement. By focusing on how you want to feel and aligning your intentions with your core values, you can create a meaningful, purpose-driven path for the year ahead. With clear intentions, actionable steps, self-compassion, and regular reflection, you'll be able to move forward with a clear, stress-free mindset—one that supports your well-being and helps you navigate the challenges and opportunities of the coming year. Embrace the journey, celebrate your progress, and let your intentions guide you toward a fulfilling and empowered new year.

Appendix: Tools and Resources

Appendix A: Holiday Budgeting Worksheets

Creating and adhering to a holiday budget is one of the most effective ways to reduce financial stress and ensure a more enjoyable holiday season. By tracking your spending, setting limits for different categories, and planning ahead, you can enjoy the holidays without the financial hangover that often follows. This appendix provides you with detailed, downloadable worksheets that will help you plan and track your holiday spending, from gifts and travel to meals and decorations.

Each worksheet is designed to guide you through every aspect of holiday budgeting, allowing you to set realistic goals, monitor your expenses, and make adjustments as needed. Whether you're preparing for a low-key family gathering or a large holiday event, these templates will help you stay organized and financially secure.

How to Use the Holiday Budgeting Worksheets

The following worksheets are organized by category, allowing you to focus on specific aspects of your holiday spending. Here's a general guide for using the templates effectively:

1. **Set Your Overall Budget:** Before you start filling out individual worksheets, determine your overall holiday budget. This is the total amount you are comfortable spending for the holiday season, based on your income, savings, and financial goals.
2. **Break Down Your Budget by Category:** Using the provided worksheets, break down your overall budget into specific categories, such as gifts, travel, food, decorations, entertainment, and charitable giving. This helps you allocate funds more intentionally and prevents over-spending in any one area.
3. **Track Your Spending:** As you make purchases or plan for upcoming expenses, record them in the corresponding worksheet. Tracking your spending helps you stay within your budget and gives you a clear picture of where your money is going.
4. **Adjust As Needed:** If you find that you're going over budget in one area, look for ways to adjust your spending in other categories. The worksheets are flexible, allowing you to make changes as you go.
5. **Review and Reflect:** At the end of the holiday season, review your worksheets to assess how well you stuck to your budget. This will help you plan more effectively for next year and make improvements where necessary.

Worksheet 1: Holiday Budget Overview

This worksheet provides a high-level overview of your holiday spending. It allows you to allocate funds to various categories and track how much you've spent in each area. Use this worksheet to monitor your overall holiday budget and ensure you're staying on track.

Category	Budgeted Amount	Actual Amount Spent	Difference
Gifts			
Travel			
Meals and Food			
Decorations			
Entertainment and Events			
Charitable Giving			
Miscellaneous			
Total			

Worksheet 2: Gift-Giving Budget

The gift-giving budget worksheet allows you to list out all the individuals or groups you plan to buy gifts for, allocate a specific budget for each, and track how much you actually spend. This helps you avoid overspending on gifts and ensures that you stay within your overall holiday budget.

Recipient	Gift Ideas	Budgeted Amount	Actual Amount Spent	Difference
Total				

Worksheet 3: Holiday Meal and Entertaining Budget

If you're hosting holiday meals or parties, this worksheet will help you budget for groceries, beverages, and other entertainment expenses. It includes sections for each meal or event, so you can plan for multiple gatherings without going over your budget.

Event/Meal	Date	Budgeted Amount	Actual Amount Spent	Difference
Total				

Worksheet 4: Travel Budget

For those who travel during the holidays, this worksheet helps you track travel-related expenses such as airfare, gas, lodging, and food. Use this worksheet to plan your trip and avoid unexpected costs.

Expense	Budgeted Amount	Actual Spent	Amount	Difference
Airfare/Train Fare				
Gas				
Lodging				
Food (while traveling)				
Activities/Entertainment				
Miscellaneous				
Total				

Worksheet 5: Holiday Decorations Budget

Decorating your home for the holidays can be fun, but it's easy to overspend on festive items. This worksheet allows you to budget for decorations, lighting, and other seasonal décor while keeping track of what you actually spend.

Item	Budgeted Amount	Actual Amount Spent	Difference
Tree			
Lights			
Ornaments			
Wreaths			
Table Décor			
Other			
Total			

Worksheet 6: Charitable Giving Budget

Many people enjoy giving back during the holidays, whether through donations to charities, gifts to those in need, or volunteering. This worksheet allows you to allocate a budget for charitable contributions and track your giving throughout the season.

Charity/Organization	Budgeted Donation	Actual Donation	Difference
Total			

Worksheet 7: Miscellaneous Holiday Expenses

The miscellaneous budget worksheet covers any additional holiday expenses that don't fit neatly into other categories, such as postage for holiday cards, wrapping supplies, or small gifts for colleagues or neighbors.

Expense	Budgeted Amount	Actual Amount Spent	Difference
Wrapping Supplies			
Postage for Cards			
Small Gifts (Neighbors, Colleagues, etc.)			
Cards			
Other			
Total			

Worksheet 8: End-of-Holiday Financial Review

This worksheet is designed to help you review your holiday spending after the season has ended. Use it to compare your planned budget with your actual spending, assess areas where you stayed on track, and identify any areas where you overspent. This reflection will help you improve your holiday budget for next year.

Category	Budgeted Amount	Actual Amount Spent	Difference
Gifts			
Travel			
Meals and Food			
Decorations			
Entertainment/ Events			
Charitable Giving			
Miscellaneous			
Total			

Conclusion

Using these holiday budgeting worksheets will help you stay organized and in control of your finances during the holiday season. By planning ahead, tracking your spending, and making adjustments as needed, you can enjoy the holidays without the burden of financial stress. Whether you're looking to cut back on spending or simply stay within a reasonable budget, these templates provide the structure you need to manage your holiday expenses effectively.

Download the full set of **Holiday Budgeting Worksheets:**

Appendix B: Family Conversation Starters: Scripts and Prompts for Easing Tension and Encouraging Positive Communication During Family Gatherings

Family gatherings during the holiday season are a time for reconnection, celebration, and togetherness. However, they can also be a source of stress and tension, especially if family members have differing viewpoints, unresolved conflicts, or strained relationships. Conversation starters and prompts can be powerful tools for easing tension, fostering positive communication, and creating a more harmonious atmosphere at family gatherings.

In this appendix, we provide a collection of conversation scripts and prompts designed to encourage meaningful dialogue, break awkward silences, and shift the focus away from potential areas of conflict. These conversation starters are thoughtfully crafted to be inclusive, engaging, and mindful of various family dynamics. Whether you're hosting a small family dinner or a large gathering, these prompts can help guide the conversation toward connection and mutual respect.

The Importance of Positive Communication at Family Gatherings

Family gatherings can sometimes bring up old wounds, disagreements, or differences of opinion. In these situations, open and positive communication is key to maintaining a peaceful and enjoyable atmosphere. Encouraging thoughtful conversation helps:

- **Ease Tension**: Conversation starters can help defuse potentially uncomfortable situations by shifting the focus toward neutral or positive topics.
- **Foster Connection**: Prompts that encourage sharing stories, experiences, or memories can help family members reconnect and strengthen their bonds.
- **Encourage Inclusivity**: Thoughtful conversation prompts ensure that everyone at the table has the opportunity to participate, helping avoid exclusion or isolation.
- **Promote Understanding**: Sharing viewpoints in a structured and respectful manner helps family members understand each other's perspectives without confrontation or argument.

Conversation Prompts for Positive Family Communication
1. Gratitude and Reflection Prompts

These prompts encourage family members to reflect on the positive aspects of their lives and express gratitude. Gratitude-based conversations can create a warm and appreciative atmosphere, helping to shift the focus away from any underlying tension.

- **"What's one thing you're grateful for this year?"**
  This simple prompt invites family members to share something they appreciate from the past year, setting a positive tone for the conversation.
- **"What was the best thing that happened to you this year?"**
  Asking about highlights from the year encourages family members to focus on positive experiences, sparking uplifting dialogue.
- **"Who has had the biggest impact on your life recently, and why?"**
  This prompt encourages deeper reflection on meaningful relationships and acts of kindness, opening the door for heartfelt conversations.

2. Family Memories and Traditions

Sharing stories from the past can be a great way to connect generations and reminisce about shared experiences. These prompts help family members recall joyful memories and reinforce family traditions.

- **"What's your favorite holiday tradition, and why is it meaningful to you?"**
  This prompt encourages family members to reflect on the traditions that matter most to them, fostering a sense of continuity and shared values.
- **"What's a funny or unexpected memory from a past holiday?"**
  Recalling funny or light-hearted memories brings laughter and joy to the conversation, helping to ease any tension in the room.
- **"What's a family tradition you'd like to start or bring back?"**
  This prompt invites creative ideas for new traditions, helping everyone feel involved in shaping future gatherings.

3. Curiosity and Learning About Each Other

Learning something new about family members can spark curiosity and build stronger connections. These prompts are designed to encourage meaningful discussions about life experiences, hobbies, and dreams.

- **"What's something you've always wanted to learn or try?"**
  This question opens the floor for family members to share their aspirations or interests, potentially leading to encouraging conversations.
- **"What's one thing most people don't know about you?"**
  This prompt can lead to surprising and fun revelations, helping family members learn more about each other and deepen their connections.
- **"What's a skill or talent you're working on right now?"**
  Sharing current goals or projects can inspire supportive conversations and allow family members to express pride in their progress.

4. Intergenerational Questions

Family gatherings often bring together people of different generations, from grandparents to grandchildren. These conversation prompts bridge the generational gap by encouraging both young and old family members to share their unique perspectives.

- **For elders: "What was a holiday like when you were younger?"**
  This prompt gives older family members an opportunity to share stories from their past, providing insight into how family traditions have evolved over time.
- **For younger family members: "What's something you're excited about for the future?"**
  This question encourages younger family members to share their hopes and dreams, allowing older family members to support and encourage them.
- **"What's one thing you've learned from someone older or younger than you?"**
  This prompt fosters mutual respect and appreciation across generations by highlighting the value of learning from each other.

5. Humor and Fun

Sometimes, a little humor is the best way to break the ice and shift the mood in a positive direction. These light-hearted prompts are designed to get everyone laughing and having fun together.

- **"If you could have any superpower, what would it be?"**
  This playful question encourages creativity and can lead to fun, light-hearted responses from family members of all ages.
- **"What's the silliest holiday tradition you've ever heard of?"**
  This prompt invites laughter and might even spark ideas for fun, new traditions.

• **"What's your most embarrassing holiday moment?"**
Sharing embarrassing moments brings humor to the conversation and can help humanize each other, creating a sense of connection and vulnerability.

6. Open-Ended and Thoughtful Prompts

For deeper and more meaningful conversations, open-ended questions allow family members to share their thoughts and perspectives on a variety of topics without feeling pressured to agree.

• **"If you could spend the holidays anywhere in the world, where would it be and why?"**
This question invites family members to share their travel dreams or favorite destinations, sparking conversations about travel, culture, and adventure.
• **"If you could give one piece of advice to your younger self, what would it be?"**
A reflective prompt like this encourages introspection and wisdom-sharing, allowing for a deeper, more heartfelt conversation.
• **"What's something you've learned this year that surprised you?"**
This prompt invites self-reflection and can lead to interesting discussions about personal growth, new experiences, or life lessons.

7. Conflict Resolution Prompts

Sometimes, family gatherings can become tense due to unresolved conflicts or differing opinions. These prompts are designed to shift the conversation toward understanding and resolution in a non-confrontational way.

• **"What's one thing we all have in common, despite our differences?"**
This prompt encourages family members to focus on shared values or interests, helping to build unity even in the face of disagreement.
• **"What's something you appreciate about someone at this table?"**
Encouraging family members to express appreciation for one another can soften any lingering tension and foster positive feelings.
• **"How can we make next year's gathering even better?"**
By focusing on improving future gatherings, this prompt shifts the focus toward collaboration and positive changes, opening the door for constructive dialogue.

Conversation Scripts for Diffusing Tension

In addition to prompts, having a few ready-made scripts can be helpful when tension arises during a family gathering. These scripts are designed to guide conversations toward resolution and understanding without escalating conflict.

1. When Political or Controversial Topics Arise

- **"I understand this is a topic we all feel strongly about, but maybe we can focus on enjoying our time together today. Let's talk about something we can all connect over."** This script acknowledges the importance of the topic while gently steering the conversation toward neutral ground.

2. When a Family Member Feels Excluded

- **"I'd love to hear your thoughts on this. What do you think?"** Inviting someone who may be feeling left out into the conversation can make them feel valued and included, shifting the dynamic toward greater inclusivity.

3. When Someone Interrupts or Speaks Over Others

- **"Let's make sure everyone has a chance to share. I'd really like to hear what you have to say."** This script politely redirects the conversation to ensure that everyone has an opportunity to speak, maintaining respect and balance.

4. When There's a Disagreement or Argument

- **"It seems like we're seeing things from different perspectives, which is totally okay. Why don't we take a break and come back to this another time when we're feeling calmer?"** This script diffuses the immediate conflict while allowing room for the conversation to be revisited in a more thoughtful way.

Tips for Facilitating Positive Conversations

Here are a few additional tips to help guide conversations in a way that fosters connection, reduces tension, and promotes inclusivity during family gatherings:

- **Lead by Example**: As a host or participant, model the type of behavior you'd like to see in others. Be open, listen attentively, and avoid interrupting or dominating the conversation.
- **Encourage Participation**: Make sure everyone has an opportunity to contribute. If someone is quieter or more reserved, gently invite them to share their thoughts.
- **Stay Neutral**: If a disagreement starts to arise, remain neutral and try to steer the conversation back to positive or neutral topics.
- **Set Ground Rules**: If necessary, set basic ground rules for the gathering, such as avoiding certain controversial topics or ensuring that everyone speaks respectfully.

Conclusion

Family gatherings are a wonderful opportunity to reconnect, build stronger bonds, and create lasting memories. By using these conversation starters, prompts, and scripts, you can help guide the conversation in a positive direction, ease tension, and encourage open communication. Whether you're discussing family traditions, sharing personal goals, or simply having fun, these tools will help ensure that everyone feels included, respected, and connected.

Appendix C: Self-Care Checklist: A Step-by-Step Guide for Maintaining Your Mental Well-Being During the Holidays

The holiday season can be a time of joy, connection, and celebration, but it can also be overwhelming and stressful. The combination of social obligations, financial pressures, disrupted routines, and high expectations often leads to emotional exhaustion and burnout. Taking care of your mental and emotional well-being during the holidays is essential to ensure that you can fully enjoy the season while maintaining balance and avoiding stress.

This **Self-Care Checklist** is designed to help you navigate the holidays with greater mindfulness and ease. It includes actionable steps to incorporate into your daily life that will help you prioritize your well-being, reduce stress, and stay grounded. By following this checklist, you can ensure that you remain physically, emotionally, and mentally healthy throughout the holiday season.

Why Self-Care is Important During the Holidays

Many people prioritize the needs of others during the holiday season, whether it's family, friends, or work obligations, often neglecting their own needs in the process. Self-care is not selfish—it's essential. When you take care of yourself, you're better equipped to handle holiday demands, maintain positive relationships, and enjoy the season fully. Key benefits of practicing self-care during the holidays include:

- **Reduced Stress**: Self-care practices, such as mindfulness, rest, and exercise, help lower stress levels and provide a buffer against the overwhelming demands of the holidays.
- **Improved Emotional Resilience**: When you're mindful of your mental health, you can better manage difficult emotions, navigate family dynamics, and cope with unexpected challenges.
- **Better Physical Health**: Maintaining healthy habits, such as balanced eating, exercise, and sleep, supports your immune system and overall well-being during the holidays.
- **More Enjoyment**: When you're not overburdened by stress, exhaustion, or burnout, you can be more present and engaged in the positive aspects of the holiday season.

How to Use the Self-Care Checklist

The checklist is broken down into several categories that address various aspects of self-care, including mental, emotional, physical, and social well-being. You can use this checklist as a daily or weekly guide to ensure that you're maintaining balance throughout the holidays. Feel free to modify the checklist to fit your individual needs and schedule, but aim to check off as many items as possible to stay grounded and centered.

Mental Well-Being Checklist

These steps are designed to help you maintain clarity, focus, and calm during the holiday season. Prioritizing mental well-being helps reduce overwhelm and increases your ability to manage holiday-related tasks and stressors.

1. Practice Mindfulness

Take at least 5-10 minutes each day to practice mindfulness, meditation, or deep breathing. This helps calm your mind, reduce anxiety, and keep you present in the moment.

- **Daily Mindfulness Practice**: Set aside time for deep breathing, meditation, or mindful reflection each day.

2. Set Realistic Expectations

Avoid overcommitting to holiday activities or creating unrealistic expectations for yourself and others. Set clear boundaries and remember that it's okay to say no to certain events or responsibilities.

- **Identify Priorities**: Make a list of the most important holiday activities and events, and let go of what isn't essential.
- **Say No When Necessary**: Politely decline invitations or tasks that would add unnecessary stress to your schedule.

3. Limit Social Media and News Consumption

Constant exposure to social media or stressful news can increase anxiety, especially during the holiday season. Limit your screen time and focus on the present.

- **Set Screen Time Limits**: Establish time limits for checking social media or news, and stick to them to avoid stress.
- **Unfollow or Mute Accounts**: Temporarily mute accounts or pages that trigger comparison, stress, or holiday-related anxiety.

4. Take Regular Breaks

Don't feel the need to constantly be "on the go" during the holidays. Take regular breaks throughout the day to rest, reflect, and recharge.

- **Short Breaks During the Day**: Step away from your tasks for 5-10 minutes to stretch, walk, or simply breathe.
- **Plan Relaxation Time**: Set aside at least 30 minutes each day to do something relaxing or enjoyable, such as reading, listening to music, or taking a bath.

Emotional Well-Being Checklist

The holidays can bring up a variety of emotions, from joy and excitement to stress and sadness. This section focuses on practices that help you maintain emotional balance and navigate the ups and downs of the season with greater ease.

1. Acknowledge Your Feelings

It's important to recognize that it's okay to feel a range of emotions during the holidays, including sadness or stress. Acknowledging your feelings rather than suppressing them helps you process emotions in a healthy way.

- **Journal or Reflect on Your Feelings**: Spend time journaling about your emotions or reflecting on how you're feeling each day.
- **Practice Self-Compassion**: Remind yourself that it's okay to feel stressed or overwhelmed and that you deserve kindness and patience.

2. Connect with Loved Ones

Stay connected with the people who bring you joy and support. Whether in person or virtually, meaningful conversations and quality time with loved ones can boost your emotional well-being.

- **Reach Out to Someone**: Call or message a friend, family member, or loved one each day to check in and maintain emotional connection.
- **Plan Intentional Time Together**: Schedule at least one gathering or call with close family or friends to catch up and share in holiday experiences.

3. Practice Gratitude

Gratitude is a powerful tool for improving emotional well-being. Reflect on the positive aspects of your life and the things you appreciate, especially during times of stress.

- **Daily Gratitude Practice**: Write down three things you're grateful for each day, whether small or significant.

- **Express Gratitude to Others**: Tell someone you appreciate them or acknowledge their kindness during the holiday season.

4. Manage Family Dynamics

Family gatherings can sometimes lead to tension or emotional discomfort. Have a plan for managing difficult conversations or relationships during the holidays.

- **Set Emotional Boundaries**: Be clear about what topics or conversations you want to avoid at family gatherings.
- **Use Conversation Starters**: Prepare positive conversation prompts (see **Appendix B**) to steer the dialogue toward constructive and enjoyable topics.

Physical Well-Being Checklist

Maintaining your physical health during the holidays is essential for both your mental and emotional well-being. The following steps will help you stay energized, healthy, and resilient throughout the season.

1. Prioritize Sleep

Getting enough sleep is essential for maintaining energy, reducing stress, and supporting overall health. Aim for 7-9 hours of sleep each night, even when holiday schedules get busy.

- **Stick to a Consistent Sleep Schedule**: Go to bed and wake up at the same time each day, even during holiday gatherings.
- **Create a Relaxing Bedtime Routine**: Incorporate calming activities, such as reading, light stretching, or meditation, into your evening routine to wind down.

2. Stay Active

Physical activity helps reduce stress, improve mood, and boost energy levels. Incorporate movement into your daily routine, even if it's just a short walk.

- **Daily Movement**: Set aside at least 20-30 minutes for physical activity each day, whether it's walking, stretching, yoga, or a workout.
- **Incorporate Family Activities**: Get the family involved in fun, active traditions, such as holiday walks, hikes, or games.

3. Eat Balanced Meals

With holiday treats and large meals, it's easy to overindulge. Balance festive eating with nutritious meals that support your overall health and well-being.

- **Eat Mindfully**: Pay attention to your body's hunger and fullness cues, and enjoy holiday treats in moderation.

- **Incorporate Nutrient-Rich Foods**: Make sure your meals include a variety of fruits, vegetables, whole grains, and lean proteins to maintain balanced nutrition.

4. Stay Hydrated

Dehydration can contribute to fatigue, headaches, and low energy levels. Drinking enough water is essential for staying energized and feeling your best during the holidays.

- **Drink Water Throughout the Day**: Aim for 8 glasses of water per day, and more if you're physically active.
- **Limit Alcohol and Sugary Drinks**: Reduce your consumption of alcohol, sugary drinks, and caffeinated beverages, as they can contribute to dehydration and energy crashes.

Social Well-Being Checklist

Holiday gatherings and social interactions are an important part of the season, but they can also be draining if not balanced properly. This section helps you navigate social commitments while protecting your energy and maintaining healthy boundaries.

1. Choose Social Events Mindfully

You don't have to attend every holiday party or event. Prioritize the gatherings that bring you joy and allow you to connect with people you care about.

- **Select Your "Must-Attend" Events**: Decide which events are most meaningful to you, and let go of the pressure to attend every gathering.
- **Limit Obligations**: Politely decline social invitations that feel like too much or would add unnecessary stress to your schedule.

2. Set Boundaries with Family and Friends

Establish clear boundaries around your time, energy, and emotional needs. It's okay to say no to social commitments that don't align with your well-being.

- **Communicate Your Boundaries**: Be open with family and friends about what you're comfortable with, whether it's in terms of time commitments, topics of conversation, or emotional energy.
- **Give Yourself Permission to Take Breaks**: If you feel overwhelmed at social events, excuse yourself for a moment to step outside or take a quiet break.

3. Balance Alone Time with Social Time

It's important to balance social gatherings with moments of solitude and rest. Make time for quiet reflection or solo activities that help you recharge.

- **Schedule "Me Time"**: Set aside at least 15-30 minutes of alone time each day to read, reflect, or engage in activities that bring you peace.

- **Engage in Low-Stress Social Interactions**: Balance large gatherings with smaller, more intimate interactions, such as coffee with a friend or a quiet evening with a loved one.

Conclusion

The holidays are a time for joy, celebration, and connection, but they can also be stressful if you don't take care of your mental and emotional well-being. By following this **Self-Care Checklist**, you can prioritize your needs, reduce holiday-related stress, and create space for relaxation, reflection, and self-compassion. Remember, the most meaningful holiday experiences come from a place of balance and well-being, so take the time to nurture yourself, just as you nurture those around you.

Appendix D: Holiday Travel Packing List: A Simple Guide to Ensure You Pack Light and Efficiently for Stress-Free Travel

The holidays often involve traveling to visit family, friends, or taking a seasonal getaway. However, packing for holiday trips can quickly become overwhelming, especially with the added stress of cold weather, gifts, and sometimes unpredictable plans. Overpacking can lead to unnecessary stress at the airport, extra baggage fees, or frustration when lugging heavy bags around. On the other hand, underpacking can leave you without essential items.

This **Holiday Travel Packing List** is designed to help you pack light and efficiently while ensuring you have everything you need for stress-free travel. Whether you're going away for a weekend or taking an extended holiday trip, this checklist will guide you through the process of planning, organizing, and packing, so you can focus on enjoying the journey.

Why Packing Efficiently Matters

Packing light and efficiently for holiday travel offers several advantages:

- **Avoids Overpacking**: With a clear plan, you'll avoid the common mistake of packing unnecessary items, reducing the size and weight of your luggage.
- **Reduces Stress**: A well-organized packing list ensures that you have all essential items, reducing last-minute anxiety and the chance of forgetting something important.
- **Saves Time**: By following an organized checklist, you'll spend less time figuring out what to bring and more time preparing for the actual trip.
- **Minimizes Costs**: Packing only what you need can help you avoid additional baggage fees, which are common during holiday air travel.
- **Increases Flexibility**: Traveling with a lighter bag gives you greater mobility and flexibility, especially during crowded holiday travel periods.

How to Use This Packing List

This guide is organized by category to help you cover all aspects of your packing, from clothing and toiletries to travel documents and gifts. Before you start packing, review the checklist to tailor it to your specific travel plans, weather conditions, and trip duration.

- **Step 1**: Review the checklist and note any items that are specific to your trip.
- **Step 2**: Use the list as you pack to check off each item as you include it.
- **Step 3**: Before leaving, review the list one final time to make sure you have everything essential.

Clothing and Accessories

Packing clothing that's versatile, comfortable, and appropriate for the weather is key to traveling light and efficiently. Prioritize items that can be mixed and matched to create multiple outfits, and stick to a neutral color palette to reduce the number of items needed.

1. Clothing Essentials

- **Weather-Appropriate Outerwear**: Pack one high-quality jacket or coat suitable for the destination's climate (e.g., a warm winter coat, rain jacket, or light jacket for mild weather).
- **Tops**: 3-5 shirts or sweaters, depending on the length of your trip. Choose layers that can be dressed up or down for different occasions.
- **Bottoms**: 2-3 pairs of pants, jeans, or skirts that coordinate with your tops. Dark colors are versatile and less likely to show dirt.
- **Undergarments**: Enough for each day of your trip, plus one extra set.
- **Socks and Tights**: Pack enough pairs for the entire trip, keeping in mind the weather (e.g., thicker socks for colder climates).
- **Sleepwear**: One set of comfortable pajamas or sleepwear.
- **Sweater or Cardigan**: A versatile layer that can be worn over various outfits for warmth.
- **Holiday Outfit (Optional)**: If you're attending a special holiday event, pack one festive outfit that doesn't require excessive care (e.g., wrinkle-free fabrics).

2. Shoes and Accessories

- **Comfortable Walking Shoes**: One pair of comfortable shoes for travel days and walking.
- **Dress Shoes (Optional)**: A pair of nicer shoes or boots if you're attending a holiday event or formal gathering.
- **Scarf, Hat, Gloves**: Pack these if traveling to a cold destination. A cozy scarf can also double as a blanket during the flight.
- **Belt**: If needed for specific outfits.

- **Jewelry (Minimal)**: Limit to essential pieces such as a pair of earrings, a watch, or a necklace. Avoid bringing expensive or valuable items.

3. Packing Tips for Clothing

- **Use Packing Cubes**: Organize your clothes by category using packing cubes to maximize space and make it easier to access your items during the trip.
- **Roll, Don't Fold**: Rolling clothes instead of folding them can save space and reduce wrinkles.
- **Limit Bulky Items**: Wear your heaviest or bulkiest items, such as boots or a coat, during travel to save space in your suitcase.

Toiletries and Personal Care

Toiletries can take up a lot of space if not planned properly. Stick to travel-sized products and essentials to minimize bulk, especially for short trips. If you're flying, remember to follow TSA liquid restrictions (3.4 ounces or 100 milliliters per container).

1. Toiletries Essentials

- **Toothbrush and Toothpaste**: Travel-sized toothpaste is perfect for short trips.
- **Shampoo and Conditioner**: Travel-sized bottles, or consider using the hotel's or family's supplies if available.
- **Body Wash or Soap**: A small bar or travel-sized body wash.
- **Face Cleanser**: Pack a gentle cleanser suitable for your skin type.
- **Deodorant**: A travel-sized stick or roll-on to save space.
- **Hairbrush or Comb**: A small or foldable brush.
- **Razor**: If you plan on shaving during your trip.
- **Moisturizer**: Travel-sized face and body moisturizer, especially important for cold or dry climates.
- **Makeup (Optional)**: Limit makeup to a few versatile items (e.g., foundation, mascara, and lipstick) that work for multiple looks.
- **Lip Balm**: Particularly important if traveling to colder climates.
- **Sunscreen**: Even in winter, sunscreen is important for sun protection.

2. Travel-Specific Toiletries

- **Hand Sanitizer**: A small bottle or wipes to stay germ-free while traveling.
- **Tissues**: A small pack of tissues for convenience.
- **Face Mask**: Depending on travel restrictions and health guidelines, pack face masks for public spaces.
- **Medication**: Any prescription medication you need, along with over-the-counter essentials like pain relievers, allergy medicine, or motion sickness tablets.

3. Packing Tips for Toiletries

- **Use a Toiletry Bag**: Keep all your personal care items in a waterproof, zippered toiletry bag for easy access and organization.
- **Reuse Travel Bottles**: Fill reusable travel-sized bottles with your favorite products to avoid buying new ones.
- **Use Multi-Purpose Products**: Pack products that serve multiple purposes, such as a moisturizer with SPF or a 2-in-1 shampoo and conditioner.

Travel Documents and Essentials

Keeping important documents and essential items organized is crucial to ensuring a smooth travel experience, especially during the busy holiday season.

1. Travel Documents

- **Passport or ID**: If traveling internationally, ensure your passport is up-to-date. For domestic travel, make sure you have a valid government-issued ID.
- **Boarding Pass**: Print your boarding pass in advance, or have it ready on your phone or app.
- **Itinerary**: Keep a printed or digital copy of your travel itinerary, including flight, hotel, and rental car details.
- **Travel Insurance (Optional)**: If you've purchased travel insurance, bring any relevant documents.
- **Emergency Contacts**: Keep a list of emergency contacts, including family members and local emergency numbers.
- **Vaccination Card (if applicable)**: Depending on your destination or airline, you may need to show proof of vaccination.

2. Money and Payment Methods

- **Cash**: Carry a small amount of cash for tips or situations where credit cards aren't accepted.
- **Credit or Debit Cards**: Make sure your cards are accepted at your destination, and notify your bank of your travel plans to avoid potential issues.
- **Travel Wallet**: Use a travel wallet or organizer to keep your cards, cash, and documents secure.

3. Electronics

- **Phone and Charger**: Don't forget your phone charger and any accessories like earbuds.
- **Portable Charger**: A portable power bank is essential for long travel days.
- **Adapter/Converter**: If traveling internationally, bring a power adapter or converter for your electronics.

- **E-Reader or Tablet**: If you plan to read or watch movies, pack a tablet or e-reader for entertainment.

Holiday-Specific Items

If you're traveling during the holidays, there are a few additional items you may want to include, especially if you're bringing gifts or participating in special holiday activities.

1. Gifts

- **Small, Portable Gifts**: Choose small, lightweight gifts that are easy to pack. Consider shipping larger gifts directly to your destination.
- **Gift Cards**: If you're worried about packing space, gift cards are a great alternative that doesn't take up any room.
- **Wrapping Paper or Gift Bags**: Consider packing foldable gift bags or purchasing wrapping supplies at your destination.

2. Holiday Decorations (Optional)

- **Small Ornaments or Decorations**: If you're celebrating at someone else's home, consider bringing a small ornament or decoration that's meaningful but easy to transport.
- **Holiday Cards**: If you haven't mailed them already, bring your holiday cards to distribute in person.

Miscellaneous Items

These are additional items you may need to bring depending on your personal preferences or specific holiday plans.

- **Reusable Water Bottle**: Stay hydrated by bringing an empty water bottle you can fill after security.
- **Snacks**: Pack healthy snacks like nuts, fruit, or granola bars for long travel days.
- **Books or Magazines**: Bring a book or magazine to read during your downtime.
- **Earplugs or Sleep Mask**: For better rest during flights or at your destination.
- **Travel Pillow**: If you're taking a long flight or car trip, a travel pillow can make the journey more comfortable.
- **Umbrella or Poncho**: Check the weather forecast and pack a compact umbrella or poncho if needed.

Packing Tips for Stress-Free Holiday Travel

1. **Pack Early**: Avoid the stress of last-minute packing by starting a few days before your trip. This gives you time to gather items and make sure nothing is forgotten.

2. **Check the Weather**: Research the weather at your destination before you pack so you can bring appropriate clothing and gear.
3. **Limit Your Luggage**: If possible, pack everything into a carry-on to avoid checked baggage fees and reduce the risk of lost luggage. For longer trips, consider packing a small suitcase and a personal item.
4. **Weigh Your Bag**: Use a luggage scale to ensure your bag meets the weight limits, especially if you're flying. This helps you avoid extra fees or the hassle of repacking at the airport.
5. **Use a Packing List**: Keep this checklist handy and use it to double-check that you've packed everything you need before leaving.

Conclusion

By following this **Holiday Travel Packing List**, you can ensure that your packing process is efficient, stress-free, and tailored to your specific holiday plans. With careful planning, you'll avoid overpacking while still bringing everything you need to enjoy your trip. Packing light and efficiently will allow you to travel more comfortably and focus on what truly matters—spending quality time with loved ones and enjoying the holiday season.

Appendix F: Further Reading & Resources: Recommended Books, Articles, and Websites for Diving Deeper into Financial, Emotional, and Mental Well-Being During the Holidays

The holiday season brings a unique mix of joy, stress, financial pressure, and emotional highs and lows. To navigate this complex time with more clarity and peace, it's essential to explore strategies and resources that promote financial stability, emotional resilience, and mental well-being. Whether you're looking to manage your holiday spending, improve communication with family, or care for your mental health, there are many excellent books, articles, and websites that can provide deeper insights and practical tips.

This appendix offers a curated list of recommended resources that will help you dive deeper into managing the holiday season with mindfulness, balance, and confidence. These books and articles cover a range of topics, including financial planning, emotional well-being, mindfulness, self-care, and managing relationships during the holidays.

1. Financial Well-Being During the Holidays

Managing your finances during the holiday season is one of the most common challenges. The pressure to spend on gifts, decorations, events, and travel can lead to financial stress or even debt. These resources will help you create a holiday budget, make smart financial decisions, and develop long-term strategies for financial well-being.

Books

- **"The Total Money Makeover" by Dave Ramsey**

  Ramsey's classic personal finance book offers straightforward advice for managing money, avoiding debt, and building financial security. While not holiday-specific, the principles in this book can be applied to create a holiday budget that aligns with your long-term financial goals.

- **"Your Money or Your Life" by Vicki Robin and Joe Dominguez**

  This personal finance classic explores the relationship between money and life satisfaction. It encourages readers to rethink their spending habits and prioritize meaningful experiences over material possessions, which is especially useful when managing holiday spending.

- **"Smart Women Finish Rich" by David Bach**

  Aimed at helping women achieve financial security, this book provides practical advice for budgeting, saving, and long-term financial planning. It includes useful strategies for managing holiday spending while staying on track with broader financial goals.

Articles

- **"How to Create a Holiday Budget You Can Stick To" (NerdWallet)**

  This article provides a step-by-step guide to creating a realistic holiday budget. It covers important tips on setting spending limits, planning for gifts and travel, and using budgeting tools to stay on track.

- **"10 Tips to Help You Avoid Holiday Debt" (Forbes)**
  Avoiding debt during the holidays is crucial for financial well-being. This article offers practical tips, including shopping early, avoiding impulse buys, and using alternative forms of gift-giving to stay within your budget.
- **"5 Holiday Budgeting Hacks to Save Money" (The Balance)**
  This article offers creative strategies for cutting costs during the holiday season, such as using cashback apps, taking advantage of seasonal sales, and prioritizing homemade gifts.

Websites

- **NerdWallet**
  nerdwallet.com
  This site provides comprehensive tools and articles on personal finance, including budgeting calculators, holiday spending tips, and strategies for managing credit card debt after the holidays.
- **The Simple Dollar**
  thesimpledollar.com
  A resource for individuals seeking financial advice, including articles on saving money during the holidays, building an emergency fund, and reducing holiday financial stress.

2. Emotional Well-Being During the Holidays

Emotional well-being is often tested during the holiday season, particularly when dealing with family dynamics, expectations, and potential feelings of loneliness or overwhelm. These resources offer insights into how to manage stress, foster positive relationships, and nurture your emotional health.

Books

- **"The Gifts of Imperfection" by Brené Brown**
  In this bestselling book, Brené Brown explores how embracing vulnerability and letting go of the need for perfection can lead to a more authentic, fulfilling life. This book is particularly useful during the holidays when perfectionism and societal pressures can heighten stress.
- **"Emotional Agility" by Susan David**
  This book teaches readers how to navigate life's challenges, including stress, anxiety, and negative emotions, with resilience and emotional flexibility. It's a valuable resource for managing difficult family dynamics and emotions during the holiday season.
- **"Self-Compassion: The Proven Power of Being Kind to Yourself" by Kristin Neff**
  This book delves into the concept of self-compassion, offering practical exercises for treating yourself with kindness and understanding—especially important during the hectic and often stressful holiday season.

Articles

- **"How to Manage Family Stress During the Holidays" (Psychology Today)**
This article provides practical tips for managing stress related to family gatherings, including setting boundaries, preparing for challenging conversations, and focusing on positive interactions.
- **"The Holiday Blues: Coping with Stress, Anxiety, and Depression" (Mayo Clinic)**
The Mayo Clinic outlines strategies for coping with the emotional challenges of the holiday season, such as combating feelings of isolation, managing expectations, and making time for self-care.
- **"How to Manage Holiday Loneliness" (Healthline)**
For those who may experience loneliness during the holidays, this article offers tips on building social connections, managing feelings of isolation, and practicing self-compassion.

Websites

- **Psychology Today**
psychologytoday.com
A resource for articles, blog posts, and expert advice on managing mental and emotional well-being, particularly during the holiday season.
- **Mindful**
mindful.org
This website offers articles and resources on mindfulness, meditation, and emotional resilience. It's a great resource for learning how to stay present and calm during holiday stress.

3. Mindfulness and Self-Care During the Holidays

The holidays can be overwhelming, making it essential to prioritize self-care and mindfulness. These resources focus on techniques for staying grounded, reducing stress, and cultivating inner peace during one of the busiest times of the year.

Books

- **"The Miracle of Mindfulness" by Thich Nhat Hanh**
A simple yet profound guide to mindfulness practice, this book helps readers stay present and fully engaged in each moment—an invaluable tool for navigating the chaos and stress of the holiday season.
- **"Radical Acceptance" by Tara Brach**
This book introduces readers to the concept of radical acceptance, the practice of embracing yourself and your life fully, even during challenging times. It's a helpful guide for managing difficult emotions and finding peace during the holidays.
- **"The Joy of Missing Out" by Tonya Dalton**
This book explores how to reclaim your time, energy, and focus by letting go of unnecessary

obligations and distractions. It's an excellent resource for anyone feeling overwhelmed by holiday commitments.

Articles

- **"10 Mindfulness Tips to Stay Present During the Holidays" (Headspace)**
  Headspace provides a list of simple mindfulness practices to help you stay calm, centered, and present during the busy holiday season.
- **"How to Practice Self-Care During the Holidays" (Verywell Mind)**
  This article explores ways to incorporate self-care into your holiday routine, including setting boundaries, managing stress, and creating personal time for relaxation and reflection.
- **"Why Self-Care is Essential During the Holidays" (Happify)**
  Happify outlines the importance of self-care and offers strategies for maintaining mental and physical health during the holiday rush, including mindfulness, exercise, and gratitude practices.

Websites

- **Headspace**
  headspace.com
  Headspace offers guided meditation, mindfulness exercises, and tips for staying calm and centered, even during hectic times like the holidays.
- **Calm**
  calm.com
  Calm provides a range of resources for stress reduction, including guided meditations, sleep aids, and relaxation techniques to help you manage holiday stress and maintain your well-being.

4. Managing Family Dynamics During the Holidays

Family dynamics can be a source of tension during the holiday season. These resources offer strategies for improving communication, setting boundaries, and managing conflicts with loved ones in a way that fosters understanding and harmony.

Books

- **"Nonviolent Communication: A Language of Life" by Marshall B. Rosenberg**
  This book teaches readers how to communicate compassionately and effectively, even in the face of conflict. The techniques can be especially helpful during holiday gatherings when tensions may run high.
- **"Crucial Conversations: Tools for Talking When Stakes Are High" by Kerry Patterson, Joseph Grenny, Ron McMillan, and Al Switzler**

This book provides strategies for having difficult conversations in a respectful and constructive way, making it an excellent resource for navigating family conflicts during the holidays.

- **"Boundaries: When to Say Yes, How to Say No to Take Control of Your Life" by Dr. Henry Cloud and Dr. John Townsend**
Setting healthy boundaries is essential for maintaining emotional well-being during the holidays. This book provides practical guidance on how to set limits without feeling guilty.

Articles

- **"How to Set Boundaries with Family During the Holidays" (The New York Times)**
This article provides advice on how to set and maintain healthy boundaries with family members during holiday gatherings, including practical tips for saying no and managing expectations.
- **"Managing Difficult Family Relationships Over the Holidays" (Harvard Business Review)**
Harvard Business Review offers insights into how to navigate challenging family dynamics, including strategies for staying calm, avoiding conflict, and fostering positive communication.
- **"How to Keep the Peace at Family Gatherings" (Real Simple)**
This article offers tips on defusing tension and keeping conversations light and positive during family holiday gatherings.

Websites

- **Greater Good Science Center**
ggsc.berkeley.edu
The Greater Good Science Center at UC Berkeley provides articles and resources on emotional well-being, positive communication, and conflict resolution, making it a valuable resource for managing family dynamics during the holidays.
- **The Gottman Institute**
gottman.com
The Gottman Institute offers research-based advice on relationships and communication, including tips for managing family stress and fostering healthy interactions during holiday gatherings.

5. Holistic Health and Wellness Resources

Maintaining a balance between physical, mental, and emotional health is key to thriving during the holiday season. These resources offer guidance on integrating holistic wellness practices into your holiday routine.

Books

- **"The Four Agreements" by Don Miguel Ruiz**
  This spiritual guide offers four principles for achieving personal freedom and peace, which can be especially helpful during the emotional and mental pressures of the holiday season.
- **"Atomic Habits" by James Clear**
  Clear's bestselling book provides a framework for building positive habits and breaking negative ones. It's useful for staying on track with health and wellness goals during the holiday season.
- **"The Self-Care Solution" by Jennifer Ashton, M.D.**
  This book outlines monthly self-care challenges to help you prioritize your health and wellness, making it an excellent resource for establishing sustainable self-care practices during the holidays.

Articles

- **"How to Stay Healthy During the Holidays" (Cleveland Clinic)**
  This article provides tips on maintaining physical health during the holiday season, including staying active, eating balanced meals, and getting enough sleep.
- **"10 Tips for Staying Balanced During the Holidays" (MindBodyGreen)**
  MindBodyGreen offers a holistic approach to staying healthy and balanced, including advice on mindfulness, nutrition, and stress management.
- **"Holiday Self-Care: How to Stay Calm and Collected" (Everyday Health)**
  Everyday Health provides practical tips for staying calm, reducing stress, and practicing self-care during the busy holiday season.

Websites

- **MindBodyGreen**
  mindbodygreen.com
  This site offers a wealth of articles and resources on holistic health, wellness, mindfulness, and nutrition, with specific tips for maintaining balance during the holidays.
- **Well + Good**
  wellandgood.com
  Well + Good provides articles, guides, and resources focused on fitness, nutrition, mental health, and overall wellness, including special content for the holiday season.

Conclusion

The holiday season can be a wonderful time for connection, celebration, and reflection, but it also presents unique challenges related to financial pressures, emotional well-being, and managing family dynamics. This **Further Reading & Resources** appendix provides you with a comprehensive selection of books, articles, and websites to help you dive deeper into these areas and navigate the holidays with more ease and confidence. Whether you're looking for advice on budgeting, tips for managing stress, or strategies for fostering positive relationships, these resources will equip you with the tools and knowledge needed to create a joyful, balanced holiday season.

<u>Message from the Author:</u>

I hope you enjoyed this book, I love astrology and knew there was not a book such as this out on the shelf. I love metaphysical items as well. Please check out my other books:

-Life of Government Benefits

-My life of Hell

-My life with Hydrocephalus

-Red Sky

-World Domination:Woman's rule

-World Domination:Woman's Rule 2: The War

-Life and Banishment of Apophis: book 1

-The Kidney Friendly Diet

-The Ultimate Hemp Cookbook

-Creating a Dispensary(legally)

-Cleanliness throughout life: the importance of showering from childhood to adulthood.

-Strong Roots: The Risks of Overcoddling children

-Hemp Horoscopes: Cosmic Insights and Earthly Healing

- Celestial Hemp Navigating the Zodiac: Through the Green Cosmos

-Astrological Hemp: Aligning The Stars with Earth's Ancient Herb

-The Astrological Guide to Hemp: Stars, Signs, and Sacred Leaves

-Green Growth: Innovative Marketing Strategies for your Hemp Products and Dispensary

-Cosmic Cannabis

-Astrological Munchies

-Henry The Hemp

-Zodiacal Roots: The Astrological Soul Of Hemp

- **Green Constellations: Intersection of Hemp and Zodiac**

-Hemp in The Houses: An astrological Adventure Through The Cannabis Galaxy

-Galactic Ganja Guide

Heavenly Hemp

Zodiac Leaves

Doctor Who Astrology

Cannastrology

Stellar Satvias and Cosmic Indicas

<u>Celestial Cannabis: A Zodiac Journey</u>

AstroHerbology: The Sky and The Soil: Volume 1

AstroHerbology:Celestial Cannabis:Volume 2

Cosmic Cannabis Cultivation

The Starry Guide to Herbal Harmony: Volume 1

The Starry Guide to Herbal Harmony: Cannabis Universe: Volume 2

Yugioh Astrology: Astrological Guide to Deck, Duels and more
Nightmare Mansion: Echoes of The Abyss
Nightmare Mansion 2: Legacy of Shadows
Nightmare Mansion 3: Shadows of the Forgotten
Nightmare Mansion 4: Echoes of the Damned
The Life and Banishment of Apophis: Book 2
Nightmare Mansion: Halls of Despair
<u>Healing with Herb: Cannabis and Hydrocephalus</u>
<u>Planetary Pot: Aligning with Astrological Herbs: Volume 1</u>
Fast Track to Freedom: 30 Days to Financial Independence Using AI, Assets, and Agile Hustles
<u>Cosmic Hemp Pathways</u>
How to Become Financially Free in 30 Days: 10,000 Paths to Prosperity
Zodiacal Herbage: Astrological Insights: Volume 1
Nightmare Mansion: Whispers in the Walls
The Daleks Invade Atlantis
Henry the hemp and Hydrocephalus

10X The Kidney Friendly Diet
Cannabis Universe: Adult coloring book
Hemp Astrology: The Healing Power of the Stars
Zodiacal Herbage: Astrological Insights: Cannabis Universe: Volume 2
<u>Planetary Pot: Aligning with Astrological Herbs: Cannabis Universes: Volume 2</u>
Doctor Who Meets the Replicators and SG-1: The Ultimate Battle for Survival
Nightmare Mansion: Curse of the Blood Moon
<u>The Celestial Stoner: A Guide to the Zodiac</u>
Cosmic Pleasures: Sex Toy Astrology for Every Sign
Hydrocephalus Astrology: Navigating the Stars and Healing Waters
Lapis and the Mischievous Chocolate Bar

Celestial Positions: Sexual Astrology for Every Sign
Apophis's Shadow Work Journal: **:** A Journey of Self-Discovery and Healing
Kinky Cosmos: Sexual Kink Astrology for Every Sign
Digital Cosmos: The Astrological Digimon Compendium
Stellar Seeds: The Cosmic Guide to Growing with Astrology
Apophis's Daily Gratitude Journal

Cat Astrology: Feline Mysteries of the Cosmos
The Cosmic Kama Sutra: An Astrological Guide to Sexual Positions
Unleash Your Potential: A Guided Journal Powered by AI Insights
Whispers of the Enchanted Grove

Cosmic Pleasures: An Astrological Guide to Sexual Kinks

369, 12 Manifestation Journal

Whisper of the nocturne journal(blank journal for writing or drawing)

The Boogey Book

Locked In Reflection: A Chastity Journey Through Locktober

Generating Wealth Quickly:

How to Generate $100,000 in 24 Hours

Star Magic: Harness the Power of the Universe

The Flatulence Chronicles: A Fart Journal for Self-Discovery

The Doctor and The Death Moth

Seize the Day: A Personal Seizure Tracking Journal

The Ultimate Boogeyman Safari: A Journey into the Boogie World and Beyond

Whispers of Samhain: 1,000 Spells of Love, Luck, and Lunar Magic: Samhain Spell Book

Apophis's guides:

Witch's Spellbook Crafting Guide for Halloween

<u>Frost & Flame: The Enchanted Yule Grimoire of 1000 Winter Spells</u>

<u>The Ultimate Boogey Goo Guide & Spooky Activities for Halloween Fun</u>

Harmony of the Scales: A Libra's Spellcraft for Balance and Beauty

The Enchanted Advent: 36 Days of Christmas Wonders

Nightmare Mansion: The Labyrinth of Screams

Harvest of Enchantment: 1,000 Spells of Gratitude, Love, and Fortune for Thanksgiving

The Boogey Chronicles: A Journal of Nightly Encounters and Shadowy Secrets

The 12 Days of Financial Freedom: A Step-by-Step Christmas Countdown to Transform Your Finances

Sigil of the Eternal Spiral Blank Journal

A Christmas Feast: Timeless Recipes for Every Meal

If you want solar for your home go here: https://www.harborsolar.live/apophisenterprises/

Get Some Tarot cards: https://www.makeplayingcards.com/sell/apophis-occult-shop

Get some shirts: https://www.bonfire.com/store/apophis-shirt-emporium/

<u>Instagrams:</u>
@apophis_enterprises,
@apophisbookemporium,
@apophisscardshop
Twitter: @apophisenterpr1 Tiktok:@apophisenterprise
Youtube: @sg1fan23477, @FiresideRetreatKingdom

H ive: @sg1fan23477

Podcast: Apophis Chat Zone: https://open.spotify.com/show/5zXbr-CLEV2xzCp8ybrfHsk?si=fb4d4fdbdce44dec

Newsletter: https://apophiss-newsletter-27c897.beehiiv.com/